4th
grd

Real Math™

Dear Student:

You'll find a lot of things in this Real Math book. You'll find stories with Mr. Sleeby, Ferdie, Portia, Manolita, Mark, and their friends whom you may remember from earlier years.

You'll find games that will give you a chance to practice and put to use many of the skills you will be learning.

You'll find stories and examples that will show you how mathematics can help you solve problems and cut down on your work.

Many of the pages you'll be reading and discussing with your class. That's because mathematics is something people often learn together and do together.

But please don't expect all fun and games. Learning should be enjoyable, but it also takes time and effort. Most of all, it takes thinking.

We hope you enjoy this book. We hope you learn a lot. And we hope you think a lot.

The Authors of Real Math

Real Math™

Stephen S. Willoughby
Carl Bereiter
Peter Hilton
Joseph H. Rubinstein

Coauthor of Thinking Story® selections Marlene Scardamalia

Real Math™ is a product of the
Open Court Mathematics and Science
Curriculum Development Center.

Richard Leffingwell, Director

Open Court   La Salle, Illinois

President and Publisher
M. Blouke Carus

Executive Vice President
Paul Carus

Education Director
Carl Bereiter

General Manager
André W. Carus

Editorial Director
Dale E. Howard

Coordinator of Editorial Services
Juanita A. Raman

Production Manager
LeRoy Ceresa

Art Director
Todd Sanders

Design James Buddenbaum
Stuart D. Paterson
Muriel Underwood

Photography Charles P. Gerity
Lew Harding

Illustration Joanna Adamska-Koperska
Dev Appleyard
Jim Cummins
David Cunningham
JoAnn Daley
Bert Dodson
Mike Eagle
Michael Haynes
Paul Hazelrigg
Ann Iosa
Dick Martin
Robert Masheris
Tak Murakami
Phill Renaud
Gene Sharp
Dan Siculan
Joel Snyder
George Suyeoka
George Ulrich

CONTENTS

UNIT IV

MULTIPLYING WHOLE NUMBERS

END-OF-UNIT SEQUENCE

UNIT V

DIVIDING WHOLE NUMBERS

END-OF-UNIT SEQUENCE

A BASKET OF APPLES

The Seedtown Apple Orchard gave Richard a basket of apples for his school. Help him estimate how many apples there are in the basket.

- Write down your best guess of how many apples there are.
- How did you make your guess?
- Do you think you have a good chance of being exactly right?

Richard's friends helped him carry away the apples.

- 10 children took 10 apples each. How many apples did they take?

There are still lots of apples left.

- Now do you know exactly how many apples there were altogether?
- Make a second guess of how many apples there were.

Then 10 more children came. They each took 10 apples. Now the basket looks like this.

- So far, 20 children have taken 10 apples each. How many apples is that?
- Make a third guess of how many apples there were.

More children came and took apples.

- So far, 30 children have taken 10 apples each. How many apples have they taken?
- How many apples do you think are left?
- Make a fourth guess of how many apples there were.

All 30 children came back. They each took another 10 apples.

- Counting both times the children took some apples, how many apples did each child take?
- How many apples have the 30 children taken altogether?
- Make a fifth guess of how many apples there were.

- Then 12 more children came. They took 10 apples each. How many is that?
- How many apples have been taken altogether?
- How many apples are left?
- How many apples were there altogether?
- Is this a guess, or are you certain?

- What was your first guess about how many apples there were?
- What was your second guess?
- What was your third guess?
- What was your fourth guess?
- What was your fifth guess?
- Did your guesses get better?

The Point Brothers make and sell pins. The pins are
packaged like this:

		Number of Pins
	one	1
There are 10 pins in a **strip**.	ten	10
There are 10 strips in a **bag**.	one hundred	100
There are 10 bags in a **box**.	one thousand	1,000
There are 10 boxes in a **case**.	ten thousand	10,000
There are 10 cases in a **shipping carton**.	one hundred thousand	100,000

6

Number of Pins

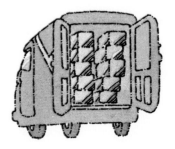

There are 10 shipping
cartons in a **vanload**.

one million   1,000,000

There are 10 vanloads
in a **truckload**.

ten million   10,000,000

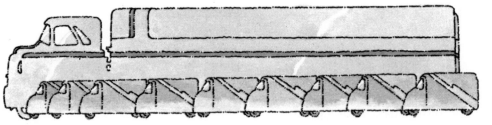

Write the number of pins. The first one has been done
for you.

1. 2 shipping cartons and 2 boxes   202,000
2. 4 cases and 8 bags
3. 3 truckloads and 6 cases
4. 4 shipping cartons, 3 boxes, and 1 strip
5. 6 vanloads, 7 cases, and 10 bags
6. 8 shipping cartons and 4 strips
7. 11 cases, 8 bags, and 12 strips
8. 1 truckload, 2 boxes, and 8 strips
9. 3 truckloads, 3 vanloads, and 9 bags
10. 11 cases and 11 strips

- How would you say each number? (For problem 1, you
  would say "two hundred two thousand.")

7

Millions			Thousands					
hundreds	tens	ones	hundreds	tens	ones	hundreds	tens	ones
	4	7	2	6	9	3	0	5

Forty-seven million, two hundred sixty-nine thousand, three hundred five

The 4 stands for 4 ten millions.	40,000,000
The 7 stands for 7 millions.	7,000,000
The 2 stands for 2 hundred thousands.	200,000
The 6 stands for 6 ten thousands.	60,000
The 9 stands for 9 thousands.	9,000
The 3 stands for 3 hundreds.	300
The 0 stands for 0 tens.	0
The 5 stands for 5 ones.	5

Write the numbers in standard form. The first one has been done for you.

1. 700 + 30 + 5   735
2. 50 + 5
3. 600 + 20 + 7
4. 1000 + 400 + 8
5. 400,000 + 50 + 7
6. 9000 + 10 + 1
7. 10,000 + 4000 + 400
8. 8000 + 10
9. 9 + 100 + 2000
10. 900,000 + 6000 + 500

11. 500,000 + 6 + 7000
12. 40 + 9 + 90,000
13. 80,000,000 + 300,000 + 9000 + 200
14. 20 + 700 + 800,000
15. 7,000,000 + 300,000 + 60,000 + 900
16. 50,000,000 + 30,000
17. 6 + 70 + 400 + 7,000,000
18. 900,000,000 + 9000 + 700
19. 1,000,000 + 80 + 1000
20. 700,000 + 7000 + 60

ROLL A NUMBER GAME

Players: 2 or more
Materials: One 0–5 cube
Object: To make the greatest 3-digit number

Rules
1. Draw lines for a 3-digit number on your paper, like this: ___ ___ ___
2. The first player rolls the cube 3 times.
3. Each time the cube is rolled, write that number in one of the 3 blanks you made. After all 3 rolls, you will have made a 3-digit number.
4. The player who makes the greatest 3-digit number is the winner of the round.

Sample Game

Number Rolled		Amy's Number	Jack's Number	Ellen's Number
3	First roll	3 ___ ___	___ 3 ___	___ 3 ___
I	Second roll	3 ___ I	___ I 3	___ 3 I
5	Third roll	3 5 I	5 I 3	5 3 I

Other Ways to Play This Game   Ellen won this round.
1. The smallest 3-digit number wins.
2. Make a 4-digit number.
3. The greatest even number wins.
4. Use a 5–10 cube. If a **10** is rolled, roll again.

Sometimes it's useful to count up. Sometimes it's useful to count down.

"26, 27, 28, ..."

5 4 3 2 1

Count up. Write the missing numbers.

1. 7, 8, 9, 10, 11, ▧ , ▧ , ▧ , ▧ , ▧ , ▧ , ▧ , 19
2. 194, 195, 196, ▧ , ▧ , ▧ , ▧ , ▧ , ▧ , ▧ , 204
3. 2987, 2988, 2989, ▧ , ▧ , ▧ , ▧ , ▧ , ▧ , ▧ , ▧ , 2998
4. 5098, 5099, ▧ , ▧ , ▧ , 5103
5. 36,571, 36,572, ▧ , ▧ , ▧ , ▧ , ▧ , ▧ , ▧ , ▧ , 36,581

Count down. Write the missing numbers.

6. 15, 14, 13, ▧ , ▧ , ▧ , ▧ , ▧ , ▧ , ▧ , ▧ , 4
7. 64, 63, 62, ▧ , ▧ , ▧ , ▧ , ▧ , ▧ , ▧ , ▧ , 53
8. 334, 333, 332, ▧ , ▧ , ▧ , ▧ , ▧ , ▧ , 325
9. 805, 804, 803, ▧ , ▧ , ▧ , ▧ , ▧ , ▧ , 796
10. 8403, 8402, 8401, ▧ , ▧ , ▧ , ▧ , ▧ , 8395

Count up or down. Write the missing numbers.

11. 13,207, 13,208, 13,209, ▧ , ▧ , ▧ , ▧ , 13,214
12. 9996, 9997, 9998, ▧ , ▧ , ▧ , ▧ , 10,003
13. 38,004, 38,003, 38,002, ▧ , ▧ , ▧ , 37,998
14. 146,236, 146,235, 146,234, ▧ , ▧ , ▧ , ▧ , 146,229
15. 999,997, 999,998, ▧ , ▧ , ▧ , ▧ , 1,000,003

ORDER GAME

Players: 2
Materials: Two 0–5 cubes, two 5–10 cubes
Object: To be the first to fill in all the boxes

Rules
1. Make a game form like the one shown.
2. Roll any 3 cubes. If you roll a **10**, roll that cube again.
3. Combine any 2 numbers rolled to make a 2-digit number. Write your first number in the START box on your game form.
4. On each turn, make a 2-digit number greater than the last number you made and write it in the next box.
5. If you cannot make a greater 2-digit number, or if you choose not to, you lose your turn.
6. The first player to fill in all the boxes on his or her game form is the winner.

Another Way to Play This Game
   Roll 4 cubes and make 3-digit
   numbers.

Can you think of other ways to play this game?

START
WIN

You can make different numbers using the digits 5, 2, and 8.
The greatest number you can make is 852.
The smallest number you can make is 258.

Copy and complete the chart.

	Use These Digits	Greatest Number	Smallest Number
1.	4, 7, 1		
2.	6, 5		
3.	3, 9		
4.	6, 7, 1		
5.	8, 3, 3		
6.	1, 9, 9		
7.	6, 9, 1, 2		
8.	7, 5, 7, 5		
9.	1, 6, 2, 2, 4		
10.	4, 3, 3, 6, 6		

You can make 6 different numbers using the digits 1, 2, and 3.
Here are the 6 numbers in order from greatest to smallest:

321   312   231   213   132   123

Write 6 different numbers in order from greatest to smallest.

11. Use the digits 4, 5, and 6.
12. Use the digits 2, 6, and 8.

ROLL A 15 GAME

Players: 2
Materials: Two 0–5 cubes, two 5–10 cubes
Object: To get the sum closer to 15

Rules
1. Roll the cubes one at a time.
2. Add the numbers as you roll. The sum of all the cubes you roll should be as close to 15 as possible.
3. You may stop after 2, 3, or 4 rolls.

If you rolled:	The sum would be:
7 and 1 and 4 and 7	19
8 and 5	13
4 and 4 and 8	16
9 and 3 and 3	15
5 and 10	15

4. The player with the sum closer to 15 wins the round. (The best score is 15; the next best scores are 14 and 16, and so on.)

Other Ways to Play This Game
1. Roll all the cubes at once.
2. Roll 2 cubes at a time.
3. Roll for a different sum.
4. Start at 20 and subtract the numbers rolled. Try to get as close to 5 as possible.

Can you think of other ways to play this game?

SLEEBY AT BAT Part 1

Work with the Thinking Story® in groups. Discuss your answers and how you figured them out. Then compare your answers with those of other groups.

Mr. Sleeby was looking for a job again. At last he was hired by a baseball team, the Lakeside Dips. The first day Mr. Sleeby came to work wearing a catcher's mask and a fielder's glove. "I'm ready to play any position," he said.

"Position?" grumbled the manager. "We didn't hire you to play ball. We hired you to be a tester."

"What's that?"

"You will test balls, bats, gloves, and so on. We want to know which ones we should buy. For a start, test these 3 kinds of bats. Find out which kind is best."

Mr. Sleeby had been watching TV. He had seen that when people want to find out which things are best, they often ask doctors. So Mr. Sleeby took the 3 bats to all the doctors in town. He asked each doctor which bat he or she thought was best.

When he was finished, Mr. Sleeby went back to the manager. This was his report: "Three doctors told me they thought the Slugger bat was best. One doctor said the Arrow looked best. Two said they liked the Champ. The other 54 doctors either said they didn't know anything about baseball bats or said they didn't want to be bothered."

"What does that tell you?" the manager asked.

"It tells me the Slugger bat is best, of course," Mr. Sleeby said.

The manager snorted. "It tells me 9 out of 10 doctors would rather not be asked," he said.

---

1. Do you agree with Mr. Sleeby that his test shows the Slugger bat is best? Why or why not?

2. What are some good things to test a bat for? List as many as you can think of.

3. Why do you think the manager said that 9 out of 10 doctors would rather not be asked about bats?

Are You Shiny or Rusty?

Very shiny   45 or more right
Shiny   40–44 right
A bit rusty   35–39 right
Rusty   Less than 35 right

Add to solve for n.

1. $5 + 3 = n$
2. $n = 6 + 2$
3. $7 + 1 = n$
4. $1 + 7 = n$
5. $n = 5 + 5$
6. $10 + 10 = n$
7. $8 + 7 = n$
8. $n = 1 + 4$

9. $6 + 5 = n$
10. $9 + 2 = n$
11. $3 + 8 = n$
12. $9 + 9 = n$
13. $6 + 4 = n$
14. $n = 4 + 6$
15. $8 + 8 = n$
16. $n = 8 + 9$

17. $1 + 9 = n$
18. $8 + 4 = n$
19. $7 + 7 = n$
20. $6 + 7 = n$
21. $9 + 5 = n$
22. $5 + 9 = n$
23. $4 + 1 = n$

24. $n = 6 + 6$
25. $10 + 9 = n$
26. $0 + 8 = n$
27. $n = 5 + 7$
28. $4 + 7 = n$
29. $n = 0 + 0$
30. $3 + 9 = n$

Add.

31. $\begin{array}{r} 6 \\ + 5 \\ \hline \end{array}$
32. $\begin{array}{r} 7 \\ + 9 \\ \hline \end{array}$
33. $\begin{array}{r} 2 \\ + 2 \\ \hline \end{array}$
34. $\begin{array}{r} 3 \\ + 7 \\ \hline \end{array}$
35. $\begin{array}{r} 2 \\ + 8 \\ \hline \end{array}$
36. $\begin{array}{r} 1 \\ + 9 \\ \hline \end{array}$

37. $\begin{array}{r} 3 \\ 5 \\ + 2 \\ \hline \end{array}$
38. $\begin{array}{r} 0 \\ 6 \\ + 9 \\ \hline \end{array}$
39. $\begin{array}{r} 8 \\ 3 \\ + 9 \\ \hline \end{array}$
40. $\begin{array}{r} 6 \\ 6 \\ + 6 \\ \hline \end{array}$
41. $\begin{array}{r} 7 \\ 8 \\ + 3 \\ \hline \end{array}$
42. $\begin{array}{r} 4 \\ 4 \\ + 4 \\ \hline \end{array}$

Add to solve for n.

43. $5 + 3 + 3 + 3 + 4 = n$
44. $7 + 1 + 3 + 4 + 3 = n$
45. $4 + 4 + 4 + 4 + 4 = n$
46. $3 + 3 + 3 + 2 + 2 = n$

47. $n = 1 + 2 + 3 + 4 + 5$
48. $n = 5 + 4 + 3 + 2 + 1$
49. $n = 3 + 3 + 3 + 3 + 3$
50. $n = 1 + 5 + 2 + 4 + 3$

Are You Shiny or Rusty?

Very shiny	45 or more right
Shiny	40–44 right
A bit rusty	35–39 right
Rusty	Less than 35 right

Subtract to solve for n.

1. $5 - 3 = n$

2. $8 - 3 = n$

3. $12 - 7 = n$

4. $18 - 9 = n$

5. $6 - 1 = n$

6. $n = 12 - 6$

7. $15 - 6 = n$

8. $n = 7 - 6$

9. $9 - 9 = n$

10. $9 - 0 = n$

11. $14 - 7 = n$

12. $n = 18 - 10$

13. $13 - 5 = n$

14. $10 - 5 = n$

15. $n = 9 - 7$

16. $8 - 6 = n$

17. $16 - 8 = n$

18. $n = 16 - 9$

19. $20 - 10 = n$

20. $14 - 7 = n$

21. $6 - 5 = n$

22. $7 - 7 = n$

23. $n = 13 - 8$

24. $11 - 8 = n$

25. $n = 11 - 8$

26. $8 - 5 = n$

27. $12 - 10 = n$

28. $n = 4 - 4$

29. $19 - 9 = n$

30. $11 - 7 = n$

Subtract.

31. $\begin{array}{r} 10 \\ -\ 5 \\ \hline \end{array}$

32. $\begin{array}{r} 6 \\ -\ 5 \\ \hline \end{array}$

33. $\begin{array}{r} 12 \\ -\ 7 \\ \hline \end{array}$

34. $\begin{array}{r} 18 \\ -\ 9 \\ \hline \end{array}$

35. $\begin{array}{r} 20 \\ -\ 10 \\ \hline \end{array}$

36. $\begin{array}{r} 13 \\ -\ 7 \\ \hline \end{array}$

37. $\begin{array}{r} 16 \\ -\ 7 \\ \hline \end{array}$

38. $\begin{array}{r} 12 \\ -\ 9 \\ \hline \end{array}$

39. $\begin{array}{r} 8 \\ -\ 8 \\ \hline \end{array}$

40. $\begin{array}{r} 10 \\ -\ 8 \\ \hline \end{array}$

41. $\begin{array}{r} 6 \\ -\ 5 \\ \hline \end{array}$

42. $\begin{array}{r} 14 \\ -\ 7 \\ \hline \end{array}$

43. $\begin{array}{r} 19 \\ -\ 10 \\ \hline \end{array}$

44. $\begin{array}{r} 4 \\ -\ 3 \\ \hline \end{array}$

45. $\begin{array}{r} 17 \\ -\ 8 \\ \hline \end{array}$

46. $\begin{array}{r} 7 \\ -\ 4 \\ \hline \end{array}$

47. $\begin{array}{r} 9 \\ -\ 5 \\ \hline \end{array}$

48. $\begin{array}{r} 16 \\ -\ 7 \\ \hline \end{array}$

49. $\begin{array}{r} 17 \\ -\ 9 \\ \hline \end{array}$

50. $\begin{array}{r} 10 \\ -\ 2 \\ \hline \end{array}$

How Fast Are You?   Are You Shiny or Rusty?

Extra fast	Very shiny 45 or more right
Very fast	Shiny 40–44 right
Fast	A bit rusty 35–39 right
Almost fast	Rusty Less than 35 right

Add or subtract to solve for n. Watch the signs.

1. $6 + 9 = n$	**9.** $n = 15 - 5$	**17.** $5 + 5 = n$	**24.** $2 + 10 = n$
2. $12 - 7 = n$	**10.** $8 + 7 = n$	**18.** $13 - 5 = n$	**25.** $7 + 3 = n$
3. $19 - 10 = n$	**11.** $0 + 0 = n$	**19.** $17 - 10 = n$	**26.** $n = 13 - 8$
4. $6 - 6 = n$	**12.** $14 - 5 = n$	**20.** $6 + 7 = n$	**27.** $1 + 1 = n$
5. $6 + 6 = n$	**13.** $n = 10 + 10$	**21.** $14 - 8 = n$	**28.** $15 - 8 = n$
6. $16 - 8 = n$	**14.** $n = 14 - 9$	**22.** $n = 7 + 5$	**29.** $4 + 8 = n$
7. $7 + 7 = n$	**15.** $n = 15 - 7$	**23.** $3 + 3 = n$	**30.** $16 - 9 = n$
8. $n = 2 + 8$	**16.** $n = 9 + 5$		

Add or subtract.

31. $\begin{array}{r} 8 \\ + 5 \\ \hline \end{array}$	**32.** $\begin{array}{r} 2 \\ + 2 \\ \hline \end{array}$	**33.** $\begin{array}{r} 15 \\ - 9 \\ \hline \end{array}$	**34.** $\begin{array}{r} 9 \\ + 9 \\ \hline \end{array}$	**35.** $\begin{array}{r} 10 \\ + 5 \\ \hline \end{array}$
36. $\begin{array}{r} 13 \\ - 6 \\ \hline \end{array}$	**37.** $\begin{array}{r} 15 \\ - 6 \\ \hline \end{array}$	**38.** $\begin{array}{r} 17 \\ - 8 \\ \hline \end{array}$	**39.** $\begin{array}{r} 4 \\ + 6 \\ \hline \end{array}$	**40.** $\begin{array}{r} 8 \\ + 6 \\ \hline \end{array}$
41. $\begin{array}{r} 8 \\ + 8 \\ \hline \end{array}$	**42.** $\begin{array}{r} 13 \\ - 9 \\ \hline \end{array}$	**43.** $\begin{array}{r} 4 \\ + 4 \\ \hline \end{array}$	**44.** $\begin{array}{r} 14 \\ - 6 \\ \hline \end{array}$	**45.** $\begin{array}{r} 13 \\ - 7 \\ \hline \end{array}$
46. $\begin{array}{r} 9 \\ + 1 \\ \hline \end{array}$	**47.** $\begin{array}{r} 3 \\ + 6 \\ \hline \end{array}$	**48.** $\begin{array}{r} 12 \\ - 9 \\ \hline \end{array}$	**49.** $\begin{array}{r} 3 \\ + 9 \\ \hline \end{array}$	**50.** $\begin{array}{r} 14 \\ - 7 \\ \hline \end{array}$

Study the map. Then answer the questions.

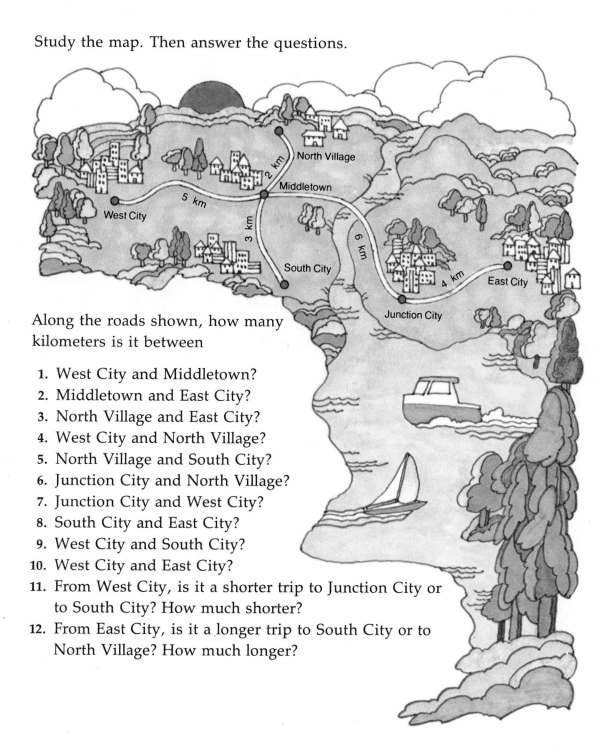

Along the roads shown, how many kilometers is it between

1. West City and Middletown?
2. Middletown and East City?
3. North Village and East City?
4. West City and North Village?
5. North Village and South City?
6. Junction City and North Village?
7. Junction City and West City?
8. South City and East City?
9. West City and South City?
10. West City and East City?
11. From West City, is it a shorter trip to Junction City or to South City? How much shorter?
12. From East City, is it a longer trip to South City or to North Village? How much longer?

19

Suppose you put a number into this function machine. The machine will add 5 to it. We say that the function rule for this machine is +5.

If you put a 3 into the machine, 8 will come out.
If you put a 5 into the machine, 10 will come out.
Copy and complete this chart for a +5 function machine.

(+5)	
In	**Out**
3	8
5	10
7	▨
9	▨
11	▨
13	▨

Copy and complete each chart. Watch the function rule.

1. (−5)

In	Out
10	5
12	7
14	9
16	
18	
20	

2. (+2)

In	Out
0	2
1	
2	
3	
4	
5	

3. (−3)

In	Out
4	
7	
10	
13	
16	
19	

4. (+10)

In	Out
40	
50	
60	
70	
80	
90	

5. (+9)

In	Out
1	
2	
3	
4	
5	
6	

6. (−4)

In	Out
14	
12	
10	
8	
6	
4	

7. (−10)

In	Out
60	
50	
40	
30	
20	
10	

8. (+7)

In	Out
2	
3	
5	
6	
8	
9	

9. (−6)

In	Out
19	
17	
15	
13	
11	
9	

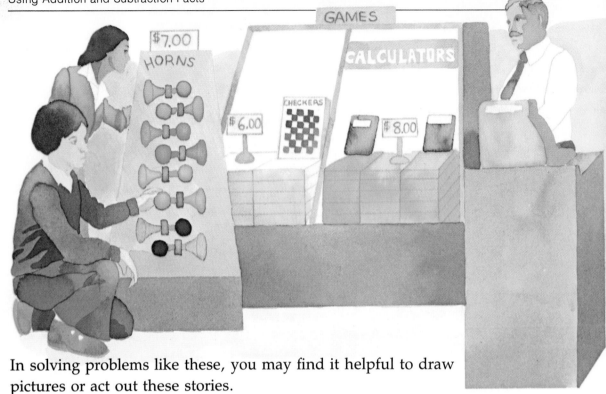

In solving problems like these, you may find it helpful to draw pictures or act out these stories.

Lydia has $18. Rob has $13.

1. Does Lydia have enough money to buy a can of tennis balls, a calculator, and a bicycle horn?

2. Suppose Rob buys a basketball and pays for it with a $10 bill. How much change should he get?

3. Lydia has already spent $5 today. If she buys a bicycle horn, how much will she have spent today?

4. Suppose Lydia buys 2 cans of tennis balls and a basketball. How much money will she have left?

5. Suppose Rob owes his mother $5 and wants to give it to her today. Would he be able to give it to her if he buys
   a. only the glove?
   b. only the game of checkers?
   c. only 2 cans of tennis balls?

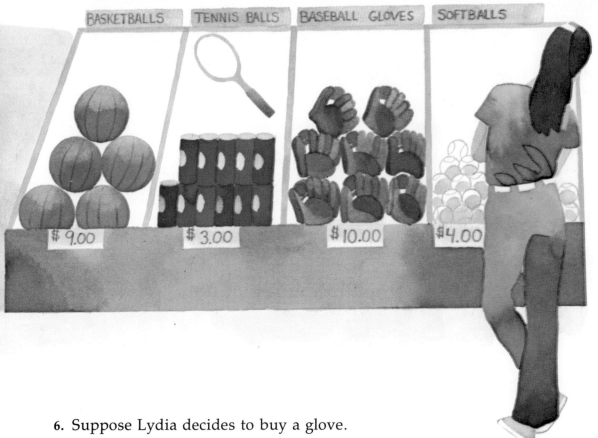

BASKETBALLS   TENNIS BALLS   BASEBALL GLOVES   SOFTBALLS

$ 9.00 $ 3.00 $ 10.00 $4.00

6. Suppose Lydia decides to buy a glove.
   a. How much money would she have left?
   b. If she then wants to buy a basketball, would she have enough money?

7. Suppose the store owner puts the gloves on sale for $6. How much has the price been lowered?

8. Suppose Rob buys a calculator and a softball. Would he be on time for the 3 o'clock softball game?

9. Lydia buys a basketball. Rob buys a checkers game and a can of tennis balls.
   a. Who spent more money?
   b. How much more?
   c. Can Rob now buy a bicycle horn?
   d. Can Lydia now buy a softball and a can of tennis balls?

23

Michael's class is doing the Numbers on the Back Activity.

The sum is 9.

What number does Michael have on his back?

In each case, write the number that Michael has on his back.

	Romi Has This Number	The Sum Is	Michael Has This Number
1.	9	14	5
2.	6	16	
3.	2	8	
4.	7	14	
5.	7	16	
6.	10	11	
7.	3	9	
8.	0	6	
9.	7	15	
10.	8	8	

Does the missing-term sentence help you solve the problem?

1. Barbara's family lives 15 kilometers from Sandy Rock $15 - n = 8$
   Park. They left home to drive to Sandy Rock Park. How
   far have they gone?

2. Susan sells hot dogs at the game. She began with $8 in $8 + n = 17$
   her pocket. Now she has $17. How much money has
   she taken in so far?

3. Ricardo's cat had a litter of kittens. He has found $n - 2 = 4$
   homes for 2 of them. He needs to find homes for the
   other 4. How many kittens were in the litter?

4. Isaac wants to buy a radio that costs $11. He has $5 + n = 11$
   earned $5. How much more money does he need?

5. Yesterday Anne bought a bag of marbles. She lost 9 $n - 9 = 9$
   playing with Jo. Now she has only 9 marbles. How
   many were in the bag?

25

Solve these problems.

1. Andy has 4¢. He wants 7¢ for milk money. How much more money does he need?

2. Betsy gave away 2 bananas. She has 6 left. How many bananas did she start with?

3. Last night Holly had 5 apples, but she ate some. How many does she have now?

4. After his birthday, Ted had 12 model rockets. He lost some and now has 9 left. How many rockets did he lose?

5. Ida picked 9 baskets of strawberries. She needs 20 to make some jam. How many more baskets must she pick?

6. After school, Ned ate 3 cookies from the plate. Now there are 5 left. How many cookies were on the plate when Ned came home from school?

7. Olga wants to do 10 math problems. She has done 6 problems. How many problems are left to do?

8. Every week Gwen runs 14 kilometers. She has run 10 kilometers so far this week. How many more kilometers does she need to run this week?

9. Yesterday Uta had 5 baseball cards and she won some. How many does she have now?

10. During band, Vanessa broke 3 clarinet reeds. Now she has 4 reeds. How many reeds did she have at the beginning of band?

The **perimeter** of a figure
is the distance around it.
To find the perimeter of
this square, add
3 + 3 + 3 + 3. The
perimeter is 12 centimeters.

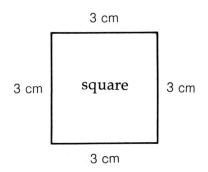

Find the perimeter.

1.

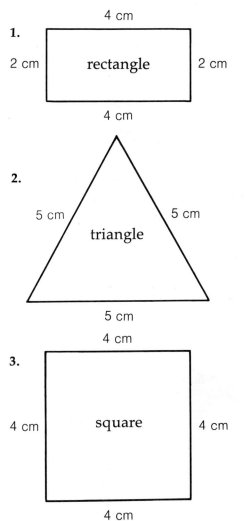

2.

3.

4.

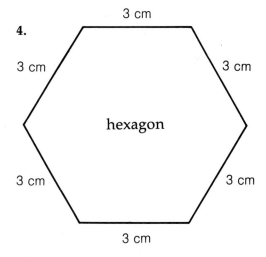

5.

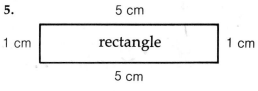

6.

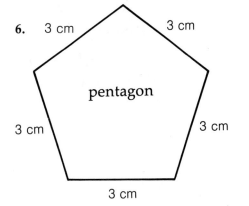

27

SLEEBY AT BAT

The manager's face turned red with anger. "I don't care what doctors say about a bat. I want to know how well a bat does what it's supposed to do. How well does it swing? How far can it hit a ball? How strong is it?"

Mr. Sleeby first set out to test the bats for hitting. He asked the pitcher to throw to him as he tested the bats. Mr. Sleeby swung at 10 pitches with the Slugger bat. He missed every time. Then he changed to the Arrow bat. He kept missing with it too. On the 24th pitch, he managed to hit a ball. The ball went hopping back to the pitcher.

"Nice hit, Mr. Sleeby," said the pitcher. "Just 10 times farther and you'd have had a home run."

Finally Mr. Sleeby tried the Champ bat.
He made 17 swings and misses. By then
the pitcher was tired of throwing to
him and quit. Mr. Sleeby reported to
the manager. "I'm proud to
say that the Arrow bat is far
better than any other for
getting hits."

1. Why does Mr. Sleeby say the Arrow bat is best? What
   do you think?

2. What are some reasons why Mr. Sleeby might have hit
   the ball with the Arrow bat and not with the others?

3. What would be a better way to find out which bat is
   best for getting hits?

4. For a home run, the ball would have to go about 120
   meters. If the pitcher is right, how far did Mr. Sleeby
   hit the ball?

Estimate the driving distances, in kilometers, between the following United States cities. For each pair of cities 4 distances are given in kilometers, but only 1 is correct. Select the correct distance.

1. New York City to Washington, D.C.
   a. 1974   **b.** 375   **c.** 1050   **d.** 35

2. New York City to Atlanta
   a. 503   **b.** 3475   **c.** 1020   **d.** 1353

3. Los Angeles to Miami
   a. 4323   **b.** 6219   **c.** 3219   **d.** 649

4. Denver to New York City
   a. 1594   **b.** 2849   **c.** 4129   **d.** 739

5. Chicago to Dallas
   a. 1475   **b.** 2138   **c.** 931   **d.** 4321

6. Chicago to Denver
   a. 976   **b.** 1201   **c.** 3011   **d.** 1603

7. Cleveland to Seattle
   a. 4975   **b.** 3232   **c.** 3778   **d.** 2178

Study the chart. Then answer the questions for those cities listed in the table.

Population Growth of 5 U.S. Cities

City	1950 Population	1960 Population	1970 Population
Cleveland, Ohio	914,808	876,050	750,879
Atlanta, Georgia	331,314	487,455	497,421
Dallas, Texas	434,462	679,684	844,401
Gary, Indiana	570,445	627,525	593,471
New York City	7,891,957	7,781,984	7,895,563

1. Name the city or cities that had a smaller population in 1970 than in 1950.

2. Name the city or cities that had a greater population in 1970 than in 1950.

3. Name the city with the largest population in 1950. In 1960. In 1970.

4. How many people lived in Dallas in 1950? Do you think your answer is exactly right?

5. Which city showed the greatest gain in population when you compare 1950 and 1970?

6. Which city showed the greatest loss in population when you compare 1950 and 1970?

7. Did any city gain in population between 1950 and 1960 and lose in population between 1960 and 1970?

Add: 225 + 389 = ?

Here's how:

$$
\begin{array}{r}
1 \\
2\,2\,5 \\
+\ 3\,8\,9 \\
\hline
4
\end{array}
$$

Start at the right.
Add the ones.
5 + 9 = 14
14 = 1 ten and 4

$$
\begin{array}{r}
1\ 1 \\
2\,2\ 5 \\
+\ 3\,8\ 9 \\
\hline
1\ 4
\end{array}
$$

Add the tens.
1 + 2 + 8 = 11   There are 11 tens.
11 tens = 1 hundred and 1 ten

$$
\begin{array}{r}
1\ 1 \\
2\,2\ 5 \\
+\ 3\ 8\,9 \\
\hline
6\ 1\ 4
\end{array}
$$

Add the hundreds.
1 + 2 + 3 = 6   There are 6 hundreds.

Remember: Start at the right. Use the same rules in
every column.

Here are more examples:

$$
\begin{array}{r}
1\,1\ \ 1\,1 \\
2\,3\,,4\,7\,5 \\
+\ 4\,8\,,6\,3\,9 \\
\hline
7\,2\,,1\,1\,4
\end{array}
\qquad
\begin{array}{r}
1\ \ \ 1 \\
4\,9\,0\,7 \\
+\ \ \ 6\,8\,5 \\
\hline
5\,5\,9\,2
\end{array}
$$

Add. Use shortcuts when you can.

1. 35   2. 50   3. 92   4. 25   5. 75   6. 63
  + 42   + 30   + 30   + 25   + 75   + 72

7. 125   8. 300   9. 499   10. 562   11. 602
  + 237   + 42   + 499   + 31   + 718

12. 100   13. 500   14. 829   15.   27   16. 325
   + 95   + 499   + 135   + 343   + 736

17. 5712   18. 15,576   19. 89,341
   + 6314   + 37,659   + 10,659

20. 1395   21. 29,324   22. 323,759,902
   + 7239   + 65,591   + 474,621,326

23. 35   24. 19   25. 31   26. 25   27. 565
     63   25   25   25   394
   + 75   36   324   25   237
                + 143   + 567   + 25   + 465

33

In each problem, 2 of the answers don't make sense, and one is correct. Choose the correct answers. Discuss your methods for finding the answers. What methods worked best?

1. 49 + 49 = ▦   a. 98   b. 198   c. 518
2. 84 + 120 = ▦   a. 204   b. 34   c. 974
3. 36 + 71 = ▦   a. 67   b. 107   c. 227
4. 125 + 237 = ▦   a. 1762   b. 222   c. 362
5. 275 + 129 = ▦   a. 104   b. 404   c. 804
6. 27 + 54 = ▦   a. 81   b. 31   c. 171
7. 48 + 71 = ▦   a. 199   b. 319   c. 119
8. 472 + 376 = ▦   a. 1028   b. 628   c. 848
9. 359 + 982 = ▦   a. 1041   b. 1341   c. 941
10. 412 + 562 = ▦   a. 974   b. 1274   c. 774
11. 73 + 793 = ▦   a. 766   b. 1066   c. 866
12. 1475 + 325 = ▦   a. 800   b. 1800   c. 2800
13. 1379 + 1682 = ▦   a. 4061   b. 2061   c. 3061
14. 2257 + 1279 = ▦   a. 3536   b. 536   c. 5536
15. 4778 + 173 = ▦   a. 951   b.) 4951   c. 4751
16. 7253 + 347 = ▦   a. 10,600   b. 7000   c.) 7600
17. 5525 + 3575 = ▦   a. 9100   b. 7100   c. 15,100

DON'T GO OVER 1000 GAME

Players: 2 or more
Materials: Two 0–5 cubes, two 5–10 cubes
Object: To get the sum closest to, but not over, 1000

Rules

1. Roll all 4 cubes. If you roll a **10**, roll that cube again.
2. Combine 3 of the numbers rolled to make a 3-digit number.
3. Roll all 4 cubes again. Make a second 3-digit number and add it to your first number.
4. You may stop after your second roll, or you may make another 3-digit number and add it to your previous sum.
5. The player whose sum is closest to, but not over, 1000 is the winner.

Sample Game

Vera rolled:	Vera wrote:		Rosalie rolled:	Rosalie wrote:
5 3 4 6	643		0 5 9 1	519
3 6 7 2	+ 327		3 7 7 1	+ 137
	970			656
	Vera stopped.		8 2 3 9	+ 329
				985
				Rosalie was the winner.

Can you think of other ways to play this game?

Subtract: 594 − 378 = ?

5 9 4 − 3 7 8	Start at the right. Subtract the ones. You can't subtract 8 from 4.

5 9̸ 4̸
− 3 7 8

Regroup the 9 tens and 4.

8 14
5 9̸ 4̸
− 3 7 8

9 tens and 4 = 8 tens and 14

8 14
5 9̸ 4̸
− 3 7 8
_____
        6

Subtract the ones.
14 − 8 = 6

8 14
5 9̸ 4̸
− 3 7 8
_____
      1 6

Subtract the tens.
8 − 7 = 1   There is 1 ten.

8 14
5 9̸ 4̸
− 3 7 8
_____
    2 1 6

Subtract the hundreds.
5 − 3 = 2   There are 2 hundreds.

```
  9 0 5
− 4 6 6
```

What do you do in a case like this?
There are no tens to regroup.

```
  89 15
  9 0 5
− 4 6 6
```

9 hundreds is the same as 90 tens.
Regroup 90 tens and 5.
90 tens and 5 = 89 tens and 15

```
  89 15
  9 0 5
− 4 6 6
  4 3 9
```

Now subtract.

Subtract. Use shortcuts when you can.

1. 35 − 23	2. 65 − 29	3. 47 − 40	4. 47 − 39	5. 93 − 87

6.
```
   425
 − 425
```
7.
```
   691
 −  25
```
8.
```
   201
 − 187
```
9.
```
   905
 − 377
```
10.
```
   391
 − 280
```

11.
```
   672
 − 314
```
12.
```
   6542
 − 3000
```
13.
```
   1000
 −    3
```
14.
```
   349,619,721
 − 218,700,399
```

Add or subtract. Use shortcuts when you can.

15. 871 − 645 18. 700 − 200 21. 901 + 675
16. 700 + 200 19. 700 − 199 22. 307 − 295
17. 770 + 199 20. 700 − 201 23. 496 − 496

ROLL A PROBLEM GAME

Players: 2 or more
Materials: One 0–5 cube
Object: To get the greatest sum

Rules

1. Use blanks to outline an addition problem on your paper, like this:

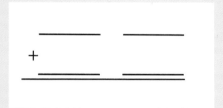

2. The first player rolls the cube 4 times.
3. Each time the cube is rolled, write that number in one of the blanks in your outline.
4. When all the blanks have been filled in, find the sum of the two 2-digit numbers.
5. The player with the greatest sum is the winner.

Other Ways to Play This Game

1. Try to get the lowest sum.
2. Add two 3-digit numbers.
3. Add three 2-digit numbers.
4. Use a 5–10 cube. If a 10 is rolled, roll again.
5. Subtract. Try to get the smallest difference, 0 or greater.

Can you think of other ways to play this game?

Add or subtract. Watch the signs.

1. 22 + 31	**2.** 63 − 41	**3.** 36 − 21	**4.** 67 + 22	**5.** 93 − 36	**6.** 27 + 49
7. 48 + 35	**8.** 82 − 57	**9.** 67 + 74	**10.** 77 − 68	**11.** 34 − 19	**12.** 83 + 28
13. 368 + 121	**14.** 529 + 310	**15.** 687 − 321	**16.** 568 − 37	**17.** 329 + 692	
18. 474 − 289	**19.** 6725 + 1235	**20.** 7925 − 2136			

21. Clara and Thomas ran for school president.
Clara got 743 votes. Thomas got 916.
   a. Who won?
   b. By how many votes?
   c. How many people voted?

SLEEBY AT BAT

"You should use one of our regular players," said the manager. "After all, we don't care how good a bat is for you. We want to know how good it is for them."

Mr. Sleeby asked Sandy Hare, leading batter for the Dips, to try the bats. First Sandy batted for a while with the Slugger bat. He had 19 hits with it. Then he batted for a while with the Arrow bat and got 20 hits. When he used the Champ bat, he had only 11 hits.

"I am happy to say that I was right," Mr. Sleeby told the manager. "The Arrow bat is by far the best for getting hits."

1. Do you agree with Mr. Sleeby that the Arrow bat was by far the best? Why or why not?

2. What are some reasons why Sandy Hare might have gotten more hits with the Arrow bat?

3. How would you change the test to make it fairer?

Amalia needs 31¢ for mailing a letter. She has these stamps:

1. Can Amalia make exactly 31¢ in postage stamps?
2. Which stamps make exactly 31¢?
3. How many postage stamps will Amalia have left?
4. What will be the total value of the stamps she has left?

These 3 children are collecting baseball cards. Peter has 643 cards, Zelda has 742, and Stan has 392.

5. How many more cards does Stan need in order to have as many as Zelda?

6. How many more cards does Peter need to have as many as Zelda?

7. Suppose Peter gives Stan 343 cards. Will Stan then have as many cards as Zelda?

8. Suppose Zelda gives Stan 200 cards. Will Stan then have as many as Zelda?

9. Challenge: How many cards would Zelda have to give to Stan for the 2 of them to have the same number?

Patty made a chart to help her find the least expensive supermarket. First she decided which brands she wanted. Can you complete the bottom line of Patty's chart?

Item	**Price (in cents)**		
	Super-Duper Supermarket	**Hi-Value Supermarket**	**Best-Buy Supermarket**
1 dozen eggs (Grade AA large)	92¢	89¢	93¢
1 liter of apple juice (Top-Core brand)	86¢	89¢	87¢
2 kilograms of potatoes	72¢	75¢	69¢
Total			

1. Which supermarket is least expensive for the 3 items listed?
2. Which supermarket is most expensive?
3. For each supermarket, write the total amount in dollars and cents.
4. Patty met Mr. O'Brien, who was going shopping. "I have to buy bread, butter, apples, and peanut butter," said Mr. O'Brien. "Do you know which supermarket will be least expensive?" he asked. Does Patty know the answer to Mr. O'Brien's question? Why or why not?

- Go comparison shopping. Make a chart like the one above. Write the names of the stores you will go to and the items you will check prices for. Then fill in your chart with the prices you find.

SLEEBY AT BAT

Mr. Sleeby tested how well the bats worked in real games. For the next 2 weeks, Sandy Hare always used the Arrow bat when he played. Al Button, second-best batter on the team, always used the Slugger bat. And Speck Tackle, a pinch hitter, used the Champ bat. Mr. Sleeby went to every game. He kept a count of what happened.

Sandy Hare batted 40 times and got 15 hits with the Arrow bat. Al Button, with his Slugger, batted 41 times and got 12 hits. Speck Tackle, using the Champ bat, batted 8 times and got 5 hits.

1. Who do you think did the best hitting? Why?

2. Does this test tell you which bat is best for getting hits? Explain.

Do you remember what these signs mean?

Here are some examples:
25 < 30 means 25 is less than 30.
10 > 7 means 10 is greater than 7.
4 + 9 = 13 means 4 plus 9 is equal to 13.

Replace ● with >, <, or = as you copy each statement
below. Think about the easiest way to answer these questions.
Discuss your methods.

1. 27 ● 19
2. 36 ● 18
3. 19 ● 79
4. 4 + 3 ● 3 + 4
5. 9 ● 19 + 10
6. 100 ● 73 + 10
7. 84 ● 73 − 10

8. 11 ● 77 + 66
9. 79 ● 77 + 10
10. 16 ● 21 + 3
11. 56 ● 40 + 20
12. 39 ● 29 + 29
13. 63 ● 33 + 23
14. 55 ● 55 − 13

15. 39 ● 52 + 49
16. 8 + 9 ● 8 − 2
17. 18 − 9 ● 18 + 3
18. 33 − 6 ● 33 − 7
19. 49 + 3 ● 49 + 5
20. 77 − 16 ● 74 − 16

21. Mr. Bajardi has $100. Does he have
enough money to pay for
a. the jacket and the pants?
b. the pants and the sweater?
c. the sweater and 3 ties?

PANTS $25   JACKETS $89 $5   SWEATERS $29

INEQUALITY GAME

Players: 2
Materials: Two 0–5 cubes, two 5–10 cubes
Object: To fill in an inequality statement correctly

Rules

1. Make one of these game forms on a sheet of paper:

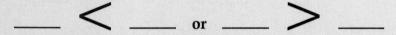

2. Roll all 4 cubes, make two 2-digit numbers, and write their sum on either side of the inequality sign. (If you roll a 🔟 , roll that cube again.)
3. The other player rolls all 4 cubes, makes two 2-digit numbers, and writes their sum in the remaining space.
4. If the inequality statement is true, the other player wins. If the inequality is false, you win.
5. Players take turns being first.

Can you think of other ways to play this game?

47

Ink has been spilled on these 2 pages. One answer is correct in each case. Decide which answer is correct.

Example: 23
              + 4

    a. 51
    b. 61
    c. 71

The sum must be at least 63. It could be as much as 72. So the correct answer must be **c,** 71.

Discuss methods for solving these problems.

1.   68
       + 2

  a.   86
  b.   96
  c. 106

2.   204
       + 7

  a.   99
  b. 279
  c. 949

3.   53
       + 330

  a.   259
  b.   863
  c. 1059

4.   2 5
       + 3

  a.   83
  b. 492
  c. 613

5.   456
       + 31

  a. 2
  b. 869
  c. 7

6.   670
       +

  a. 6532
  b. 7413
  c. 9705

7. 87
   − 3█

   a. 51
   b. 64
   c. 92

8. 82
   − 3█

   a. 46
   b. 56
   c. 66

9. 100
   − 7█

   a. 15
   b. 25
   c. 35

10. 74█
   − 283

   a. 406
   b. 582
   c. 462

11. 8█
   − 3█5

   a. 482
   b. 607
   c. 758

12. 30█
   − ███

   a. 206
   b. 317
   c. 402

13. 812
   − 368

   a. 4█
   b. 5█
   c. 6█

14. 7904
   − 6█

   a. 1250
   b. 725
   c. 76

15. 3406
   − 759

   a. █757
   b. █747
   c. █647

SLEEBY AT BAT Part 5

One day when Al Button was batting, his Slugger bat broke. "That proves Slugger bats are no good," he said. "Let's use Arrow bats."

The manager said, "Not so fast. I want a better test." He told Mr. Sleeby to take 10 of each kind of bat and test how strong they were.

Mr. Sleeby carried all the bats off in a wagon. He kept going until he found a big rock. Then he took each bat and hit it against the rock. Not one of the bats broke. "All of the bats are strong," Mr. Sleeby told the manager.

"Give them a harder test," said the manager.

Mr. Sleeby went back and found a bigger rock. He hit each bat against the rock. Again, none of them broke.

"Give them a harder test yet," said the manager.

Mr. Sleeby went out again with his wagon full of bats. On the street he stopped to watch a crew tearing down a building. The workers had a crane, which swung a huge steel ball back and forth. When the steel ball hit a wall, the wall crashed down. Mr. Sleeby put all the bats on the ground. He asked the workers, "Would you try to break these bats with your steel ball?"

"Are you sure you want us to do that?" asked one of the workers.

"Yes," said Mr. Sleeby. "I'm giving the bats a test."

The steel ball came crashing down on the bats. Pieces of wood flew into the air.

Later Mr. Sleeby reported to the manager. "The bats are all alike. They all passed the easy tests and they all failed the hard test."

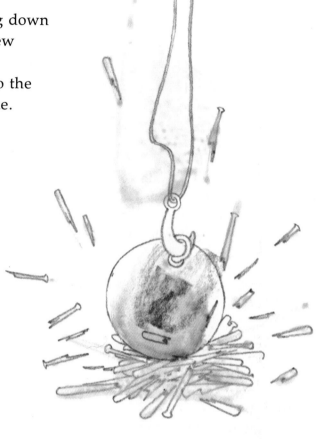

1. How many bats did Mr. Sleeby test?

2. Why should he have to test so many bats? Why not 1 of each kind?

3. Was the second test harder than the first? Explain.

4. Is Mr. Sleeby right that the bats are all alike? If some are stronger, how could you find out?

Sometimes you don't need an exact answer. Select the best answer for each problem. You don't have to do the calculations.

1. The zipper was invented in 1891. About how many years ago was that?
   a. About 40   b. About 120   c. About 90

2. George Washington was born in 1732. About how many years ago was that?
   a. About 250   b. About 100   c. About 500

3. Christopher Columbus reached America in 1492. About how many years ago was that?
   a. About 500   b. About 250   c. About 100

4. The American Declaration of Independence was signed in 1776. About how many years ago was that?
   a. About 100   b. About 200   c. About 300

5. In 1976, the population of Detroit, Michigan, was 1,314,206 and the population of Chicago, Illinois, was 3,074,084. About how many more people lived in Chicago than in Detroit?
   a. About 176,000   b. About 1,760,000   c. About 17,600,000

6. In 1973, the United States minted $74,067,700 worth of
   50-cent pieces (half dollars). About how many coins is
   that?

   a. About 148,000,000   **b.** About 37,000,000   **c.** About 5,000,000

7. In 1978, the number of kilometers of railroad track in
   Canada was 71,503; in Mexico, it was 19,680. About
   how many more kilometers of track did Canada have
   than Mexico?

   a. 5200   **b.** 52,000   **c.** 520

8. 741,272 aircraft took off or landed at Chicago's O'Hare
   Field and 516,558 aircraft took off or landed at Atlanta
   International Airport during 1977. About how many
   more aircraft flew into or out of O'Hare than Atlanta
   International?

   a. 230,000   **b.** 23,000   **c.** 203,000

9. The air distance between Boston, Massachusetts, and
   Seattle, Washington, is 4016 kilometers. The air
   distance between Boston and Los Angeles, California,
   is 3131 kilometers. Boston is about how much farther
   away from Seattle than it is from Los Angeles?

   a. 90 kilometers   **b.** 710 kilometers   **c.** 900 kilometers

1. About how full is the fuel tank?
   a. $\frac{1}{2}$ full   b. $\frac{1}{3}$ full   c. $\frac{3}{4}$ full

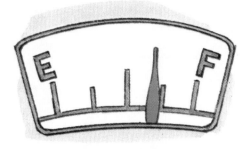

2. About how full is the glass?
   a. $\frac{1}{4}$ full   b. $\frac{1}{2}$ full   c. $\frac{2}{3}$ full

3. About how much of the bookshelf is empty?
   a. $\frac{1}{8}$ b. $\frac{1}{3}$ c. $\frac{1}{2}$

4. About how much of the pie is left?
   a. $\frac{1}{6}$ b. $\frac{1}{16}$ c. $\frac{1}{3}$

5. About how much of this triangle is colored?
   a. $\frac{1}{2}$ b. $\frac{2}{3}$ c. $\frac{3}{4}$

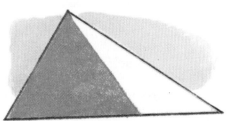

6. The length of the short stick is about what fraction of the length of the long stick?
   a. $\frac{1}{8}$ b. $\frac{1}{4}$ c. $\frac{1}{3}$

Which statements do not make sense?

1. $\frac{1}{2}$ of the students in Diana's class are girls and $\frac{2}{3}$ are boys.

2. $\frac{1}{2}$ of the students in John's class are boys, and $\frac{3}{4}$ of the students are wearing sneakers.

3. Eric tossed a coin 12 times. $\frac{1}{2}$ of the tosses turned up heads. $\frac{1}{4}$ of the tosses turned up tails.

4. Sandra is using a recipe that makes 3 servings. Only 2 people will be eating, so Sandra is using $\frac{2}{3}$ the amount given for each ingredient.

5. There are 10 fireplace logs in a bundle. If 5 logs are burned, $\frac{1}{2}$ of the bundle is left.

6. In $\frac{1}{2}$ hour, Joe, Betty, and Sam planted a small flower garden. If they started at 9:00 A.M., they must have worked until 10:30 A.M.

7. A spinner has 6 parts of the same size.
   a. $\frac{1}{2}$ of the area of the spinner is red.
   b. If you spin the spinner many times, you would land on red about $\frac{1}{2}$ the time.

8. The bottom half of this bottle holds more juice than the top half.

20 cm

20 cm

9. Fran ate $\frac{1}{2}$ of her birthday cake on Monday, $\frac{1}{2}$ on Tuesday, and $\frac{1}{2}$ on Wednesday.

dollar

one dollar = 100 cents
1 dollar = 100¢

half dollar

one half dollar = 50 cents
$\frac{1}{2}$ of 100¢ = 50¢

quarter

one quarter dollar = 25 cents
$\frac{1}{4}$ of 100¢ = 25 cents

dime

one-tenth dollar = 10 cents
$\frac{1}{10}$ of 100¢ = 10 cents

Write the amount as a fraction of a dollar. Then write how many cents.

	Coins	Fraction of a Dollar	Cents
1.		$\frac{2}{4}$	50¢
2.			
3.			
4.			
5.			

- How many quarters are in one dollar?
- How many quarters are in one half dollar?
- How many dimes are in one dollar?
- How many dimes are in one half dollar?
- Which would you rather have, 10 dimes or 4 quarters?

1. Miss Wing is driving to a town 100 kilometers from her home. She has 40 kilometers left to go. Is she halfway there yet?

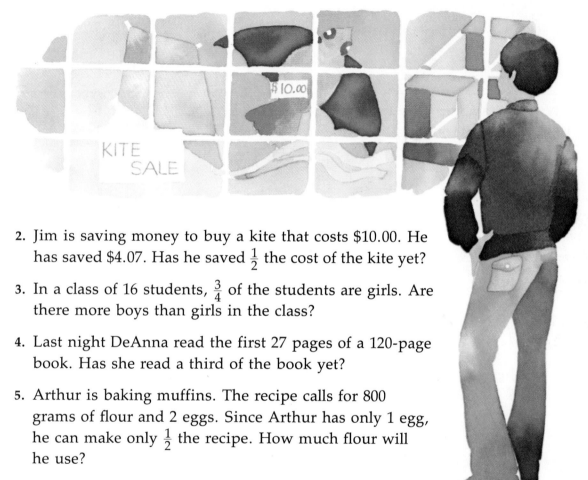

$10.00

KITE
SALE

2. Jim is saving money to buy a kite that costs $10.00. He has saved $4.07. Has he saved $\frac{1}{2}$ the cost of the kite yet?

3. In a class of 16 students, $\frac{3}{4}$ of the students are girls. Are there more boys than girls in the class?

4. Last night DeAnna read the first 27 pages of a 120-page book. Has she read a third of the book yet?

5. Arthur is baking muffins. The recipe calls for 800 grams of flour and 2 eggs. Since Arthur has only 1 egg, he can make only $\frac{1}{2}$ the recipe. How much flour will he use?

6. Maureen cut her pie into 8 equal slices. 7 slices were eaten. Is more than $\frac{1}{4}$ of the pie left?

7. The gas tank on Mr. Lee's car holds 84 liters. He just put in 64 liters of gas to fill the tank. About how full was the tank before filling?
   a. About $\frac{1}{4}$ full   b. About $\frac{1}{2}$ full   c. About $\frac{3}{4}$ full

8. A bicycle that usually sells for $100 is on sale for $72. Is that more than $\frac{1}{4}$ off the regular price?

1 dollar = $1.00

50¢ = $0.50

Write the amount shown in cents, then in dollars and cents. The first one has been done for you.

1.		35¢	$0.35
2.			
3.			
4.			
5.			
6.			
7.			
8.			

25¢ = $0.25   10¢ = $0.10   5¢ = $0.05   1¢ = $0.01

Write the amount in dollars and cents.

1. 10 cents = ▮
2. 2 dimes = ▮
3. 4 dimes and 7 cents = ▮
4. 8 dimes and 6 cents = ▮
5. 8 cents = ▮

6. 1 dollar and 2 dimes = ▮
7. 3 dollars and 4 dimes = ▮
8. 6 dollars and 3 cents = ▮
9. 1 dollar, 3 dimes, and 6 cents = ▮
10. 3 dollars, 6 dimes, and 2 cents = ▮

Replace ● with >, <, or = as you copy each statement.

11. $4.00 ● $3.48
12. $6.00 ● $5.98
13. $3.28 ● $3.28
14. $2.80 ● $0.28
15. $0.97 ● $97

16. $9.43 ● $19.43
17. $11.11 ● $1.11
18. $96 ● $96.00
19. $0.04 ● $4.04
20. $38.95 ● $40

MONEY ROLL GAME

Players: 2
Materials: One 0–5 cube, one 5–10 cube
Object: To make a number for the greater amount of money

Rules

1. Use blanks, a decimal point, and a dollar sign to outline an amount of money on your paper, like this: $___ ___.___ ___
2. Players take turns rolling either cube.
3. Each time a cube is rolled, both players write that number in one of the blanks in their outlines.
4. The player who makes the number for the greater amount of money is the winner.

Sample Game

Number rolled:	Peggy wrote:	Joyce wrote:
3	$___ ___.___ 3 ___	$___ ___.___ 3
7	$___ ___.3 7	$___ 7 ___.___ 3
8	$8 ___.3 7	$___ 7 8.___ 3
6	$8 6.3 7	$6 7.8 3

Peggy was the winner.

Other Ways to Play This Game

1. Make a number for the smaller amount of money.
2. Use only a 0–5 cube.
3. Use only a 5–10 cube.
4. Use 10 cards or slips of paper numbered 0 through 9 instead of cubes. Players take turns drawing cards from a container.

Rose had $1.29. Then she found a $5 bill. When she told Dan, he said, "I can tell you how much money you have altogether." Then he added like this: "You had $1.29, and the 5 more you found makes $1.34 in all."

"That can't be," said Rose. "You should be more careful when you add numbers with decimal points."

• Why doesn't Dan's answer make sense?

Then Rose added like this:

$$\begin{array}{r} \$1.29 \\ +\ \ 5.00 \\ \hline \$6.29 \end{array}$$

"I guess that answer makes more sense," said Dan. "But you added zeros to $5 to make it $5.00."

"That's right," said Rose. "But whether I write $5 or $5.00, it's still 5 dollars."

In each problem, 2 of the answers are clearly wrong and 1 is correct. Choose the correct answers.

1. $2.98 + $4   a. $3.02   b. $6.98   c. $3.38
2. $3.05 − $1.50   a. $1.55   b. $2.90   c. $4.55
3. $6.75 + $1.25   a. $7.00   b. $6.90   c. $8.00
4. $0.50 + $0.47   a. $9.70   b. $97   c. $0.97
5. $0.37 − $0.12   a. $25   b. $0.25   c. $0.49
6. $3.98 + $0.45   a. $4.43   b. $3.43   c. $4.75

When you add numbers, like 475 and 137, you line them up like this:

$$\begin{array}{r} 475 \\ + \ 137 \\ \hline \end{array}$$

You add ones to ones, tens to tens, and so on.

When you add amounts of money like $4.75 and $1.37, you line up the decimal points.

$$\begin{array}{r} \$4.75 \\ + \ \ 1.37 \\ \hline \end{array}$$

You add cents to cents, dimes to dimes, dollars to dollars, and so on.

When you subtract numbers, like 178 from 342, you line them up like this:

$$\begin{array}{r} 342 \\ - \ 178 \\ \hline \end{array}$$

You subtract ones from ones, tens from tens, and so on.

When you subtract amounts of money, like $1.78 from $3.42, you line up the decimal points.

$$\begin{array}{r} \$3.42 \\ - \ \ 1.78 \\ \hline \end{array}$$

You subtract cents from cents, dimes from dimes, dollars from dollars, and so on.

Here are 2 examples to help you.

A. $65.47 + $39.80
Remember to line up the decimal points:

$$\begin{array}{r} \$ \ 65.47 \\ + \ \ \ \ 39.80 \\ \hline \$105.27 \end{array}$$

B. $14.98 + $17
You can write $17 as $17.00 to help you line up the decimal points:

$$\begin{array}{r} \$14.98 \\ + \ \ 17.00 \\ \hline \$31.98 \end{array}$$

Add or subtract. Use shortcuts when you can.

1. $15 + $3.98
2. $0.25 + $0.75
3. $19.99 − $9.99
4. $5.98 + $3.15
5. $2.00 − $1.25
6. $11.99 − $0.49
7. $5.37 + $43
8. $6.35 − $1.27
9. $13.98 − $1.39

The **balance** in a bank book tells you how much money
you have. When you take out money, it's called a **withdrawal.**
When you put in money, it's called a **deposit.**

Alicia had $62.93 in her bank account. She
made a withdrawal of $18.50. What is her
balance now?

$62.93 — old balance
− 18.50 — withdrawal
$44.43 — new balance

Ronnie had $146.50 in his bank account.
Then he made a deposit of $25.95. What is
his balance now?

$146.50 — old balance
+ 25.95 — deposit
$172.45 — new balance

Lian, Bernie, Laurel, Gloria, Jeb, and Jess also have bank
accounts. This chart shows deposits and withdrawals
made this week. Write the new balance for each child.

		Old Balance	Deposit	Withdrawal	New Balance
1.	Lian	$32.50	$3.25	—	
2.	Bernie	$75.00	—	$20.00	
3.	Laurel	$65.98	$5.93	—	
4.	Gloria	$32.76	$11.78	—	
5.	Jeb	$107.98	—	$15.32	
6.	Jess	$10.75	—	$5.00	

SLEEBY AT BAT

"Since you can't tell what kind of bat is best," said the manager, "we'll buy the cheapest ones. Find out what the best deal is for buying 20 new bats."

This is what Mr. Sleeby found out:

1. Slugger bats cost $5 each.
2. Arrow bats cost $6 each, but if you buy 4 you get 1 extra bat free.
3. Champ bats are 2 for $11, but if you buy a dozen or more you get a $15 discount. That is, you get $15 back.

Mr. Sleeby told his friend Mark, "I get all mixed up trying to figure out how much 20 bats will cost."

Mark had some play money. Using the play money, they were able to find the cheapest way to buy 20 bats.

1. How much will 20 Sluggers cost? 20 Arrows?
   20 Champs?

2. What kind of bat is cheapest if you buy 20 of them?

3. You may be surprised to know that Mr. Sleeby bought 20
   bats for $90. Can you figure out how he did that?

SANDWICHES

Hamburger (100 grams)..........50¢
Super hamburger (200 grams) 75¢
Bologna sandwich ....40¢

SALADS

Potato salad..............20¢
Lettuce and tomato........25¢
Bean salad................15¢

DRINKS

Milk............15¢
Juice............20¢

DESSERTS

Apple pie........35¢
Gelatin..........15¢
Ice cream.......20¢

All prices include tax.

Donna wants to eat something different for lunch each day. But she can spend only $1.25 or less on lunch. She also wants to buy at least 1 sandwich, 1 salad, 1 dessert, and 1 drink each day.

Donna has made a chart so that she can plan her lunches for the week. She knows what she will buy on Monday, and she has selected a sandwich for Tuesday.

Help Donna plan her menu for the rest of the week. Copy and complete the chart.

Day	Sandwich	Salad	Dessert	Drink	Total Price
Monday	Hamburger, 50¢	Potato salad, 20¢	Apple pie, 35¢	Milk, 15¢	$1.20
Tuesday	Super hamburger, 75¢				
Wednesday					
Thursday					
Friday					

Count up or down. Write the missing numbers.

1. 47, 48, 49, ▨, ▨, ▨, ▨, ▨, 55
2. 5494, 5493, 5492, ▨, ▨, ▨, ▨, 5487
3. 666, 667, 668, ▨, ▨, ▨, ▨, ▨, 674
4. 26,549, 26,548, 26,547, ▨, ▨, ▨, ▨, 26,542

Add or subtract to solve for n. Watch the signs.

5. $17 - 7 = n$ 8. $n = 6 + 8$ 11. $15 - 6 = n$
6. $8 + 9 = n$ 9. $n = 7 + 9$ 12. $14 - 8 = n$
7. $12 - 6 = n$ 10. $n = 5 + 8$ 13. $7 + 7 = n$

Solve for n.

14. $8 + n = 12$ 16. $14 = n + 5$ 18. $5 + n = 10$
15. $n - 7 = 10$ 17. $9 = 17 - n$ 19. $n - 10 = 6$

Add or subtract. Watch the signs.

20. $87 - 46$ 21. $49 + 73$ 22. $492 + 764$

23.   63,587,304   24.   30,942,176   25.   27   26.   95
    − 24,069,253   + 58,417,926   62   106
                                             + 48   + 247

Replace ● with =, >, or <.

27. $4.75 ● $3.89   29. $5.62 ● $5.62
28. $21.31 ● $36.57   30. $18.99 ● $25.47

Add or subtract.

31. $3.50 + $4.61   33. $8.03 - $3.99
32. $5.00 - $3.21   34. $9.68 + $17.97

Find the perimeter.

35.

3 cm

1 cm   1 cm

3 cm

36.

1 cm

3 cm

3 cm

1 cm

37.

3 cm   3 cm

3 cm

38. About how full is the gas tank?
   a. Completely full   **b.** $\frac{3}{4}$ full   **c.** $\frac{1}{2}$ full

39. About how full is the pitcher?
   a. $\frac{3}{4}$ **b.** $\frac{1}{3}$ **c.** $\frac{1}{2}$

40. About what fraction of the spinner is red?
   a. About $\frac{1}{3}$ **b.** About $\frac{1}{2}$ **c.** About $\frac{2}{3}$

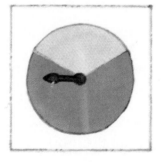

Solve these problems.

41. The car Miss Simon wants to buy costs about $6000. She has saved about $1500. About how much more money does she need?

42. Yesterday Sabina bought a bicycle for $98. Today she bought a basket for it for $13. Jane bought the same kind of bicycle with a basket for $109. Who paid less for her bicycle and basket?

43. Ahmed is 11 years old. He is 4 years older than his brother and 6 years older than his sister. How old is his brother?

44. Rona ran around the track 17 times in one direction and 6 times in the other direction. How many times did she run around the track?

Distances from New York City

City	Distance (kilometers)
Alexandria, Egypt	8,034
Bombay, India	13,175
Colón, Panama	3,178
Istanbul, Turkey	8,064
Lisbon, Portugal	4,717
Paris, France	4,830
Rome, Italy	6,500
St. John's, Newfoundland	1,740
Shanghai, China	14,643

Use the table to choose the best answer.

45. About how far is it from Bombay to New York?
   a. About 5000 kilometers (km)   b. About 8000 km   c. About 13,000 km

46. About how much farther is it from New York to
   Istanbul than from New York to Paris?
   a. About 1500 km   b. About 3000 km   c. About 5000 km

47. About how far is it from Alexandria to New York to
   Shanghai?
   a. About 16,000 km   b. About 8000 km   c. About 22,500 km

48. About how far is it from Bombay to New York to
   Colón?
   a. About 14,500 km   b. About 16,000 km   c. About 18,000 km

49. About how much farther is it from Lisbon to New
   York than from Lisbon to St. John's?
   a. About 1500 km   b. About 3000 km   c. Not enough information

50. About how far is it from Rome to New York and back
   to Rome again?
   a. About 22,500 km   b. About 9500 km   c. About 13,000 km

Solve for n. Remember to watch the signs.

1. $5 + 8 = n$
2. $n = 5 + 8$
3. $n = 7 + 9$
4. $2 + 8 = n$

5. $n = 4 + 4$
6. $17 - 8 = n$
7. $n = 14 - 6$
8. $n = 12 - 9$

9. $18 - 8 = n$
10. $n = 12 - 10$
11. $8 + 3 = n$
12. $14 - 9 = n$

13. $n = 8 + 8$
14. $8 - 8 = n$
15. $n = 16 - 9$
16. $n = 16 - 10$

17. $8 + n = 13$
18. $15 = 8 + n$
19. $4 + n = 8$
20. $12 = 6 + n$

21. $6 + n = 15$
22. $n - 5 = 10$
23. $4 = n - 9$
24. $9 = 18 - n$

25. $10 = 13 - n$
26. $10 = 17 - n$
27. $8 + n = 14$
28. $8 + n = 8$

29. $14 - n = 6$
30. $14 = n + 9$
31. $10 = n - 8$
32. $10 = n - 7$

Add.

33.
$$\begin{array}{r} 7 \\ 9 \\ 6 \\ + 5 \\ \hline \end{array}$$

34.
$$\begin{array}{r} 6 \\ 8 \\ 3 \\ + 2 \\ \hline \end{array}$$

35.
$$\begin{array}{r} 5 \\ 4 \\ 6 \\ + 3 \\ \hline \end{array}$$

36.
$$\begin{array}{r} 3 \\ 5 \\ 8 \\ + 1 \\ \hline \end{array}$$

37.
$$\begin{array}{r} 1 \\ 3 \\ 5 \\ + 7 \\ \hline \end{array}$$

38.
$$\begin{array}{r} 9 \\ + 2 \\ \hline \end{array}$$

39.
$$\begin{array}{r} 5 \\ + 6 \\ \hline \end{array}$$

40.
$$\begin{array}{r} 8 \\ + 9 \\ \hline \end{array}$$

41.
$$\begin{array}{r} 5 \\ + 9 \\ \hline \end{array}$$

42.
$$\begin{array}{r} 3 \\ + 9 \\ \hline \end{array}$$

43.
$$\begin{array}{r} 7 \\ + 6 \\ \hline \end{array}$$

Add.

44. $5 + 7 + 3 = n$
45. $8 + 6 + 4 = n$
46. $3 + 5 + 2 = n$

47. $9 + 7 + 3 = n$
48. $8 + 3 + 7 + 4 = n$
49. $5 + 9 + 8 + 1 = n$

50. $6 + 7 + 5 = n$
51. $3 + 2 + 9 + 4 = n$
52. $7 + 4 + 7 + 3 = n$

Add.

1.	2.	3.	4.	5.
56 + 97	83 + 46	186 + 39	39 + 208	346 + 287

6.	7.	8.	9.	10.
470 + 208	3408 + 2697	210 + 25	798 + 300	3461 + 2879

Subtract.

11.	12.	13.	14.	15.
793 − 200	92 − 67	607 − 289	573 − 381	491 − 268

16.	17.	18.	19.	20.
60 − 37	589 − 280	260 − 173	3508 − 809	6379 − 370

Add or subtract. Watch the signs.

21.	22.	23.	24.
593 + 248	28 + 7	43,572 − 1,281	53,408,761 + 721,508

25.	26.	27.	28.
3,472,694 + 5,309,721	61,204 − 34,561	793 + 291	804,721 − 712,438

Find the missing digit.

29.	30.	31.	32.
4 0 7 − 2 2 9 1 ▓ 8	6 0 2 − 3 4 5 2 5 ▓	3 2 1 − 2 8 5 ▓ 6	7 7 5 − 3 9 1 3 ▓ 4

33.	34.	35.	36.
4 3 7 − 3 2 8 1 ▓ 9	5 8 1 − 4 3 7 1 4 ▓	8 6 2 − 3 9 2 4 ▓ 0	3 4 9 − 1 7 8 1 ▓ 1

71

Add or subtract. Watch the signs.

1. $2.30 + 5.40	**2.** $6.81 + 7.93	**3.** $3.75 + 4.25	**4.** $5.25 − 3.75
5. $18.75 + 14.50	**6.** $4.73 − 3.98	**7.** $18.75 − 14.50	**8.** $6.00 − 1.75

Replace ⬤ in each statement below with =, >, or <.

9. $6.38 ⬤ $4.98 **12.** $5.05 ⬤ $5.05 **15.** $3.76 ⬤ $4.00

10. $5.11 ⬤ $5.51 **13.** $7.00 ⬤ $6.97 **16.** $4.00 ⬤ $4

11. $5.05 ⬤ $5.50 **14.** $8.95 ⬤ $8.59 **17.** $23.70 ⬤ $2.37

18. After school, Miguel, Billy, and Tracy ate some of the cake Billy's father had baked. About how much of the cake did they eat?

  a. About $\frac{1}{4}$ **b.** About $\frac{1}{2}$ **c.** About $\frac{3}{4}$

19. The United Fund drive in Westville has a goal of $50,000. This sign shows how much money has been raised so far. About what fraction of the goal has been raised so far?

  a. About $\frac{1}{5}$ **b.** About $\frac{2}{5}$ **c.** About $\frac{3}{5}$

20. Becky put all her comic books in a stack. So did Lisa. The height of Becky's stack is about what fraction of the height of Lisa's stack?

  a. About $\frac{1}{3}$ **b.** About $\frac{1}{2}$ **c.** About $\frac{1}{8}$

Write the amount as a fraction of a dollar. Then write it as cents.

	Coins	Fraction of a Dollar	Cents
1.		$\frac{3}{4}$	75¢
2.			
3.			
4.			

Solve these problems.

5. Franklin wants to swim 20 laps in the pool. If he swims 11, has he swum more than $\frac{1}{2}$ of them?

6. Hannah has walked 6 blocks from her house toward her aunt's house. There are 13 blocks between their houses. About what part of the distance has she walked?
   a. About $\frac{1}{4}$ b. About $\frac{3}{4}$ c. About $\frac{1}{2}$

7. There are 1000 meters in a kilometer. How many meters are there in 2 kilometers?

8. There are 1000 grams in a kilogram. How many grams are there in 2 kilograms?

9. Juan weighs 47 kilograms. His father weighs 76 kilograms. What is the difference in their weights?

Planet	Distance from the Sun (in millions of kilometers)
Mercury	58
Venus	108
Earth	299
Mars	456
Jupiter	778
Saturn	1429
Uranus	2863
Neptune	4491
Pluto	5879

Use the table to choose the best answer.

1. How far is Earth from the sun?
   a. 58 million kilometers (km)   b. 299 million km   c. 778 million km

2. Which of these planets is farthest from the sun?
   a. Mars   b. Earth   c. Pluto

3. About how much farther from the sun is Pluto than Uranus?
   About   a. 1000 million km   b. 3000 million km   c. 5000 million km

4. About how much farther from the sun is Jupiter than Earth?
   About   a. 500 million km   b. 700 million km   c. 900 million km

5. About how much farther from the sun is Pluto than Mercury?
   About   a. 1 million km   b. 10 million km   c. 5800 million km

6. About how much farther from the sun is Uranus than Saturn?
   About   a. 1400 million km   b. 2800 million km   c. 4200 million km

7. About how much farther from the sun is Jupiter than Mars?
   About   a. 100 million km   b. 200 million km   c. 300 million km

Lynn completed a survey about the birthdays of all the students at Oakwood School. She recorded the results on a chart. But she lost about half of the chart when her dog chewed it up. Study what is left of Lynn's chart.

Give exact answers to these questions.

Month	Number of Student Birthdays
January	15
February	18
March	13
April	20
May	17
June	16

1. How many students have birthdays in
   a. February?   b. June?

2. Name a month in which exactly 17 students have birthdays.

3. How many more students have birthdays in February than in January?

4. How many students have birthdays during the first 3 months of the year?

Make good guesses about the answers to these questions.

5. About how many students have birthdays in
   a. August?   b. September?

6. About how many students have birthdays during the second half of the year?

7. About how many students do you think there are in Oakwood School?

• Make up some questions that can be answered from the chart. Ask a friend to answer them.
• Make a similar chart for your school or class. See how well you can estimate the number of birthdays in the whole year from the number in the first half of the year (January through June).

75

Count up or down. Write the missing numbers.

1. 526, 525, 524, ■, ■, ■, ■, ■, 518
2. 207, 208, 209, ■, ■, ■, ■, 214
3. 85, 84, 83, ■, ■, ■, ■, ■, ■, 76

Add or subtract to solve for n.
Watch the signs.

4. $n = 8 + 9$	10. $17 - 9 = n$	16. $10 = 19 - n$
5. $n = 13 - 6$	11. $n = 8 + 6$	17. $6 + n = 13$
6. $6 + 9 = n$	12. $11 - 2 = n$	18. $n - 14 = 3$
7. $7 + 8 = n$	13. $n = 16 - 9$	19. $5 + n = 18$
8. $n = 8 - 3$	14. $n = 9 + 5$	20. $14 - 5 = n$
9. $5 + 9 = n$	15. $3 + 9 = n$	21. $17 = n + 5$

Watch the signs.

22.   45
    + 38

23.   927
    − 359

24.   271
    + 899

25.   4789
    + 2228

26.   4789
    − 2228

27.   12,021
    − 2,867

28.   36
      49
    + 82

29.   329
      472
    + 605

30.   405
      328
    + 82

Replace ● with =, >, or <.

31. $6.58 ● $3.27
32. $5.05 ● $5.05
33. $11.22 ● $13.08
34. $14.00 ● $14

Add or subtract.

35. $7.05 − $6.88
36. $86.41 + $3.98
37. $6.00 − $2.50
38. $122.67 + $8.05

Find the perimeter.

39.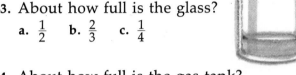
2 cm   2 cm

2 cm

40.
4 cm

1 cm   1 cm

4 cm

41.
2 cm

1 cm   1 cm   1 cm

2 cm

42. About how much of the rectangle is colored?

  a. $\frac{1}{4}$ **b.** $\frac{1}{2}$ **c.** $\frac{7}{8}$

43. About how full is the glass?

  a. $\frac{1}{2}$ **b.** $\frac{2}{3}$ **c.** $\frac{1}{4}$

44. About how full is the gas tank?

  a. $\frac{1}{4}$ **b.** $\frac{1}{2}$ **c.** $\frac{3}{4}$

Solve these problems.

45. The talking movie was invented in 1927. The telephone was invented 51 years earlier. In what year was that?

46. There were 12 people who finished a 10,000-meter race. Charlene finished third. How many people finished behind her?

47. Eddy weighs 37 kilograms. 2 years ago he weighed 31 kilograms. How much weight did he gain in those 2 years?

48. Chicago, Illinois, is about 460 kilometers from St. Louis, Missouri. About how far is a round trip between these cities?

Theodore Roosevelt was born in 1858. Franklin Roosevelt was born in 1882.

49. Who was older in 1890?
50. How old was Franklin Roosevelt in 1890?

UNIT II   MULTIPLICATION AND DIVISION

George knows his birthday is 8 weeks from today.

He wants to know how many days that is.

He starts counting on the calendar,
"1, 2, 3, 4, 5, 6, 7, 8, 9, . . ."

"I know a better way," Sharon says. "Add 7 and 7 and 7,
and so on until you've added eight 7s."

$7 + 7 + 7 + 7 + 7 + 7 + 7 + 7 = ?$

- Do you know a quicker way?
- Do you remember what 8×7 is?

There are 7 days in a week.

1. How many days are there in 8 weeks? $8 \times 7 = n$
2. How many days are there in 7 weeks? $7 \times 7 = n$
3. How many days are there in 6 weeks? $6 \times 7 = n$
4. How many days are there in 5 weeks? $5 \times 7 = n$
5. How many days are there in 9 weeks? $9 \times 7 = n$

What is the area of the rectangle?
Area = 3 × 5 square centimeters

5 cm

3 cm   3 cm

5 cm

Let's turn the rectangle on its side.
Area = 5 × 3 square centimeters

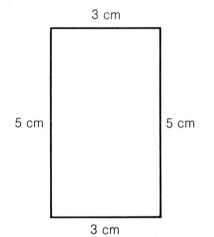

3 cm

5 cm   5 cm

3 cm

• Did the area of the rectangle change?

• Does 3 × 5 = 5 × 3?

• What is 3 × 5?

• What is 5 × 3?

Rule: The order in which 2 numbers are multiplied
makes no difference to the answer.

Multiply. Compare the problems in each pair.

1. 2 × 5 = n   2. 1 × 8 = n   3. 10 × 4 = n   4. 5 × 5 = n   5. 9 × 0 = n
   5 × 2 = n   8 × 1 = n   4 × 10 = n   5 × 5 = n   0 × 9 = n

6. 3 × 4 = n   7. 3 × 9 = n   8. 5 × 8 = n   9. 6 × 9 = n   10. 7 × 9 = n
   4 × 3 = n   9 × 3 = n   8 × 5 = n   9 × 6 = n   9 × 7 = n

81

There are 7 days in a week.

1. How many days are there in 2 weeks? $2 \times 7 = n$
2. How many days are there in 1 week? $1 \times 7 = n$
3. How many days are there in 0 weeks? $0 \times 7 = n$

There are 5 fingers on a hand.

4. How many fingers are there on 2 hands? $2 \times 5 = n$
5. How many fingers are there on 1 hand? $1 \times 5 = n$
6. How many fingers are there on 0 hands? $0 \times 5 = n$

- State a rule for multiplying by 2.

- State a rule for multiplying by 1.

- State a rule for multiplying by 0.

7×10 is 7 tens, or 70. 3×10 is 3 tens, or 30.

7. $6 \times 10 = n$ 9. $10 \times 6 = n$
8. $9 \times 10 = n$ 10. $10 \times 9 = n$

- State a rule for multiplying by 10.

Multiply to solve for n.

1. $0 \times 5 = n$ 8. $4 \times 10 = n$ 15. $6 \times 2 = n$
2. $5 \times 0 = n$ 9. $2 \times 9 = n$ 16. $10 \times 2 = n$
3. $8 \times 1 = n$ 10. $9 \times 2 = n$ 17. $1 \times 9 = n$
4. $1 \times 8 = n$ 11. $1 \times 10 = n$ 18. $7 \times 0 = n$
5. $2 \times 7 = n$ 12. $10 \times 0 = n$ 19. $0 \times 8 = n$
6. $7 \times 2 = n$ 13. $5 \times 10 = n$ 20. $8 \times 10 = n$
7. $10 \times 4 = n$ 14. $2 \times 8 = n$ 21. $7 \times 2 = n$

Multiply.

22. $\begin{array}{r} 7 \\ \times\, 1 \\ \hline \end{array}$ 23. $\begin{array}{r} 6 \\ \times\, 2 \\ \hline \end{array}$ 24. $\begin{array}{r} 7 \\ \times\, 10 \\ \hline \end{array}$ 25. $\begin{array}{r} 10 \\ \times\, 8 \\ \hline \end{array}$

26. $\begin{array}{r} 10 \\ \times\, 2 \\ \hline \end{array}$ 27. $\begin{array}{r} 8 \\ \times\, 0 \\ \hline \end{array}$ 28. $\begin{array}{r} 5 \\ \times\, 2 \\ \hline \end{array}$ 29. $\begin{array}{r} 2 \\ \times\, 8 \\ \hline \end{array}$

For many people, 2 of the hardest multiplication facts to remember are $7 \times 8 = 56$ and $7 \times 6 = 42$. Try to remember them!

30. $\begin{array}{r} 8 \\ \times\, 7 \\ \hline \end{array}$ 31. $\begin{array}{r} 7 \\ \times\, 6 \\ \hline \end{array}$ 32. $\begin{array}{r} 7 \\ \times\, 8 \\ \hline \end{array}$ 33. $\begin{array}{r} 6 \\ \times\, 7 \\ \hline \end{array}$

$7 \times 8 = ?$

The multiplication table is a short way to list the multiplication facts. To find 7×8, look in the row marked 7 and the column marked 8.

- What number do you find there?
- Did you expect to find 56?

Use the table to find these facts.

1. $8 \times 7 = n$ 3. $7 \times 7 = n$
2. $7 \times 6 = n$ 4. $8 \times 8 = n$

X	0	1	2	3	4	5	6	7	8	9	10
0	0	0	0	0	0	0	0	0	0	0	0
1	0	1	2	3	4	5	6	7	8	9	10
2	0	2	4	6	8	10	12	14	16	18	20
3	0	3	6	9	12	15	18	21	24	27	30
4	0	4	8	12	16	20	24	28	32	36	40
5	0	5	10	15	20	25	30	35	40	45	50
6	0	6	12	18	24	30	36	42	48	54	60
7	0	7	14	21	28	35	42	49	56	63	70
8	0	8	16	24	32	40	48	56	64	72	80
9	0	9	18	27	36	45	54	63	72	81	90
10	0	10	20	30	40	50	60	70	80	90	100

On the multiplication table, compare the columns marked 5 and 10.
- What is 4×10?   What is 4×5?
- What is 6×10?   What is 6×5?
- What is 8×10?   What is 8×5?

X	0	1	2	3	4	5	6	7	8	9	10
0	0	0	0	0	0	0	0	0	0	0	0
1	0	1	2	3	4	5	6	7	8	9	10
2	0	2	4	6	8	10	12	14	16	18	20
3	0	3	6	9	12	15	18	21	24	27	30
4	0	4	8	12	16	20	24	28	32	36	40
5	0	5	10	15	20	25	30	35	40	45	50
6	0	6	12	18	24	30	36	42	48	54	60
7	0	7	14	21	28	35	42	49	56	63	70
8	0	8	16	24	32	40	48	56	64	72	80
9	0	9	18	27	36	45	54	63	72	81	90
10	0	10	20	30	40	50	60	70	80	90	100

To multiply 8×10, you can write 8 with a 0 after it. To multiply 8×5, you can write $\frac{1}{2}$ of 8 (which is 4) with a 0 after it. This is because 5 is $\frac{1}{2}$ of 10.

Try to do these problems without looking at the table.

5. $2 \times 5 = n$ 7. $4 \times 5 = n$ 9. $6 \times 5 = n$ 11. $8 \times 5 = n$
6. $10 \times 5 = n$ 8. $5 \times 6 = n$ 10. $5 \times 8 = n$ 12. $5 \times 10 = n$

To do 7×5 isn't so easy. But here's a way: You know that 6×5 is 30. Now add 1 more 5 to make 7×5. That's 30 and 5 more, which is 35.

Try to do these problems without looking at the table.

13. $3 \times 5 = n$ **15.** $5 \times 5 = n$ **17.** $7 \times 5 = n$ **19.** $9 \times 5 = n$

14. $5 \times 7 = n$ **16.** $5 \times 1 = n$ **18.** $5 \times 9 = n$ **20.** $5 \times 3 = n$

On the multiplication table compare the 9 and 10 columns.

- What is 7×10?   What is 7×9?
  Is it $70 - 7$?
- What is 8×10?   What is 8×9?
  Is it $80 - 8$?

X	0	1	2	3	4	5	6	7	8	9	10
0	0	0	0	0	0	0	0	0	0	0	0
1	0	1	2	3	4	5	6	7	8	9	10
2	0	2	4	6	8	10	12	14	16	18	20
3	0	3	6	9	12	15	18	21	24	27	30
4	0	4	8	12	16	20	24	28	32	36	40
5	0	5	10	15	20	25	30	35	40	45	50
6	0	6	12	18	24	30	36	42	48	54	60
7	0	7	14	21	28	35	42	49	56	63	70
8	0	8	16	24	32	40	48	56	64	72	80
9	0	9	18	27	36	45	54	63	72	81	90
10	0	10	20	30	40	50	60	70	80	90	100

To find 7×9, you can find 7×10 and then subtract 7.
To find 8×9, you can find 8×10 and then subtract 8.

- What can you do to find 6×9?

Now try these.

21. $9 \times 8 = n$ **24.** $9 \times 7 = n$ **27.** $7 \times 9 = n$ **30.** $5 \times 9 = n$

22. $4 \times 9 = n$ **25.** $9 \times 9 = n$ **28.** $9 \times 6 = n$ **31.** $3 \times 9 = n$

23. $9 \times 2 = n$ **26.** $6 \times 9 = n$ **29.** $8 \times 9 = n$ **32.** $9 \times 1 = n$

What happens when you add up $9 \times 8 = 72$
the digits in the answer to 9×8? $7 + 2 = 9$ The sum of the digits is 9.

33. Add up the digits in each answer for problems 22 through 32.

1. Copy and complete this multiplication table.

How many facts do you know?

- Do you know the 0, 1, 2, and 10 facts? If you do, cross off the 0, 1, 2, and 10 columns and the 0, 1, 2, and 10 rows.
- Do you know the 5 and 9 facts? If you do, cross off the 5 and 9 rows and columns.

If you do not know these facts, practice them!

X	0	1	2	3	4	5	6	7	8	9	10
0	0	0									
1		1									
2		2	4	6		10	12	14			
3				9	12	15		21			
4								28	32		
5									40		
6								42	48		
7								49			
8							48	56			
9							54				
10							60	70			

Do you remember these?

2. $7 \times 8 = n$ **4.** $8 \times 7 = n$

3. $6 \times 7 = n$ **5.** $7 \times 6 = n$

There are 121 facts listed on the multiplication table.

- How many do you know?
- How many are left to learn?

Help a friend learn the facts.

Are You Shiny or Rusty?

Very shiny	45 or more right
Shiny	40–44 right
A bit rusty	35–39 right
Rusty	Less than 35 right

Multiply to solve for n.

1. $5 \times 8 = n$
2. $4 \times 9 = n$
3. $7 \times 8 = n$
4. $6 \times 7 = n$
5. $10 \times 5 = n$
6. $7 \times 0 = n$
7. $8 \times 9 = n$
8. $6 \times 9 = n$
9. $10 \times 6 = n$
10. $5 \times 6 = n$

11. $0 \times 8 = n$
12. $1 \times 8 = n$
13. $2 \times 8 = n$
14. $7 \times 2 = n$
15. $2 \times 9 = n$
16. $8 \times 7 = n$
17. $7 \times 6 = n$
18. $5 \times 5 = n$
19. $9 \times 9 = n$
20. $9 \times 10 = n$

21. $5 \times 4 = n$
22. $7 \times 5 = n$
23. $2 \times 5 = n$
24. $9 \times 5 = n$
25. $0 \times 9 = n$
26. $1 \times 9 = n$
27. $3 \times 9 = n$
28. $2 \times 2 = n$
29. $2 \times 4 = n$
30. $2 \times 7 = n$

31. $1 \times 5 = n$
32. $5 \times 3 = n$
33. $5 \times 9 = n$
34. $9 \times 2 = n$
35. $9 \times 3 = n$
36. $9 \times 4 = n$
37. $9 \times 8 = n$
38. $10 \times 7 = n$
39. $10 \times 8 = n$
40. $2 \times 6 = n$

Multiply.

41. $\begin{array}{r} 9 \\ \times\ 6 \\ \hline \end{array}$
42. $\begin{array}{r} 2 \\ \times\ 1 \\ \hline \end{array}$
43. $\begin{array}{r} 9 \\ \times\ 7 \\ \hline \end{array}$
44. $\begin{array}{r} 2 \\ \times\ 6 \\ \hline \end{array}$
45. $\begin{array}{r} 5 \\ \times\ 2 \\ \hline \end{array}$

46. $\begin{array}{r} 5 \\ \times\ 7 \\ \hline \end{array}$
47. $\begin{array}{r} 5 \\ \times\ 10 \\ \hline \end{array}$
48. $\begin{array}{r} 10 \\ \times\ 5 \\ \hline \end{array}$
49. $\begin{array}{r} 0 \\ \times\ 10 \\ \hline \end{array}$
50. $\begin{array}{r} 2 \\ \times\ 0 \\ \hline \end{array}$

A **right angle** looks like this:

These are right angles: These are not right angles:

- Can you find some right angles in your classroom?
- Can you find some angles in your classroom that are not right angles?

A triangle that has a right angle is called a **right triangle.**

These are
right triangles:

These are not
right triangles:

The ancient Greeks found
something very interesting
about right triangles. They
found it by looking at squares
on the sides of the triangles.
Look at this triangle and the
3 squares. See if you find
anything interesting.

3 cm

5 cm

4 cm

1. What is the area of the red square?
2. What is the area of the blue square?
3. What is the area of the red square
   plus the area of the blue square?
4. What is the area of the green square?

Each small box is 1 square centimeter.

- Does the triangle have a right angle?
- What is the area of the red square?
- What is the area of the blue square?
- What is the area of the red square plus the area of the blue square?
- What is the area of the green square?
  (Hint: Count the square centimeters. Pair the half squares to make whole squares.)

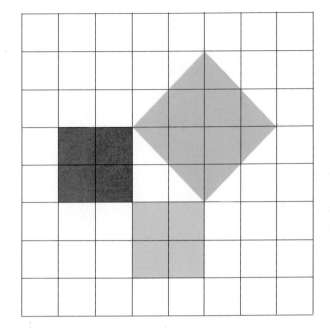

Using graph paper, try this experiment yourself.

To find the area of a square, multiply the length of a side by itself.

Complete the charts.

	Length of Side	Area of Square
1.	1 cm	▦
2.	2 cm	▦
3.	3 cm	▦
4.	4 cm	▦
5.	5 cm	▦

	Length of Side	Area of Square
6.	6 cm	▦
7.	7 cm	▦
8.	8 cm	▦
9.	9 cm	▦
10.	10 cm	▦

ADD THE PRODUCTS GAME

Players: 2 or more
Materials: Two 0–5 cubes
Object: To score a total of 50 or more

Rules
1. Take turns rolling both cubes.
2. On each turn, find the product of the 2 numbers you roll.
3. Add the product to your last score.

If your score was:	And you rolled:	Your new score would be:
12	3 2	18
36	4 0	36
25	5 1	30

4. The first player whose score totals 50 or more is the winner.

Other Ways to Play This Game

1. Use one 0–5 and one 5–10 cube. Try to score a total of 150 or more.
2. Use two 5–10 cubes. Try to score a total of 450 or more.

Can you think of other ways to play this game?

Multiples of 3 can be found by counting by 3s from a product you know.

Example: $3 \times 7 = n$ Let's say you know that $3 \times 6 = 18$.
Then 3×7 is 18 and 3 more.
So $3 \times 7 = 18 + 3 = 21$.

Multiples of 6 can be found by doubling multiples of 3, since 6 is twice 3.

Example: $6 \times 7 = n$ Let's say you know that $3 \times 7 = 21$.
Then 6×7 is twice 3×7.
So $6 \times 7 = 21 + 21 = 42$.

Multiples of 4 can be found by doubling multiples of 2.

Example: $4 \times 7 = n$ Let's say you know that $2 \times 7 = 14$.
Then 4×7 is twice 2×7.
So $4 \times 7 = 14 + 14 = 28$.

Multiples of 8 can be found by doubling multiples of 4.

Example: $8 \times 9 = n$ Let's say you know that $4 \times 9 = 36$.
Then 8×9 is twice 4×9.
So $8 \times 9 = 36 + 36 = 72$.

Multiply.

1. $4 \times 3 = n$	7. $4 \times 6 = n$	13. $6 \times 4 = n$	19. $8 \times 4 = n$
2. $3 \times 6 = n$	8. $6 \times 6 = n$	14. $9 \times 4 = n$	20. $6 \times 8 = n$
3. $7 \times 3 = n$	9. $7 \times 6 = n$	15. $8 \times 7 = n$	21. $9 \times 8 = n$
4. $8 \times 3 = n$	10. $8 \times 6 = n$	16. $4 \times 7 = n$	22. $8 \times 0 = n$
5. $9 \times 3 = n$	11. $9 \times 6 = n$	17. $4 \times 5 = n$	23. $5 \times 8 = n$
6. $3 \times 9 = n$	12. $5 \times 6 = n$	18. $8 \times 8 = n$	24. $10 \times 8 = n$

MONEY MATTERS

Portia and Mark had the idea of starting a club. Manolita, Ferdie, and Willy joined it. They needed a clubhouse. Mr. Breezy said they could use a shed in his backyard, but they would have to get a new door for it.

"How much will a door cost?" Portia asked.

"You should be able to get a used door for about $10," said Mr. Breezy.

Where could they get $10? "Let's put on a show," said Ferdie. "We'll make people pay money to see it."

Everyone thought that was a good idea. The children found funny clothes to wear. They made a stage by laying an old door on top of some boxes. They cut up pieces of paper and made ten $1 tickets.

Ten people came to the show. Portia sang. Mark told jokes. Manolita did magic tricks. Ferdie danced. And Willy sold tickets. Everyone liked the show. When it was over, the children rushed to Willy's ticket booth.

"I sold every ticket," Willy said proudly.

"How much money do we have?" the others asked.

"Ten cents," said Willy.

"Just a minute," said Mark. "We made ten $1 tickets. You said you sold all of them."

"That's right," said Willy. "I sold them for a penny apiece. Here's the money."

"A penny apiece!" they all shouted. "Tickets were supposed to be a dollar apiece!"

"Nobody told me that," Willy said. "I charged what I thought they were worth. I didn't think a little piece of paper was worth a dollar. I figured each ticket cost us about a penny. So that's what I charged."

The children all sat down sadly on their stage. "Now we'll never get a door," Ferdie moaned.

"Yes, we will," said Mark.

1. How much money would the children have made if Willy had sold all the tickets for the amount planned?

2. Perhaps they wouldn't have made any money at all if Willy had asked as much as he was supposed to for the tickets. How could that be?

3. Do you agree with Willy that it wouldn't be fair to sell tickets for a dollar when they cost only about a penny to make? Why or why not?

4. How could Mark be so sure they will get a door?

How Fast Are You?

Extra fast
Very fast
Fast
Almost fast

Are You Shiny or Rusty?

Very shiny	45 or more right
Shiny	40–44 right
A bit rusty	35–39 right
Rusty	Less than 35 right

Multiply to solve for n.

1. $5 \times 3 = n$	9. $4 \times 4 = n$	17. $4 \times 6 = n$	25. $n = 3 \times 6$
2. $n = 4 \times 5$	10. $10 \times 7 = n$	18. $6 \times 7 = n$	26. $10 \times 1 = n$
3. $8 \times 2 = n$	11. $n = 4 \times 3$	19. $n = 9 \times 2$	27. $6 \times 7 = n$
4. $5 \times 10 = n$	12. $3 \times 1 = n$	20. $1 \times 8 = n$	28. $n = 6 \times 10$
5. $n = 2 \times 7$	13. $n = 2 \times 8$	21. $8 \times 5 = n$	29. $9 \times 5 = n$
6. $7 \times 1 = n$	14. $7 \times 8 = n$	22. $n = 7 \times 0$	30. $8 \times 8 = n$
7. $0 \times 8 = n$	15. $5 \times 0 = n$	23. $3 \times 7 = n$	
8. $n = 2 \times 5$	16. $n = 6 \times 5$	24. $5 \times 7 = n$	

Multiply.

31.	32.	33.	34.	35.
5	9	7	9	9
$\times 5$	$\times 8$	$\times 8$	$\times 6$	$\times 9$

36.	37.	38.	39.	40.
8	5	6	7	6
$\times 9$	$\times 9$	$\times 7$	$\times 7$	$\times 6$

41. 0×6	43. 2×7	45. 5×3	47. 3×9	49. 8×3
42. 9×4	44. 4×7	46. 9×7	48. 6×8	50. 8×4

On your paper, circle the answers that took you a long
time and the ones you got wrong. Make flash cards for
these facts and practice them.

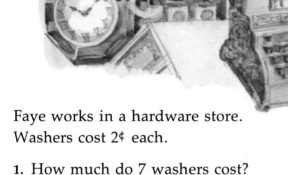

Faye works in a hardware store.
Washers cost 2¢ each.

1. How much do 7 washers cost?

2. How much do 9 washers cost?

3. Faye made a chart so she won't have to multiply each time she sells washers. Her chart looks like this:

Washer Chart

	0	1	2	3	4	5	6	7	8	9	10
×2	0	2	4								

Copy and complete the chart.

4. Brass nails also cost 2¢ each. Faye decides to make a nail chart. What will it look like? Do you think she should make the chart?

5. Small springs cost 7¢ each. Make a chart for springs like Faye's chart for washers.

6. Lag bolts cost 7¢ each. Either make a chart for lag bolts or write what you could use instead.

7. Sets of hooks and eyes cost 9¢ each. Make a hook-and-eye chart.

8. Make a chart for sandpaper that costs 10¢ a sheet.

Copy and complete the charts.

1. (×5)

In	Out
1	5
2	▓
3	▓
4	▓
5	▓

2. (×2)

In	Out
0	▓
2	▓
4	▓
6	▓
8	▓

3. (×4)

In	Out
0	▓
2	▓
4	▓
6	▓
8	▓

4. (×3)

In	Out
8	▓
7	▓
6	▓
5	▓
4	▓

5. (×6)

In	Out
8	▓
7	▓
6	▓
5	▓
4	▓

6. (×10)

In	Out
3	▓
9	▓
6	▓
4	▓
2	▓

7. (×7)

In	Out
0	▓
2	▓
4	▓
6	▓
8	▓

8. (×8)

In	Out
8	▓
4	▓
2	▓
1	▓
0	▓

9. (×9)

In	Out
9	▓
8	▓
7	▓
6	▓
5	▓

What is the area of each rectangle?

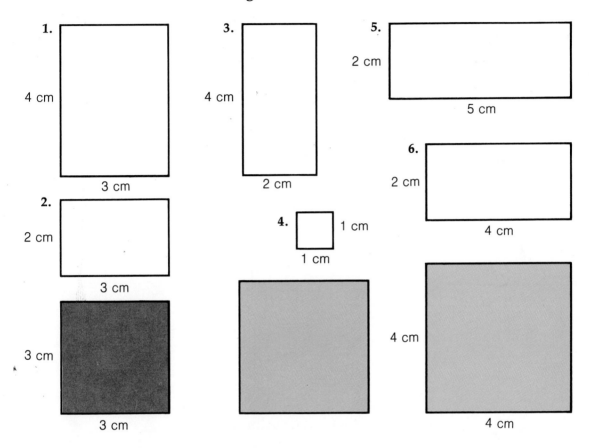

1. 4 cm, 3 cm

2. 2 cm, 3 cm

3. 4 cm, 2 cm

4. 1 cm, 1 cm

5. 2 cm, 5 cm

6. 2 cm, 4 cm

3 cm, 3 cm

4 cm

4 cm, 4 cm

7. What is the area of the red square?
8. What is the area of the blue square?

Each side of the green square is between 3 and 4 centimeters long.

9. Can the area of the green square be less than 9 square centimeters?
10. Can the area of the green square be more than 16 square centimeters?
Trace the green square. Compare its area with the areas of the red and blue squares.

97

Albert is thinking of a rectangle. He says: "It is at least 4 centimeters long, but no more than 5 centimeters long. It is at least 1 centimeter wide, but no more than 2 centimeters wide."

Albert can't be thinking of this rectangle, because it is less than 4 cm long.

He can't be thinking of this rectangle, because it is more than 2 cm wide.

He might be thinking of this rectangle.

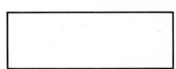

Which of these rectangles can be the one Albert is thinking of? Write **yes** or **no** for each one. Use a centimeter ruler to measure.

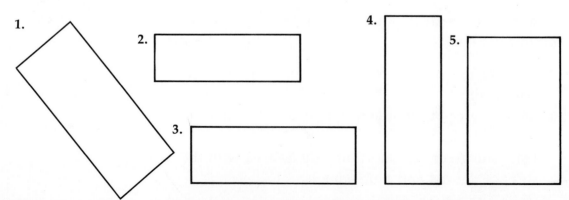

98

Elena and Danny had an argument about whose garden was bigger. They decided to measure. Elena's garden is at least 9 meters long, but no more than 10 meters long. It is at least 6 meters wide, but no more than 7 meters wide.

1. Draw a picture of the smallest garden Elena might have.
2. What is the smallest area Elena's garden could be?
3. Draw a picture of the largest garden Elena might have.
4. What is the largest area Elena's garden could be?

Danny's garden is at least 8 meters long, but no more than 9 meters long. It is at least 7 meters, but no more than 8 meters, wide.

5. Draw a picture of the smallest garden Danny might have.
6. What is the smallest area Danny's garden could be?
7. Draw a picture of the largest garden Danny might have.
8. What is the largest area Danny's garden could be?
9. Can you tell whose garden has the greater area, Elena's or Danny's?

Complete this chart about other children's gardens.

	Whose Garden	Length (meters)		Width (meters)		Area (square meters)	
		At Least	No More Than	At Least	No More Than	At Least	No More Than
10.	Anita's	9	10	4	5	36	▨
11.	Larry's	7	8	7	8	▨	▨
12.	Celia's	8	9	5	6	▨	▨
13.	Jesse's	6	7	5	6	▨	▨

MONEY MATTERS   Part 2

Mr. Mudanza wondered why there were $1 bills, $2 bills, $5 bills, and $10 bills, but not $3, $4, $6, $7, $8, and $9 bills. "I think I could change that a little," he said.

The next day he went to a bookstore to buy a book that cost $6. "Here's a $6 bill," he said to the clerk.

"Something is wrong with this bill," said the clerk. "It's thicker and stiffer than it should be. It says $5 on one side and $1 on the other. This is a fake bill! Police! Police!"

"Calm down," said Mr. Mudanza. "You wanted $6 and I gave you $6. I don't know what you're so worried about. By the way, I think I'll take this magazine, too. How much is it?"

"It's $1."

"Then give me back my $6 bill and I'll give you $7," said Mr. Mudanza.

The clerk was glad to give Mr. Mudanza back his $6 bill. But the clerk was not glad when Mr. Mudanza said, "Here's a $7 bill instead."

"This bill is worse then the other one," said the clerk. "It's even thicker and stiffer. And it still says $5 on one side and $1 on the other side. You can't tell me this makes $7!"

"Not everything shows," said Mr. Mudanza. "Why do you think the $7 bill is thicker than the $6 bill?"

1. How did Mr. Mudanza make his $6 bill?

2. Why was his $6 bill thinner than his $7 bill?

3. Challenge question: What are 5 different ways that Mr. Mudanza could make a $20 bill?

4. Detective question: How could Mr. Mudanza make a $7 bill that was no thicker than the $6 bill he made?

5. Do you think it would be a good idea to have $3, $4, $6, $7, $8, and $9 bills in addition to the bills we already have? Why or why not? What about $99 bills?

How Fast Are You?

Extra fast
Very fast
Fast
Almost fast

Are You Shiny or Rusty?

Very shiny	45 or more right
Shiny	40–44 right
A bit rusty	35–39 right
Rusty	Less than 35 right

Multiply to solve for n.

1. $6 \times 10 = n$
2. $4 \times 3 = n$
3. $6 \times 0 = n$
4. $3 \times 5 = n$
5. $6 \times 9 = n$
6. $2 \times 2 = n$
7. $5 \times 7 = n$
8. $3 \times 6 = n$

9. $9 \times 8 = n$
10. $5 \times 6 = n$
11. $6 \times 6 = n$
12. $2 \times 7 = n$
13. $4 \times 6 = n$
14. $10 \times 10 = n$
15. $6 \times 8 = n$
16. $7 \times 7 = n$

17. $2 \times 8 = n$
18. $5 \times 2 = n$
19. $7 \times 6 = n$
20. $7 \times 9 = n$
21. $8 \times 7 = n$
22. $2 \times 4 = n$
23. $7 \times 1 = n$

24. $3 \times 9 = n$
25. $3 \times 3 = n$
26. $8 \times 9 = n$
27. $9 \times 9 = n$
28. $0 \times 3 = n$
29. $5 \times 9 = n$
30. $9 \times 2 = n$

Multiply.

31.
$$\begin{array}{r} 5 \\ \times\ 0 \\ \hline \end{array}$$

32.
$$\begin{array}{r} 4 \\ \times\ 4 \\ \hline \end{array}$$

33.
$$\begin{array}{r} 2 \\ \times\ 3 \\ \hline \end{array}$$

34.
$$\begin{array}{r} 4 \\ \times\ 2 \\ \hline \end{array}$$

35.
$$\begin{array}{r} 1 \\ \times\ 8 \\ \hline \end{array}$$

36.
$$\begin{array}{r} 6 \\ \times\ 7 \\ \hline \end{array}$$

37.
$$\begin{array}{r} 10 \\ \times\ 2 \\ \hline \end{array}$$

38.
$$\begin{array}{r} 7 \\ \times\ 8 \\ \hline \end{array}$$

39.
$$\begin{array}{r} 0 \\ \times\ 9 \\ \hline \end{array}$$

40.
$$\begin{array}{r} 9 \\ \times\ 7 \\ \hline \end{array}$$

41.
$$\begin{array}{r} 8 \\ \times\ 6 \\ \hline \end{array}$$

42.
$$\begin{array}{r} 2 \\ \times\ 6 \\ \hline \end{array}$$

43.
$$\begin{array}{r} 8 \\ \times\ 8 \\ \hline \end{array}$$

44.
$$\begin{array}{r} 7 \\ \times\ 5 \\ \hline \end{array}$$

45.
$$\begin{array}{r} 5 \\ \times\ 8 \\ \hline \end{array}$$

46.
$$\begin{array}{r} 4 \\ \times\ 9 \\ \hline \end{array}$$

47.
$$\begin{array}{r} 5 \\ \times\ 5 \\ \hline \end{array}$$

48.
$$\begin{array}{r} 6 \\ \times\ 5 \\ \hline \end{array}$$

49.
$$\begin{array}{r} 3 \\ \times\ 7 \\ \hline \end{array}$$

50.
$$\begin{array}{r} 5 \\ \times\ 4 \\ \hline \end{array}$$

Susan's class is doing the Missing Factor Activity.

The product is 15.

What number does Susan have on her back?

In each case, write the number that Susan has on her back.

	Ed Has This Number	The Product Is	Susan Has This Number
1.	3	24	8
2.	6	18	
3.	9	45	
4.	5	50	
5.	4	36	
6.	7	49	
7.	2	18	
8.	10	10	
9.	1	8	
10.	0	0	

Look at problem 10 again. Can you tell which number Susan has? What numbers might she have?

Does the missing-term sentence help you solve the problem?

1. Gina earns $3 each time she mows her aunt's grass. How many times will she have to mow grass to earn the $15 she needs for a new tennis racquet?

   $n \times 3 = 15$

2. Jorge made 8 trips around the park on his bike. He rode a total of 24 kilometers. How long is each trip around the park?

   $8 \times n = 24$

3. A machine at Krispy Kreme Doughnuts cuts holes in the middle of 9 doughnuts every minute. How many minutes will it take the machine to cut holes in 90 doughnuts?

   $n \times 9 = 90$

4. Grant had $7 when he went to the ball game. He had $3 when he got home. How much did he spend?

   $7 - n = 3$

5. Each day, Katy listens to her radio for 4 hours. A battery will last in the radio for about 36 hours. About how many days can Katy listen to her radio before the battery goes dead?

   $4 \times n = 36$

6. Jared baked 21 cookies. He takes 3 cookies in his lunch every day. For how many days will he have cookies in his lunch?

   $3 \times n = 21$

Solve these problems.

1. Stacey is inviting 28 friends to her birthday party.
   a. She has 4 days to write all the invitations. If she writes 6 invitations each day, will she finish in time?
   b. If she writes 7 each day, will she finish in time?
   c. If she writes 8 each day, will she finish in time?

2. Every day, Tanya uses 4 slices of bread for her lunch sandwiches. A loaf of bread has 20 slices. How many days can Tanya make sandwiches from 1 loaf of bread?

3. Each day, Craig knits 10 centimeters on the scarf he's making. He wants the scarf to be 1 meter (100 centimeters) long. How many days will it take Craig to make his scarf?

Solve for n.

4. $9 \times n = 27$	10. $n \times 10 = 60$	16. $6 \times n = 30$
5. $3 \times n = 0$	11. $72 = 9 \times n$	17. $n \times 6 = 54$
6. $20 = n \times 10$	12. $48 = 8 \times n$	18. $7 \times n = 42$
7. $6 \times n = 48$	13. $n \times 8 = 72$	19. $3 \times n = 27$
8. $32 = n \times 8$	14. $5 \times n = 35$	20. $45 = n \times 5$
9. $5 \times n = 25$	15. $6 \times n = 36$	21. $81 = n \times 9$

1. Keith earns $3 each hour. Today he earned $18. How many hours did he work today?

2. María has to work only 3 hours to earn $18. How much does she earn each hour?

3. 8 children want to share 24 cookies equally. How many cookies should each child get?

4. When the Crickets and the Grasshoppers play football, they can score only by getting touchdowns and kicking extra points. Frankie Footer is the extra-point kicker for the Cricket football team. She never misses, so each time they get a touchdown, the Crickets get 7 points. Today they scored 42 points. How many touchdowns did they get?

5. Paul Fumbletoes kicks extra points for the Grasshopper football team. He always misses, so each touchdown is worth only 6 points. How many touchdowns do the Grasshoppers need to score 42 points?

6. In a game between the Crickets and the Grasshoppers, the final score was 56 to 54.
   a. Which team won?
   b. How many touchdowns did the winning team score?
   c. How many touchdowns did the losing team score?

Division is the opposite of multiplication, just as subtraction is the opposite of addition.

1. $8 + 6 = 14$, so $14 - 6 = ?$
2. $8 \times 6 = 48$, so $48 \div 6 = ?$
3. $56 = 7 \times 8$, so $56 \div 8 = ?$
4. $49 = 7 \times 7$, so $? = 49 \div 7$

Divide.

5. $10 \div 10 = n$ **11.** $72 \div 9 = n$ **17.** $63 \div 7 = n$
6. $20 \div 5 = n$ **12.** $35 \div 7 = n$ **18.** $n = 56 \div 8$
7. $n = 5 \div 1$ **13.** $72 \div 8 = n$ **19.** $64 \div 8 = n$
8. $n = 14 \div 7$ **14.** $60 \div 6 = n$ **20.** $80 \div 10 = n$
9. $42 \div 7 = n$ **15.** $n = 30 \div 5$ **21.** $n = 100 \div 10$
10. $40 \div 8 = n$ **16.** $45 \div 9 = n$ **22.** $81 \div 9 = n$

You know that the sign $\div$ means "divided by."

$\overline{)}$ is another symbol that has to do with division.

$\overline{)}$ means that division is to take place.

Example: $7\overline{)56}$
This means that we are going to divide 56 by 7. Write the answer as shown:

$$7\overline{)\overset{8}{56}}$$

Divide.

23. $5\overline{)50}$ **25.** $10\overline{)90}$ **27.** $3\overline{)21}$ **29.** $2\overline{)0}$

24. $7\overline{)63}$ **26.** $5\overline{)30}$ **28.** $5\overline{)40}$ **30.** $5\overline{)25}$

107

MONEY MATTERS

Mark, Portia, Willy, and Ferdie were all collecting coins. One day they got together to see who had the most money.

Mark had a stack of quarters that was 4 centimeters high.

Willy had a stack of dimes. It was about as high as Mark's stack.

Portia had a stack of nickels. Her stack was about twice as high as Mark's stack.

Ferdie had a stack of pennies. His stack was 4 times as high as Mark's stack.

Ferdie was excited. "I have the most because my stack is the highest."

"I have the most because quarters are worth the most," said Mark.

"I have the most because dimes are so thin," said Willy. "If you count my dimes and Mark's quarters, you'll find that I have more coins than he does."

Portia said, "I think I have the most. Don't forget that my stack is very high and I have nickels."

1. Copy and complete the bar graph to show the heights of the 4 stacks of money.

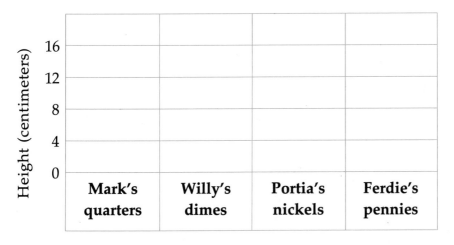

2. Superdetective questions: Who has the largest amount of money? The second largest amount of money? The third largest amount? And who has the smallest amount?

Add or subtract. Watch the signs.

1. $8 + 7 = n$.
2. $16 - 7 = n$
3. $10 - 10 = n$
4. $9 + 8 = n$

5. $12 = 3 + n$
6. $14 = 7 + n$
7. $n = 12 - 7$
8. $8 = n + 3$

9. $10 = 20 - n$
10. $18 - n = 9$
11. $16 - 0 = n$
12. $10 + n = 18$

Add or subtract. Use shortcuts when you can.

13. $\begin{array}{r} 25 \\ + 37 \\ \hline \end{array}$

16. $\begin{array}{r} 1000 \\ - 500 \\ \hline \end{array}$

19. $\begin{array}{r} 8216 \\ - 3216 \\ \hline \end{array}$

22. $\begin{array}{r} 250 \\ + 150 \\ \hline \end{array}$

14. $\begin{array}{r} 92 \\ - 35 \\ \hline \end{array}$

17. $\begin{array}{r} 76 \\ + 28 \\ \hline \end{array}$

20. $\begin{array}{r} 1711 \\ - 1699 \\ \hline \end{array}$

23. $\begin{array}{r} 800 \\ - 750 \\ \hline \end{array}$

15. $\begin{array}{r} 671 \\ - 234 \\ \hline \end{array}$

18. $\begin{array}{r} 197 \\ + 803 \\ \hline \end{array}$

21. $\begin{array}{r} 7345 \\ - 28 \\ \hline \end{array}$

24. $\begin{array}{r} 800 \\ - 799 \\ \hline \end{array}$

Multiply or divide. Watch the signs.

25. $9 \times 4 = n$
26. $64 \div 8 = n$
27. $8 \times 7 = n$
28. $18 \div 9 = n$

29. $28 \div 4 = n$
30. $27 \div 3 = n$
31. $10 \times 9 = n$
32. $8 \times n = 56$

33. $9 \div n = 3$
34. $42 = n \times 7$
35. $36 = 4 \times n$
36. $100 = n \times 10$

37. $81 \div 9 = n$
38. $63 \div n = 9$
39. $5 = 45 \div n$
40. $42 \div 6 = n$

41. $n \times 8 = 32$
42. $n \times 8 = 40$
43. $9 \times n = 63$
44. $9 \times n = 90$

45. $24 \div n = 6$
46. $24 \div n = 4$
47. $n \times 3 = 21$
48. $54 \div n = 9$

Sasha, Tina, Vicky, and Liza hunted for treasure on the beach. When they found valuable things, they sold them. Sometimes they found money. At the end of each week they divided all their money equally. Use play money to act out what they did.

1. The first week, they found some shells and coral. They sold these for $27. They also found $5 in cash.
   a. How much money did they get altogether?
   b. How much money should each girl get?

2. The second week, they found more shells and an old coin. They sold these for $31. They also found $5 in cash.
   a. How much money did they get altogether?
   b. How much money should each of them get?

3. The third week, they found some driftwood and 3 old bottles. They sold these for $23. They also found $7 in cash.
   a. How much money did they get altogether?
   b. How much money should each of them get?

There are several good answers to the last question. Each person can get $7, leaving $2. They can put the $2 in the fund for next week. Or they can divide it equally. Each person would get an extra half dollar (50 cents). Or they could spend the $2 on something they all can use, such as a water jug or a metal detector.

7 children want to divide 56 cents equally.
How much will each child get?

$$7\overline{)56}^{8}$$

7 children want to divide 57 cents equally.
How much will each child get?

$$7\overline{)57}$$

After each child gets 8 cents, there is still 1 cent left over. Sometimes we wish to divide a whole number of things equally but cannot do so without something left over, or remaining. We can write:

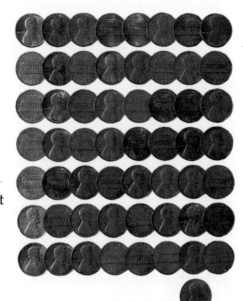

$$7\overline{)57}^{8\ R1}$$

When we read this answer, we say, "8 remainder 1."

6 children want to divide 40 cents equally.
How much will each child get? How much will be left over?

$$6\overline{)40}^{6\ R4}$$

Each child gets 6 cents, and there are 4 cents remaining.

Divide. Watch for remainders.

1. $8\overline{)48}$ 5. $5\overline{)37}$ 9. $3\overline{)29}$ 13. $6\overline{)63}$ 17. $9\overline{)47}$

2. $8\overline{)51}$ 6. $7\overline{)43}$ 10. $6\overline{)36}$ 14. $8\overline{)34}$ 18. $5\overline{)45}$

3. $9\overline{)54}$ 7. $3\overline{)26}$ 11. $5\overline{)47}$ 15. $10\overline{)85}$ 19. $7\overline{)54}$

4. $9\overline{)58}$ 8. $10\overline{)46}$ 12. $4\overline{)38}$ 16. $2\overline{)15}$ 20. $4\overline{)26}$

Divide.

1. 4)30	**6.** 6)20	**11.** 4)19	**16.** 9)56	**21.** 5)28
2. 7)29	**7.** 5)22	**12.** 8)39	**17.** 7)56	**22.** 6)34
3. 8)43	**8.** 2)15	**13.** 5)17	**18.** 3)16	**23.** 10)41
4. 5)38	**9.** 9)73	**14.** 5)25	**19.** 2)12	**24.** 8)12
5. 4)36	**10.** 10)26	**15.** 6)50	**20.** 1)8	**25.** 7)51

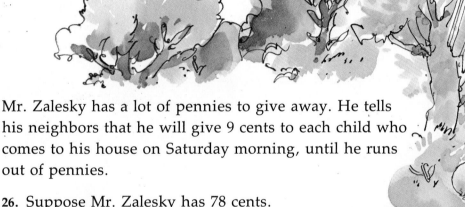

Mr. Zalesky has a lot of pennies to give away. He tells his neighbors that he will give 9 cents to each child who comes to his house on Saturday morning, until he runs out of pennies.

26. Suppose Mr. Zalesky has 78 cents.
 a. How many children will get 9 cents?
 b. How many cents will be left?

27. Suppose Mr. Zalesky has 83 cents.
 a. How many children will get 9 cents?
 b. How many cents will be left?

28. Suppose he has 63 cents.
 a. How many children will get 9 cents?
 b. How many cents will be left?

29. Suppose he has 97 cents.
 a. How many children will get 9 cents?
 b. How many cents will be left?

MONEY MATTERS

Mr. Sleeby is very honest, but sometimes he forgets to pay for things. One day he had $2.00 when he went out shopping. He bought a carton of eggs, some nails, and a mousetrap. When he got home, he had $1.10 left.

"I think I forgot to pay someone," he said. "Let's see. The eggs were marked 90¢. The mousetrap was marked 40¢. And the bag of nails was marked 50¢."

Mr. Sleeby told Loretta the Letter Carrier about his problem. She said, "Since you forgot to pay for something, then it must be the eggs."

"I'm amazed that you can tell what I forgot, just by looking at the eggs," said Mr. Sleeby. But he took Loretta's word for it and went to pay the grocer 90¢.

"What's this for?" asked the grocer. "I know that you paid for those eggs yesterday. I remember you gave me a $2 bill."

"This is very confusing," said Mr. Sleeby. As he walked along the street, he counted his money again.

"What's the matter, Mr. Sleeby?" asked a woman. She was watching him from the door of her hardware shop. "Are you worrying about the 90¢ you owe me?"

1. If Mr. Sleeby had paid for everything, how much money would he have left?

2. Why would Loretta the Letter Carrier think Mr. Sleeby had forgotten to pay for the eggs? Why didn't she guess the nails or the mousetrap?

3. How could Mr. Sleeby owe the woman at the hardware shop 90¢?

4. Why did Loretta give Mr. Sleeby the wrong answer to his problem?

A MEDICAL PROBLEM

Act out and discuss this story. As you turn to similar stories (those having purple color bars), follow the same routine.

Brenda and her friends like to visit Mrs. Martin, the dog trainer.

"May we help feed your dogs?" the children asked.

"Yes," said Mrs. Martin. "But first I have to mix some medicine in their food. All the dogs have sore throats from barking so much. You can help me figure out how much medicine to mix in. How much is $4 \times 3 + 2$?"

"It's 14," said Brenda, Timmy, and Cindy.

"It's 20," said Elise and Tom.

The children argued about which answer was right, but they couldn't decide. Finally Cindy said, "Why don't you tell us the whole problem?"

"It doesn't seem like a very hard problem," Mrs. Martin said. "I have to give 4 spoonfuls of medicine to each dog. I have 3 black dogs and 2 brown dogs. That is $4 \times 3 + 2$, right?"

"Now we know what the right answer is," they all said.

- How could Brenda, Timmy, and Cindy have gotten the answer 14?
- How could Elise and Tom get 20?
- Which is the right answer to Mrs. Martin's problem? Why?
- Can you think of a way to ask the question about 4, 3, and 2 so that people would know which way to answer it?

Here is a way to write the problem that means add 3 and 2, then multiply by 4:

$$4 \times (3 + 2)$$

Here is a way to write the problem that means multiply 4×3 and then add 2:

$$(4 \times 3) + 2$$

Rule: Do the operations inside the parentheses first.

$$4 \times (3 + 2) = 4 \times 5 = 20$$
$$(4 \times 3) + 2 = 12 + 2 = 14$$

There is another rule we will use: If a problem can be worked from left to right, we won't have to put in parentheses. Mrs. Martin had to put in parentheses, because the way to get the right answer is to calculate this:

$$4 \times (3 + 2)$$

Here are some examples that show how these rules work.

a. $4 \times 3 + 2 = 12 + 2 = 14$
b. $(6 - 3) \times 6 + 1 = 3 \times 6 + 1 = 18 + 1 = 19$
c. $3 \times 4 \times (7 - 5) - 6 = 3 \times 4 \times 2 - 6 = 24 - 6 = 18$
d. $(4 \times 7) + (4 \times 3) = 28 + 12 = 40$

We do operations inside the parentheses first.

Examples

a. $40 \div (5 + 3) = 40 \div 8 = 5$

b. $(40 \div 5) + 3 = 8 + 3 = 11$

c. $12 - (8 - 3) = 12 - 5 = 7$

d. $(12 - 8) - 3 = 4 - 3 = 1$

e. $7 \times (5 + 4) = 7 \times 9 = 63$

f. $(7 \times 5) + 4 = 35 + 4 = 39$

g. $32 \div (8 \div 2) = 32 \div 4 = 8$

h. $(32 \div 8) \div 2 = 4 \div 2 = 2$

Solve for n. Watch the parentheses. Watch the signs.

1. $24 \div (6 \div 2) = n$

2. $(24 \div 6) \div 2 = n$

3. $28 - (8 \div 4) = n$

4. $(28 - 8) \div 4 = n$

5. $7 \times (4 + 6) = n$

6. $(7 \times 4) + 6 = n$

7. $16 + (7 + 5) = n$

8. $(16 + 7) + 5 = n$

9. $16 - (7 - 5) = n$

10. $(16 - 7) - 5 = n$

11. $(2 \times 3) \times 3 = n$

12. $2 \times (3 \times 3) = n$

13. $(18 \div 6) \div 3 = n$

14. $18 \div (6 \div 3) = n$

15. $(25 - 12) - (20 - 7) = n$

16. $4 \times (6 - 6) = n$

For each problem below, see how many different answers you can get by putting parentheses in different places. The first 2 have been done for you.

17. $5 + 4 \times 3 = n$

$(5 + 4) \times 3 = 27$

$5 + (4 \times 3) = 17$

There are 2 answers.

18. $2 \times 10 \div 2 = n$

$(2 \times 10) \div 2 = 10$

$2 \times (10 \div 2) = 10$

There is 1 answer.

19. $17 - 10 + 1 = n$

20. $16 + 3 \times 2 = n$

21. $2 \times 3 \times 4 = n$

22. $2 \times 3 + 4 = n$

23. $16 \div 4 \times 2 = n$

24. $12 - 2 \times 6 = n$

25. $4 \times 6 \div 3 = n$

26. $16 - 4 \times 2 = n$

27. $12 - 2 \times 3 = n$

CUBO

Players: 2 or more
Materials: Two 0–5 cubes, two 5–10 cubes
Object: To score as close to 21 as possible

Rules
1. Roll all 4 cubes on each turn.
2. Use any combination of the 4 operations (addition, subtraction, multiplication, and division) on the numbers rolled. Use the number on each cube once and only once. (If 2 cubes have the same number, you must use both.)

If you rolled:	You could make these numbers:	By doing these operations, for example:
	19	6 − 3 = 3; 3 × 6 = 18; 18 + 1 = 19
3, 6, 6, 1	23	3 × 6 = 18; 18 + 6 = 24; 24 − 1 = 23
	21	6 − 1 = 5; 5 × 3 = 15; 15 + 6 = 21
	21	6 − 3 = 3; 6 + 1 = 7; 3 × 7 = 21

3. The player who scores 21 or closest to it is the winner of the round.

Other Ways to Play This Game

1. Make the goal a number other than 21.
2. Use different combinations of cubes.
3. Use more than or fewer than 4 cubes.

1. Mike received $6.75 on his birthday. 3 days later he got a belated birthday card with $3 in it. How much money did Mike receive altogether for his birthday?

2. The Circle K Ranch is 5 kilometers wide. What is the area of the ranch?

3. Melissa has 35 customers on her paper route. She began her route with 35 papers and now has 10 left. How many more papers does she have to deliver?

4. Jeff has a room shaped like a rectangle. It is 4 meters long and 3 meters wide. What is the area of the floor in Jeff's room?

5. Last spring the ecology club planted 108 tree seedlings. 19 seedlings didn't survive the cold winter. How many trees made it through the winter?

6. Robin can ride 1 kilometer on her bike in about 4 minutes. About how long will it take her to ride to Green Lake, a distance of 8 kilometers?

7. In 1950, the population of the state of Minnesota was 2,982,483. In 1960, the population was 3,413,864. About how many people moved to Minnesota between 1950 and 1960?

8. Burt wants to put new carpeting in his room. He measured the floor and found that it is a square with sides 4 meters long. He can buy a rectangular piece of carpet that is 8 meters long and 3 meters wide. If he cuts up the carpet, does he have enough to cover his floor completely?

9. The balance in Alice's bank account was $78.27. She withdrew $49.56 to buy a new bicycle. What is the present balance in her account?

10. Bobby's mother bought 8 cans of juice for a party. Each can serves 7 people. How many people can she serve with the juice she bought?

11. Sheila has invited 26 people to a party. She wants to give each person a party hat. Hats come in packages of 10. How many packages does she need to buy?

12. Manuel saved $27 to spend on vacation. He wants to spend the same amount each of the 3 weeks of his vacation. How much should he spend each week?

Multiply.

1. 9×6 3. 8×7 5. 7×5 7. 9×3

2. 3×6 4. 5×8 6. 9×8 8. 4×5

Divide. Don't forget remainders.

9. $9 \overline{)18}$ 11. $4 \overline{)36}$ 13. $7 \overline{)56}$ 15. $3 \overline{)26}$

10. $6 \overline{)59}$ 12. $7 \overline{)21}$ 14. $4 \overline{)37}$ 16. $4 \overline{)32}$

17. $10 \div 2$ 18. $27 \div 9$ 19. $49 \div 7$ 20. $15 \div 3$

Add or subtract to solve.

21. $\begin{array}{r} 7 \\ + 5 \\ \hline \end{array}$ 22. $\begin{array}{r} 12 \\ - 9 \\ \hline \end{array}$ 23. $\begin{array}{r} 6 \\ + 3 \\ \hline \end{array}$ 24. $\begin{array}{r} 6 \\ - 3 \\ \hline \end{array}$

25. $\begin{array}{r} 15 \\ - 5 \\ \hline \end{array}$ 26. $\begin{array}{r} 8 \\ + 7 \\ \hline \end{array}$ 27. $\begin{array}{r} 7 \\ + 6 \\ \hline \end{array}$ 28. $\begin{array}{r} 9 \\ - 5 \\ \hline \end{array}$

Solve for n. Watch the signs.

29. $n - 4 = 12$ 31. $6 \times 8 = n$ 33. $n = 36 + 25$ 35. $25 \div 5 = n$

30. $n = 14 - 13$ 32. $4 = 20 \div n$ 34. $7 + n = 23$ 36. $8 \times 5 = n$

Add or subtract. Watch the signs.

37. $\begin{array}{r} 73 \\ + 96 \\ \hline \end{array}$ 38. $\begin{array}{r} 97 \\ - 38 \\ \hline \end{array}$ 39. $\begin{array}{r} 24 \\ + 56 \\ \hline \end{array}$

Add or subtract. Watch the signs.

| **40.** | 605
$-\ 416$ | **41.** | 860
$+\ 320$ | **42.** | 197
$-\ \ 45$ |

43. Erica bought 8 pencils. They cost 9¢ each. She gave the storekeeper 75¢. How much change should she get?

44. a. What is the area of a rectangular garden that is 8 meters long and 6 meters wide?
   b. Is the area of this garden larger or smaller than the area of a garden that is 7 meters long and 7 meters wide?

45. About what is the length of a string that is made by tying two 9-meter strings together?

46. William paid 48¢ for 6 plums. How much did each plum cost?

47. A kite string is about 65 meters long. Another string that is about 75 meters long is tied to it. About how long is the combined string?

48. Mrs. Sandina knows that the area of her rug is between 50 and 60 square meters and that the length of the rug is 9 meters. She also knows that the width of the rug is a whole number of meters. What is the width?

49. Teresa has 47 apples to give to 5 children.
   a. How many apples will each child get?
   b. How many apples will be left over?

50. Vance has 47 apples. He wants to give an equal number of apples to each of 4 children. But he also wants to keep at least 10 for himself.
   a. How many would he give to each child?
   b. How many would he keep for himself?

Solve for n.

1. $2 \times 10 = n$ 6. $4 \times n = 28$ 11. $6 \times 8 = n$

2. $n = 8 \times 9$ 7. $5 \times 9 = n$ 12. $n = 5 \times 5$

3. $5 \times 9 = n$ 8. $64 = 8 \times n$ 13. $1 \times n = 7$

4. $n \times 7 = 35$ 9. $9 \times n = 54$ 14. $6 \times 5 = n$

5. $24 = 4 \times n$ 10. $80 = n \times 10$ 15. $3 \times n = 18$

Solve for n. Watch the parentheses. Watch the signs.

16. $4 \times (3 + 5) = n$ 21. $17 - (9 - 5) = n$

17. $n = (3 \times 5) + (3 \times 4)$ 22. $n = (4 + 8) - 3$

18. $6 + (5 \times 2) = n$ 23. $6 \times (8 - 5) = n$

19. $(17 - 9) - 5 = n$ 24. $8 \times (2 + 7) = n$

20. $n = 4 \times (3 - 1)$ 25. $n = 5 + (3 \times 4)$

Solve for n. Watch the signs.

26. $n = 24 - 8$ 29. $n \div 3 = 7$ 32. $n \times 7 = 63$

27. $7 \times n = 56$ 30. $56 - n = 18$ 33. $n = 82 - 39$

28. $8 + 3 = n$ 31. $15 + 6 = n$ 34. $n + 18 = 97$

Divide to solve for n.

35. $15 \div 3 = n$ 38. $n = 35 \div 7$ 41. $24 \div 8 = n$

36. $n = 27 \div 9$ 39. $n = 72 \div 9$ 42. $n = 54 \div 9$

37. $30 \div 10 = n$ 40. $49 \div 7 = n$ 43. $42 \div 6 = n$

Divide. Watch the remainders.

44. $7\overline{)49}$ 47. $5\overline{)40}$ 50. $6\overline{)24}$ 53. $8\overline{)68}$

45. $7\overline{)39}$ 48. $7\overline{)50}$ 51. $3\overline{)24}$ 54. $4\overline{)35}$

46. $8\overline{)72}$ 49. $5\overline{)36}$ 52. $6\overline{)18}$ 55. $2\overline{)11}$

Solve these problems.

56. Andrew bought 3 pencils for 9¢ each at the department store. How much did they cost altogether?
57. Julia sells apples at a fruit stand. Today she sold 7 apples for 8¢ each. How much money did she take in?

Kevin wants to buy 35 marbles. They come in bags of 10.

58. How many bags should he buy?
59. How many extra marbles will he have?

60. Spiders have 8 legs, and beetles have 6 legs. How many legs do 8 spiders have?

A cotton shirt costs $15. Ties cost $3.

61. How much do 2 cotton shirts cost?
62. How much do 2 shirts and 4 ties cost?

Patricia's garden is square. It measures 6 meters on each side.

63. What is the area of the garden?
64. What is the perimeter of the garden?

65. Dennis wants to buy 2 erasers that cost 15¢ each. How much change should he get if he gives the storekeeper 2 quarters?

There are 3 rows of bunks in Mr. Fink's cabin. Each row has 9 bunks.

66. How many bunks are there in the cabin?
67. If each bunk has a top bed and a bottom bed, how many people can sleep in the cabin?

Use the information in these charts to make up questions.
Exchange questions with a friend and solve them.

For example: 1. Which stadium has the most seats?
2. In which stadium is it easiest to hit a home run?
3. How many more seats are there in
   Riverfront Stadium than in Wrigley Field?

National League Stadiums

Team	Stadium	Home-Run Distances (meters)			Seating Capacity
		Left Field	Center Field	Right Field	
Atlanta Braves	Atlanta–Fulton County Stadium	101	123	101	52,194
Chicago Cubs	Wrigley Field	108	122	108	37,741
Cincinnati Reds	Riverfront Stadium	101	123	101	59,963
Houston Astros	Astrodome	109	124	104	45,000
Los Angeles Dodgers	Dodger Stadium	101	120	101	56,000
Montreal Expos	Olympic Stadium	99	123	99	59,511
New York Mets	Shea Stadium	108	125	108	55,300
Philadelphia Phillies	Veterans Stadium	101	124	101	58,651
Pittsburgh Pirates	Three Rivers Stadium	102	122	102	50,230
St. Louis Cardinals	Busch Memorial Stadium	101	126	101	50,222
San Diego Padres	San Diego Stadium	101	128	101	48,443
San Francisco Giants	Candlestick Park	102	125	102	58,000

American League Stadiums

Team	Stadium	Home-Run Distances (meters)			Seating Capacity
		Left Field	Center Field	Right Field	
Baltimore Orioles	Memorial Stadium	94	125	94	52,860
Boston Red Sox	Fenway Park	96	128	92	33,502
California Angels	Anaheim Stadium	112	123	112	43,250
Chicago White Sox	Comiskey Park	107	136	107	44,492
Cleveland Indians	Municipal Stadium	98	122	98	76,713
Detroit Tigers	Tiger Stadium	104	134	99	53,676
Kansas City Royals	Royals Stadium	101	125	101	40,762
Milwaukee Brewers	Milwaukee County Stadium	110	123	110	54,187
Minnesota Twins	Metropolitan Stadium	112	123	110	45,919
New York Yankees	Yankee Stadium	118	123	108	57,545
Oakland A's	Oakland–Alameda County Coliseum	101	122	101	50,000
Seattle Mariners	Kingdome	96	125	96	59,059
Texas Rangers	Arlington Stadium	113	122	113	41,097
Toronto Blue Jays	Exhibition Stadium	101	122	101	43,737

Multiply.

1. 9×9 **3.** 6×5 **5.** 0×9 **7.** 8×9
2. 8×0 **4.** 7×3 **6.** 9×3 **8.** 7×5

Divide. Don't forget remainders.

9. $5 \overline{)\, 40}$ **11.** $7 \overline{)\, 42}$ **13.** $2 \overline{)\, 15}$ **15.** $6 \overline{)\, 24}$
10. $5 \overline{)\, 38}$ **12.** $6 \overline{)\, 39}$ **14.** $8 \overline{)\, 65}$ **16.** $4 \overline{)\, 32}$

Add or subtract to solve.

17. $6 + 8$ **19.** $12 - 2$ **21.** $13 - 8$ **23.** $15 - 7$
18. $11 - 5$ **20.** $9 + 9$ **22.** $10 + 5$ **24.** $7 + 9$

Solve for n. Watch the signs.

25. $16 \div 4 = n$ **29.** $8 \times 7 = n$ **33.** $42 \div 7 = n$
26. $n \times 7 = 28$ **30.** $n \times 8 = 24$ **34.** $13 + 28 = n$
27. $n = 49 \div 7$ **31.** $42 - n = 6$
28. $3 \times n = 27$ **32.** $n + 8 = 17$

Solve. Watch the signs.

35. $\begin{array}{r} 54 \\ -\ 36 \\ \hline \end{array}$ **36.** $\begin{array}{r} 83 \\ +\ 17 \\ \hline \end{array}$ **37.** $\begin{array}{r} 207 \\ -\ 68 \\ \hline \end{array}$

38. $\begin{array}{r} 39 \\ +\ 38 \\ \hline \end{array}$ **39.** $\begin{array}{r} 465 \\ -\ 190 \\ \hline \end{array}$ **40.** $\begin{array}{r} 7300 \\ -\ 480 \\ \hline \end{array}$

Find the perimeter.

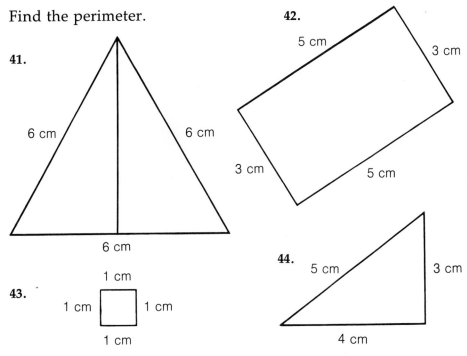

41.

6 cm   6 cm

6 cm

42.

5 cm   3 cm

3 cm   5 cm

43.

1 cm

1 cm   1 cm

1 cm

44.

5 cm   3 cm

4 cm

45. Cookbooks cost $6 each. How much do 4 cookbooks cost?

46. Jill has 20 marbles. She wants to put 5 in each bag. How many bags will she need?

47. Lewis planted 9 seeds. 3 of them sprouted. How many didn't sprout?

48. The top of Allison's desk is 2 meters wide and 3 meters long. What is the area of the desk top?

49. Kareem needs 30 hamburger buns for a picnic. They come in packages of 8. How many packages should he buy?

50. Katherine's classroom has 6 rows of desks. Each row has 5 desks. How many desks are there in the classroom?

UNIT III GRAPHING AND FUNCTIONS
TOPICS IN GEOMETRY

Graph City

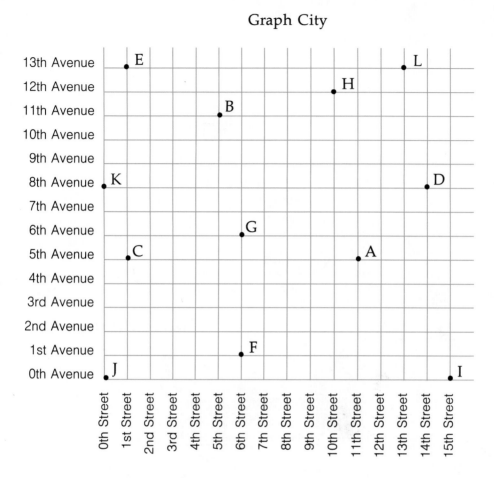

Look at the map of Graph City.

If you went to the corner of 11th Street and 5th Avenue, where would you be? The point is labeled A.

- Where is point B?
- Suppose a friend in Graph City asked you to meet her at the corner of 11th and 5th. Where would you go?
- If your friend didn't go to the same place you went, where do you think she might be?
- What would you do about it?

132

Suppose the people of Graph City agree always to give the street name first and the avenue name second.

1. Where is the corner of 11th and 5th?

2. Where is the corner of 5th and 11th?

3. How many blocks would you have to walk to get from 11th and 5th to 5th and 11th? (You must not cut across blocks.)

4. Is there more than one way to get from 11th and 5th to 5th and 11th by walking only 12 blocks?
See how many ways you can find.

5. Suppose you don't cut across blocks and you don't walk in a wrong direction on purpose.
   a. Do all ways of getting from 11th and 5th to 5th and 11th require walking exactly 12 blocks?
   Is there a shorter way?
   b. What must you do to make the path longer?

6. How many blocks would you have to walk to get from 8th and 8th to 8th and 8th?

7. How many blocks would you have to walk to get from 4th and 7th to 6th and 3rd?

Give the location of these points on the map of Graph City (always give the street name first and the avenue name second).

8. A 11th and 5th	12. E	16. I
9. B	13. F	17. J
10. C	14. G	18. K
11. D	15. H	19. L

You may remember that the people in Graph City say "11th and 5th" as a short way to say "the corner of 11th Street and 5th Avenue."

Here's an even shorter way: (11, 5)

You can use this way for the graph on page 135. For example, to tell where point B is, you can write (3, 8).

• How would you tell where point E is?

The two numbers that tell the location of a point on a graph are called the **coordinates** of that point.

The coordinates of point B are (3, 8).
The coordinates of point E are (13, 2).

The "sideways" coordinate is given first. The "up-and-down" coordinate is given second.

1. What are the coordinates of point M?
2. What are the coordinates of point A?
3. What are the coordinates of point X?
4. What are the coordinates of point Z?

Solve these riddles by writing the correct letter for each of the coordinates.

5. What did the acorn say when it grew up?

(0, 5), (13, 2), (1, 2), (8, 3), (13, 2), (0, 12), (10, 7), (8, 12)

or

(0, 5), (13, 2), (13, 2)   (7, 10), (8, 3)   (6, 6)

(0, 12), (10, 7), (13, 2), (13, 2)

6. Which president of the United States would you have gone to if your clothes needed mending?

    (0, 12), (6, 6), (8, 12), (11, 12), (1, 2), (10, 7)

7. Which 2 presidents of the United States had the same names as cars?

    (2, 1), (1, 2), (10, 7), (14, 10) and

    (11, 12), (7, 10), (13, 5), (5, 13), (1, 2), (11, 12), (13, 5)

8. What kind of sand is found at the bottom of the Pacific Ocean?

    (5, 2), (13, 2), (0, 12)   (3, 10), (6, 6), (13, 5), (14, 10)

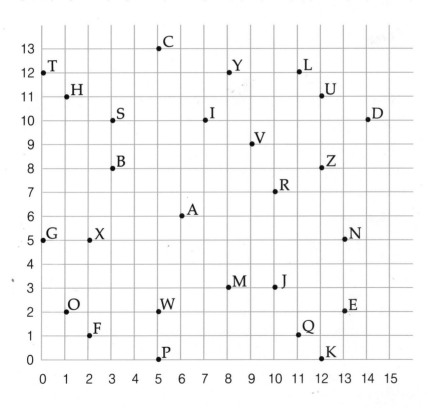

Make up your own riddles or questions. Ask a friend to solve them.

This function machine does something to numbers that are put into it. If you put in a 7, a 12 will come out. We will write that like this:

7 ⟋ (?) ⟍ 12

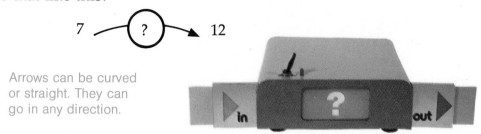

Arrows can be curved or straight. They can go in any direction.

If we put in a 10, a 15 will come out.

10 ⟍ (?) ⟋ 15

This set of arrow operations shows what happens when we put in 0, 4, 9, and 25.

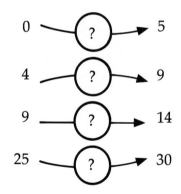

0 ⟍ (?) ⟋ 5

4 ⟋ (?) ⟍ 9

9 ⟶ (?) ⟶ 14

25 ⟍ (?) ⟋ 30

- What do you think will come out if you put in 100?
- What do you think the function machine is doing?

The function rule for this machine is **add 5.** We will write the add 5 function like this:

⟋ (+5) ⟍

Find a function rule for each set of arrow operations.

1.

3 → (?) → 10

6 → (?) → 13

8 → (?) → 15

1 → (?) → 8

2.

3 → (?) → 6

4 → (?) → 8

5 → (?) → 10

1 → (?) → 2

3.

4 → (?) → 12

5 → (?) → 15

7 → (?) → 21

0 → (?) → 0

4.

8 → (?) → 6

5 → (?) → 3

2 → (?) → 0

3 → (?) → 1

5.

10 → (?) → 5

20 → (?) → 15

5 → (?) → 0

6 → (?) → 1

6.

8 → (?) → 4

4 → (?) → 2

2 → (?) → 1

0 → (?) → 0

7.

9 → (?) → 3

12 → (?) → 4

30 → (?) → 10

3 → (?) → 1

8.

5 → (?) → 5

8 → (?) → 8

126 → (?) → 126

3 → (?) → 3

9.

3 → (?) → 27

5 → (?) → 45

1 → (?) → 9

8 → (?) → 72

The rule for a certain function machine is +4. If you put the number 7 into the machine, what number will come out?

Here's another way to ask the same question:

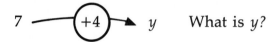

7 —— (+4) —▲ y What is y?

In each case, tell what y is.

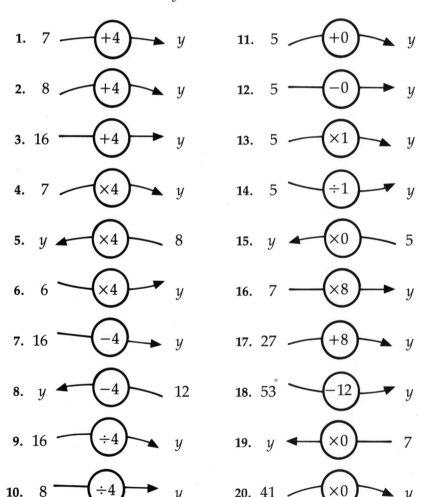

1. 7 —— (+4) —▲ y

2. 8 —— (+4) —▲ y

3. 16 —— (+4) —▶ y

4. 7 —— (×4) —▲ y

5. y ◀— (×4) —— 8

6. 6 —— (×4) —▶ y

7. 16 —— (−4) —▶ y

8. y ◀— (−4) —— 12

9. 16 —— (÷4) —▲ y

10. 8 —— (÷4) —▶ y

11. 5 —— (+0) —▲ y

12. 5 —— (−0) —▶ y

13. 5 —— (×1) —▲ y

14. 5 —— (÷1) —▶ y

15. y ◀— (×0) —— 5

16. 7 —— (×8) —▶ y

17. 27 —— (+8) —▲ y

18. 53 —— (−12) —▶ y

19. y ◀— (×0) —— 7

20. 41 —— (×0) —▲ y

The rule for a certain function machine is +4. If the number that comes out is 10, what number was put into the machine?

Here's another way to ask the same question:

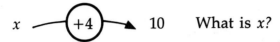

x — (+4) → 10   What is x?

In each case, tell what x is.

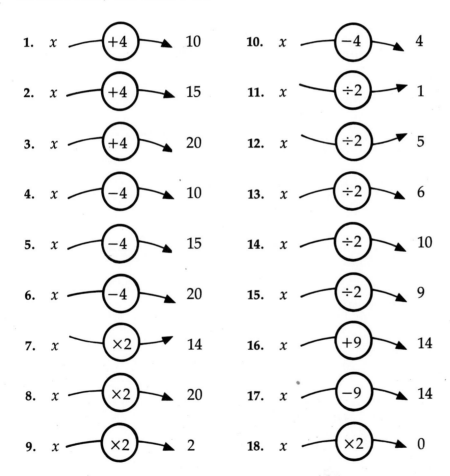

1. x — (+4) → 10   10. x — (−4) → 4

2. x — (+4) → 15   11. x — (÷2) → 1

3. x — (+4) → 20   12. x — (÷2) → 5

4. x — (−4) → 10   13. x — (÷2) → 6

5. x — (−4) → 15   14. x — (÷2) → 10

6. x — (−4) → 20   15. x — (÷2) → 9

7. x — (×2) → 14   16. x — (+9) → 14

8. x — (×2) → 20   17. x — (−9) → 14

9. x — (×2) → 2   18. x — (×2) → 0

Look at these function machines.

If you put 5 into this machine, you get out 15.

This machine does the opposite. If you put in 15, you get out 5.

Because these machines do opposite things, we say that

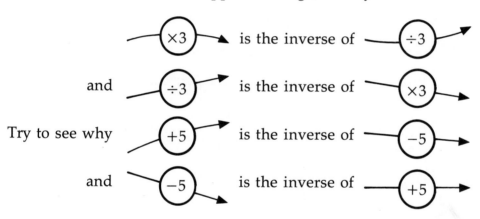

×3 is the inverse of ÷3

and ÷3 is the inverse of ×3

Try to see why +5 is the inverse of −5

and −5 is the inverse of +5

Write the inverse arrow operation.

1.

2.

3.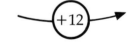

4.

5.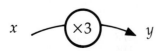

6.

7. Suppose a function machine followed this rule:

x ──(×3)──▸ y

What number could you put in to get out 21?

Inverse arrow operations can help you find what number went into a machine.

Example: x 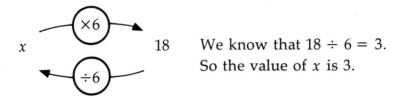 18   What is x?

Use the inverse arrow operations.

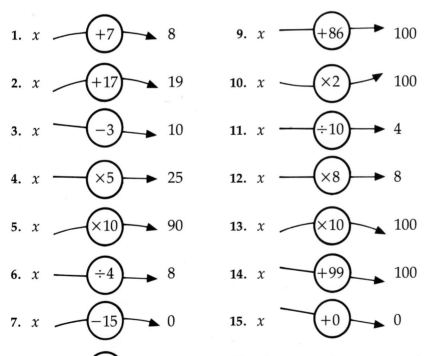

x 18   We know that $18 \div 6 = 3$.
So the value of x is 3.

Use inverse arrow operations, if they help you, to find the value of x.

1. x —(+7)→ 8

2. x —(+17)→ 19

3. x —(−3)→ 10

4. x —(×5)→ 25

5. x —(×10)→ 90

6. x —(÷4)→ 8

7. x —(−15)→ 0

8. x —(×0)→ 0

9. x —(+86)→ 100

10. x —(×2)→ 100

11. x —(÷10)→ 4

12. x —(×8)→ 8

13. x —(×10)→ 100

14. x —(+99)→ 100

15. x —(+0)→ 0

Think! Can x have more than 1 value? Can you solve problem 8?

141

Look at this function machine.
It works according to this rule:
If you put in 7, then 12 comes out.

$x \longrightarrow \boxed{+5} \longrightarrow y$

Let's write that pair of numbers like this: (7, 12)

The first number in the pair (7) is the one that went in.
The second number in the pair (12) is the one that came out.

A pair of numbers written this way, (7, 12), is called an **ordered pair.** We call it that because the order is important to show which number is which.

We can list other ordered pairs for the +5 function machine.
   If we put in 3, then 8 comes out: (3, 8)
   If we put in 9, then 14 comes out: (9, 14)
   And so on.
In this way, we can say that a function machine produces ordered pairs of numbers.

Copy each list of ordered pairs, but replace the x or y with the correct number.

1. $x \longrightarrow \boxed{+5} \longrightarrow y$ (7, 12), (12, y), (15, y), (0, y), (x, 7)

142

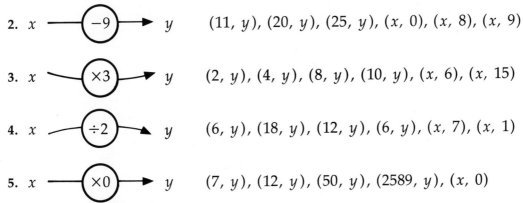

2. x —(−9)→ y (11, y), (20, y), (25, y), (x, 0), (x, 8), (x, 9)

3. x —(×3)→ y (2, y), (4, y), (8, y), (10, y), (x, 6), (x, 15)

4. x —(÷2)→ y (6, y), (18, y), (12, y), (6, y), (x, 7), (x, 1)

5. x —(×0)→ y (7, y), (12, y), (50, y), (2589, y), (x, 0)

- Suppose problem 5 included the ordered pair (x, 7).
  What would your answer be?

Here's a secret code to help you solve the riddles below.

A	B	C	D	E	F	G	H	I	J	K	L	M
26	25	24	23	22	21	20	19	18	17	16	15	14

N	O	P	Q	R	S	T	U	V	W	X	Y	Z
13	12	11	10	9	8	7	6	5	4	3	2	1

Use function rules to help solve the riddles. Find the
value of x or y in each ordered pair. Then use the code to
find what letter each value stands for.

1. What's a noisy group of people?

   Use this function rule: x —(+3)→ y

   (23, y)   (12, y), (x, 15), (3, y), (20, y)
   (21, y), (6, y), (9, y), (x, 7), (x, 26)

2. What's another name for a police chief?

   Use this function rule: x —(−5)→ y

   (31, y)   (12, y), (17, y), (x, 6)   (x, 19), (x, 7), (16, y)

THE LOST ISLAND OF ADDONIA   Part 1

After their ship sank, Ferdie, Portia, Manolita, and Mark spent 3 days on a raft. Then their raft drifted to the shore of a green island. A woman and a little girl came down to meet them.

"Welcome to Addonia," said the woman.

"Thank you," said Portia. "How far is it to the nearest library? I haven't had anything to read for 3 days."

"The library is 10 kilometers from here," said the girl.

"That's right," said the woman. "It's 43 kilometers from here."

"Wait a minute," said Mark. "Something's crazy here." An old man was sitting on a rock near them. Mark asked him, "Who is telling the truth about how far the library is?"

"They both are," said the old man. "The library is exactly 86 kilometers from here." When he saw how puzzled the children looked, the old man smiled.

"I guess you don't know how we do things here in Addonia," he said. "We have a secret way of saying numbers. It protects us from spies.

But you children don't look like spies. I'll tell you the secret. Whenever we say a number, we always add our age to it."

"You mean," said Manolita, "that if it was 2 o'clock, I'd have to say it was 11 o'clock, because I'm 9 years old?"

"That's right," said the old man. "And I would say it's 85 o'clock."

---

1. If you wanted to talk about 6 things in Addonia, what number would you say instead?

2. If a 10-year-old wanted 10 cents, what would the child have to ask for?

3. A 12-year-old child in Addonia said, "There are 17 people in my family." How many are there really?

4. A detective question: How old is the old man?

5. A superdetective question: How far is it to the library?

Use inverse operations to find the values of x in the ordered pairs.

1. x 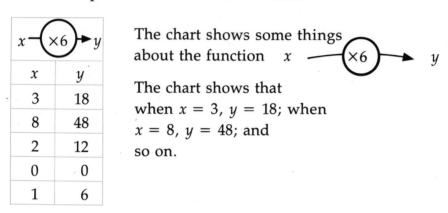 y $(x, 5), (x, 7), (x, 15), (x, 205), (x, 73)$

2. x ⊘-5⊘ y $(x, 5), (x, 25), (x, 30), (x, 35), (x, 45)$

3. x ⊘÷8⊘ y $(x, 1), (x, 3), (x, 8), (x, 9), (x, 10)$

This is a completed function machine chart.

x—⊘×6⊘→y

x	y
3	18
8	48
2	12
0	0
1	6

The chart shows some things about the function x —⊘×6⊘→ y

The chart shows that when $x = 3$, $y = 18$; when $x = 8$, $y = 48$; and so on.

Copy and complete these charts.

4. x—⊘×4⊘→y

x	y
1	4
▨	8
6	▨
▨	12
10	▨

5. x—⊘+3⊘→y

x	y
▨	7
2	▨
5	▨
▨	25
6	▨

6. x—⊘×8⊘→y

x	y
0	▨
▨	24
2	▨
1	8
▨	32

7. $x \rightarrow (+7) \rightarrow y$

x	y
8	
30	
	27
6	
	107

8. $x \rightarrow (\times 6) \rightarrow y$

x	y
3	
	54
10	
	48
7	

9. $x \rightarrow (-3) \rightarrow y$

x	y
	5
	10
	9
24	
3	

10. $x \rightarrow (\times 7) \rightarrow y$

x	y
7	
0	
10	
	14
	21

11. $x \rightarrow (-4) \rightarrow y$

x	y
	15
	21
	72
	3
	19

12. $x \rightarrow (+6) \rightarrow y$

x	y
	25
	35
	45
	55
	65

13. $x \rightarrow (\times 10) \rightarrow y$

x	y
	100
	200
	300
	400
	500

14. $x \rightarrow (-10) \rightarrow y$

x	y
	100
	200
	300
	400
	500

Find the function rules before you complete these charts.

15. $x \rightarrow (?) \rightarrow y$

x	y
2	
	20
6	12
0	
12	18

16. $x \rightarrow (?) \rightarrow y$

x	y
100	
3	3
2	
7	
25	25

17. $x \rightarrow (?) \rightarrow y$

x	y
3	9
20	60
5	15
	27
	30

18. $x \rightarrow (?) \rightarrow y$

x	y
6	0
20	
5	0
31	
12	

147

THE LOST ISLAND OF ADDONIA   Part 2

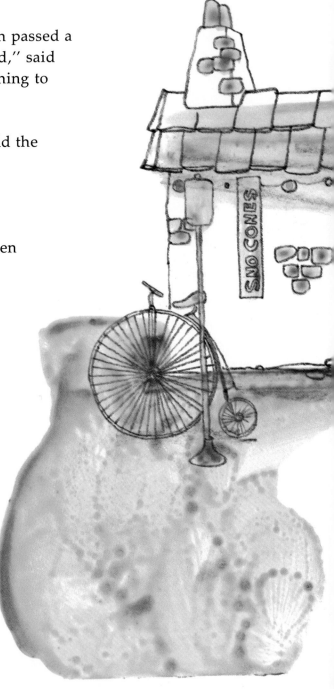

On the way to the library, the children passed a hamburger stand. "Let's get some food," said Ferdie. "It's true we haven't had anything to read for 3 days. But we haven't had anything to eat, either."

"Give us 4 hamburgers," Ferdie told the cook.

"I'm not sure I can make so few hamburgers," said the cook.

"He's right," Mark said. "One hamburger apiece isn't very much when we're so hungry. Let's get 3 apiece."

"All right," said Ferdie. "Make us 12 hamburgers."

"I think I know how many that is," said the cook. He made them 4 hamburgers.

"Where are the others?" Ferdie asked.

"You ordered only 26, didn't you?" the cook said.

"I give up," said Ferdie. "There's no way to get what you want in this country."

"Let me try," said Manolita. She said to the cook, "You see how many hamburgers you made for us? Please make that many again and then make that many again."

"I wish you children would make up your minds," said the cook. "Twenty-third you say 23 things and 24th you say something else."

1. Why couldn't the cook make the 4 hamburgers Ferdie asked for?

2. How old was the cook?

3. How would you say the last thing that the cook said? Say it our way, not the Addonian way.

4. A detective question: How old did the cook think Ferdie was?

FUNCTION GAME

Players: 2 or more
Materials: Two 0–5 cubes, two 5–10 cubes
Object: To score closest to 100 without going over

Rules

1. Make a blank function machine chart like the one shown.
2. The first player rolls all 4 cubes to get the values of x. Write all 4 values of x in your chart.
3. Select a function and write it in the blank circle at the top of your chart.
4. Using your function rule, find the values of y.
5. Find the sum of all the values of y.
6. The player with the sum closest to, but not over, 100 wins the round.

x	y
Sum	

Sample Game

Numbers Rolled	Mario's Chart	Anna's Chart	JoAnn's Chart

Mario's Chart — $x \to (\times 4) \to y$

x	y
5	20
4	16
6	24
8	32
Sum	92

Anna's Chart — $x \to (+18) \to y$

x	y
5	23
4	22
6	24
8	26
Sum	95

JoAnn's Chart — $x \to (+20) \to y$

x	y
5	25
4	24
6	26
8	28
Sum	103

Anna was the winner of the round.

150

In each problem, 2 of the answers are clearly wrong and
1 is correct. Choose the correct answer.

1. 409   a. 2197   8.   597   a. 1119
    + 618   b. 517   − 522   b. 175
               c. 1027   c. 75

2. 756   a. 438   9.   543   a. 365
    − 318   b. 1074   − 178   b. 165
               c. 108   c. 665

3. 4195   a. 128   10. 1618   a. 20,940
    − 3167   b. 1028   + 9322   b. 8030
               c. 7278   c. 10,940

4. 522   a. 2595   11. 241   a. 166
    + 973   b. 1495   − 75   b. 316
               c. 1005   c. 66

5. 5376   a. 8637   12. 233   a. 400
    + 3261   b. 837   + 167   b. 690
               c. 12,637   c. 190

6. 4603   a. 8257   13. 537   a. 1023
    − 4346   b. 1257   + 386   b. 623
               c. 257   c. 923

7. 180   a. 416   14. 2102   a. 533
    + 436   b. 616   − 1569   b. 3683
               c. 896   c. 293

1. Copy the list of ordered pairs, but replace each x or y with the correct number.

x ⟶ $\boxed{+2}$ ⟶ y $(0, y), (7, y), (10, y), (x, 3), (x, 5), (x, 10)$

2. Make a graph. Use the ordered pairs you found in problem 1 as coordinates of points on your graph. Remember that the first (or x) number tells how far to go to the right. The second (or y) number tells how far to go up. Does your graph look like this?

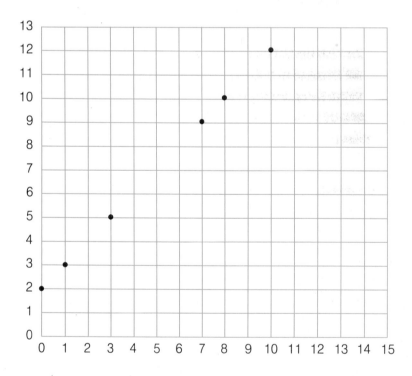

3. Do you notice anything interesting about the 6 points on your graph? Check with a ruler to see if they are all on the same straight line.

Look at your graph, but don't do any calculations for problems 4 and 5.

4. Think about the point that has 4 as its first coordinate.
   a. Where do you think the point ought to be?
   b. What is its second coordinate?
   c. If 4 were put into a +2 function machine, what would come out?

5. Copy each ordered pair, but replace each x or y with the number you believe would make the point fall on the line.
   a. $(2, y)$ b. $(x, 11)$ c. $(x, 8)$ d. $(11, y)$

Copy each list of ordered pairs, but replace each x or y with the correct number. Then graph each set of ordered pairs.

6. x —(−3)→ y $(5, y), (4, y), (x, 0), (x, 5), (10, y), (x, 10)$

7. x —(÷2)→ y $(4, y), (6, y), (20, y), (x, 4), (x, 8), (10, y)$

8. x —(×0)→ y $(1, y), (3, y), (0, y), (10, y), (5, y), (9, y)$

9. x —(+0)→ y $(1, y), (3, y), (0, y), (x, 9), (x, 12), (x, 8)$

10. x —(×1)→ y $(1, y), (3, y), (0, y), (x, 9), (x, 12), (x, 8)$

- Compare your graphs for problems 9 and 10.

Suppose you are graphing this function:

And let's say you are using these 5 ordered pairs:

x	y
0	0
1	8
2	16
3	24
4	32

Then you might think that you would need long, skinny graph paper.

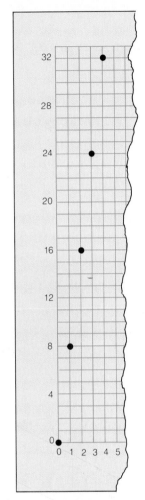

But there is another way to fit the 5 points on your graph paper.

And you don't need a funny shape.

You can let each space in the up-and-down direction stand for more than 1 unit.

In the graph on the right, each up-and-down space stands for 4 units. All the points fit.

- Make your own graph of these points. But let each up-and-down space stand for 8 units. Do the points fit?

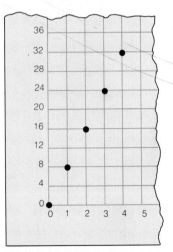

154

When you make a graph, think ahead. Make sure your graph will fit on your paper.

Copy and complete each chart. Then graph each set of ordered pairs.

---

1. $x \rightarrow \boxed{\times 5} \rightarrow y$

x	y
0	▦
2	▦
4	▦
6	▦
8	▦

2. $x \rightarrow \boxed{\times 7} \rightarrow y$

x	y
0	▦
3	▦
5	▦
7	▦
9	▦

3. $x \rightarrow \boxed{\times 10} \rightarrow y$

x	y
0	▦
2	▦
5	▦
7	▦
10	▦

---

4. $x \rightarrow \boxed{\div 10} \rightarrow y$

x	y
0	▦
20	▦
50	▦
70	▦
100	▦

5. $x \rightarrow \boxed{\div 5} \rightarrow y$

x	y
0	▦
10	▦
20	▦
30	▦
40	▦
50	▦

6. $x \rightarrow \boxed{- 10} \rightarrow y$

x	y
60	▦
50	▦
40	▦
30	▦
20	▦
10	▦

These 2 function machines have been put together.
A number *(x)* goes into the first machine.
The number that comes out *(n)* goes into the second machine.
Then a third number *(y)* comes out.
This is called a **composite function machine.**

Here's how to write what this composite function
machine does:

x ──(×3)──► n ──(+5)──► y

Suppose you put 6 into the first machine.
What would come out of the second machine?

6 ──(×3)──► n ──(+5)──► y What is *y?*

First decide what *n* is.   Then decide what *y* is.

6 ──(×3)──►$\overset{18}{n}$──(+5)──► y 6 ──(×3)──►$\overset{18}{n}$──(+5)──►$\overset{23}{y}$

You can do all this a short way:

6 ──(×3)──► n ──(+5)──► y *n* is 18; *y* is 23.

Find the value of y.

1. $7 \rightarrow (+3) \rightarrow n \rightarrow (\times 8) \rightarrow y$

2. $7 \rightarrow (\times 8) \rightarrow n \rightarrow (+3) \rightarrow y$

3. $4 \rightarrow (+7) \rightarrow n \rightarrow (\times 1) \rightarrow y$

4. $5 \rightarrow (\times 5) \rightarrow n \rightarrow (-5) \rightarrow y$

5. $20 \rightarrow (-16) \rightarrow n \rightarrow (\times 3) \rightarrow y$

6. $9 \rightarrow (\div 3) \rightarrow n \rightarrow (+2) \rightarrow y$

7. $15 \rightarrow (\div 5) \rightarrow n \rightarrow (\times 4) \rightarrow y$

8. $4 \rightarrow (\times 3) \rightarrow n \rightarrow (\div 2) \rightarrow y$

9. $4 \rightarrow (\div 2) \rightarrow n \rightarrow (\times 3) \rightarrow y$

10. $145 \rightarrow (-100) \rightarrow n \rightarrow (\div 5) \rightarrow y$

11. $16 \rightarrow (+5) \rightarrow n \rightarrow (-5) \rightarrow y$

12. $8 \rightarrow (\times 4) \rightarrow n \rightarrow (\div 4) \rightarrow y$

13. $6 \rightarrow (\times 2) \rightarrow n \rightarrow (\div 3) \rightarrow y$

14. $5 \rightarrow (+5) \rightarrow n \rightarrow (\times 2) \rightarrow y$

15. $18 \rightarrow (\div 6) \rightarrow n \rightarrow (\times 3) \rightarrow y$

16. $3 \rightarrow (+3) \rightarrow n \rightarrow (\times 4) \rightarrow y$

17. $24 \rightarrow (\div 4) \rightarrow n \rightarrow (\times 9) \rightarrow y$

18. $56 \rightarrow (\div 7) \rightarrow n \rightarrow (\times 6) \rightarrow y$

19. $200 \rightarrow (-100) \rightarrow n \rightarrow (\div 10) \rightarrow y$

20. $9 \rightarrow (\times 5) \rightarrow n \rightarrow (+10) \rightarrow y$

157

Karen opened a lemonade stand. She decided to charge 3¢ for each glass of lemonade, plus a 1¢ handling charge.

So if you bought 1 glass of lemonade, Karen would charge you 3¢ plus a 1¢ handling charge—a total of 4¢.

If you bought 2 glasses, she would charge you 6¢ for the 2 glasses plus the 1¢ handling charge—a total of 7¢.

To help her figure out what to charge, she started to make this function chart.

x	y
1	4
2	7
3	▨
4	▨
5	▨
6	▨

1. Help Karen. Copy and complete the chart. Then graph the ordered pairs.

2. Connect the points on your graph. Do they all lie in a straight line?

3. Look at your graph. How much would Karen charge somebody who bought 9 glasses of lemonade? (You may have to extend your graph.)

4. Devon and Brad each wanted a glass of lemonade. Brad had an idea. "Devon," he said. "Let me buy 2 glasses and we will share them." Why did Brad think that was a good idea?

Suppose a number was put into this composite function and 23 came out. What number was put in? In other words, if y is 23, what is x?

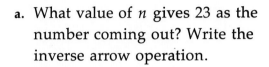

a. What value of n gives 23 as the number coming out? Write the inverse arrow operation.

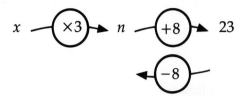

b. $23 - 8 = 15$
So n is 15.

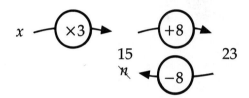

c. What value of x gives 15 as the value of n?
Write the inverse arrow operation.
$15 \div 3 = 5$
So when y is 23, x is 5.
Let's check this:
$5 \times 3 = 15$, $15 + 8 = 23$. That checks.

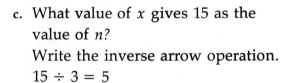

You don't have to write all the steps.
You can just write this: n is 15, x is 5.

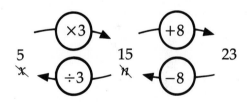

Use inverse operations to find the value of x.

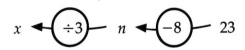

THE LOST ISLAND OF ADDONIA Part 3

The 4 children came to the Addonia Public School. "Let's go in here," Portia said. "Maybe this is where the library is."

Inside the school a mathematics class was going on. "Remember," said the teacher, "every triangle has 37 sides. What's the rule, Joan?"

"A triangle has 11 sides," said a girl in the front row.

"Very good, Joan. And how many sides does a square have?"

"A square has 13 sides," said Joan.

"I'm afraid that's wrong," said the teacher. "Henry, how many sides does a square have?"

"A square has 13 sides," said Henry.

"That's right," said the teacher. "And now let's welcome our 38 visitors from America."

1. How could Joan be wrong when she said a square has 13 sides and Henry be right when he said the same thing?

2. What should Joan have said about the number of sides a square has?

3. How old is Joan?

4. How old is Henry?

5. How old is the teacher?

6. Superdetective questions: How old would Joan say that Henry is? How old would Henry say that Joan is? Why would they say the same number?

Use inverse operations to replace each x with the correct number. Then make a graph for each set of ordered pairs.

1. x ──(×2)──▶ y $(x, 2), (x, 10), (x, 20), (x, 0), (x, 16)$

2. x ──(+7)──▶ y $(x, 9), (x, 17), (x, 27), (x, 7), (x, 8)$

3. x ──(−9)──▶ y $(x, 9), (x, 7), (x, 3), (x, 8), (x, 5)$

4. x ──(÷6)──▶ y $(x, 6), (x, 3), (x, 8), (x, 7), (x, 9)$

5. x ──(×2)──▶ n ──(+7)──▶ y $(x, 9), (x, 17), (x, 27), (x, 7)$

6. x ──(×3)──▶ n ──(−5)──▶ y $(x, 1), (x, 7), (x, 10), (x, 25)$

7. x ──(−5)──▶ n ──(×3)──▶ y $(x, 0), (x, 15), (x, 6), (x, 12)$

8. x ──(+6)──▶ n ──(÷2)──▶ y $(x, 6), (x, 5), (x, 7), (x, 3)$

9. x ──(÷3)──▶ n ──(−3)──▶ y $(x, 2), (x, 4), (x, 1), (x, 3)$

10. x ──(−7)──▶ n ──(×4)──▶ y $(x, 28), (x, 20), (x, 16), (x, 12)$

11. a. Pick a number between 0 and 10 for the value of x.

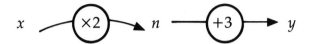

Make an ordered pair of the number you used for x and the value of y.

b. Find 2 more ordered pairs for the same function.

c. Graph the 3 ordered pairs you have found.

d. Look at your graph. Pick a point that has 4 as its first (sideways) coordinate and is on the same line as the other 3 points. What is the second coordinate of the point you picked?

e. Look at your graph. Pick a point that has 15 as its second (up-and-down) coordinate and is on the same line as the other points. What is the first coordinate of the point you picked?

f. Replace x and y in the ordered pairs with the correct numbers:

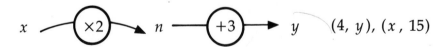

• Did you use the graph to find x in the second ordered pair?

THE LOST ISLAND OF ADDONIA — Part 4

At last the children came to the library. Portia found a book to read. It was called *Goldilocks and the 48 Bears*. When Portia went to check out the book, the librarian said, "Books are not free in Addonia. You will have to pay 46¢ a day to take this book out."

"That's too much money," said Portia. "I can't pay that."

"It's not too much," said an old woman. "You should be happy to pay 73¢ a day for such a fine book."

"That's right," said a young boy. "Why, 9¢ a day is not very much. We all pay that."

"I can't figure out anything here," said Portia. "I want to go home."

"If you think things are bad here," said the librarian, "you should see what it's like in Subtractia."

1. About how much does it really cost to take a book out
   of the Addonia Library?

2. Could it cost 1¢ a day?

3. Could it cost more than 10¢ a day?

4. A detective question: How old is the person who wrote
   the book Portia wants to read?

Watch the signs.

1. $n + 6 = 16$ 3. $n - 17 = 35$ 5. $n \div 3 = 7$
2. $56 \div n = 7$ 4. $7 \times 5 = n$ 6. $n + 9 = 31$

Add or subtract.

7. $\begin{array}{r} 1589 \\ + 2496 \\ \hline \end{array}$
8. $\begin{array}{r} 329 \\ - 167 \\ \hline \end{array}$
9. $\begin{array}{r} 1720 \\ + 2679 \\ \hline \end{array}$
10. $\begin{array}{r} \$4.27 \\ - 1.79 \\ \hline \end{array}$
11. $\begin{array}{r} \$13.56 \\ + \quad 8.82 \\ \hline \end{array}$

12. Which pie has been cut into pieces that are $\frac{1}{6}$ its size?
13. Which pie has been cut into pieces that are $\frac{1}{5}$ its size?
14. Which pie has **more** pieces?
15. Which pie has **bigger** pieces?

Solve for n. Watch the signs.

16. $n = 8 + 7$ 19. $n \times 8 = 32$ 22. $n \div 10 = 7$
17. $n = 8 \times 7$ 20. $24 \div n = 8$ 23. $n - 8 = 39$
18. $8 + n = 31$ 21. $n \div 3 = 8$ 24. $56 = 7 \times n$

Watch the signs.

25. $\begin{array}{r} 63 \\ + 9 \\ \hline \end{array}$
26. $\begin{array}{r} 63 \\ - 9 \\ \hline \end{array}$
27. $\begin{array}{r} 73 \\ - 19 \\ \hline \end{array}$
28. $9\overline{)32}$
29. $\begin{array}{r} 536 \\ + 800 \\ \hline \end{array}$

30. $\begin{array}{r} 5137 \\ - 2428 \\ \hline \end{array}$
31. $\begin{array}{r} 3000 \\ - 1998 \\ \hline \end{array}$
32. $\begin{array}{r} \$2.16 \\ + 3.04 \\ \hline \end{array}$
33. $\begin{array}{r} \$81.07 \\ - 17.28 \\ \hline \end{array}$
34. $\begin{array}{r} \$ 4.07 \\ + 26.90 \\ \hline \end{array}$

For each function rule, follow these steps:

A. Find 4 ordered pairs of numbers.

B. Graph the 4 points.

C. Try to draw a line through all 4 points.

1.

2.

3.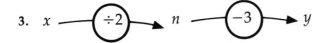

4.

5. x ⟶ ×2 ⟶ y

6.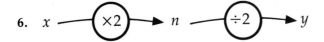

Compare your answers for problems 1 through 6 with the answers of others in your class.

- Did you choose the same numbers?
- Are the 4 points on your graphs the same?
- Are the lines on your graphs the same?

Are You Shiny or Rusty?

Very shiny   45 or more right
Shiny   40–44 right
A bit rusty   35–39 right
Rusty   Less than 35 right

Solve for n. Watch the signs.

1. $40 \div n = 8$
2. $n - 7 = 10$
3. $7 \times 9 = n$
4. $n + 9 = 17$
5. $n \div 3 = 7$
6. $n = 4 + 7$
7. $24 = n \times 8$
8. $13 - 9 = n$
9. $n \div 5 = 9$

10. $n \times 5 = 30$
11. $8 + n = 15$
12. $n - 2 = 9$
13. $n + 8 = 14$
14. $3 \times 9 = n$
15. $n = 72 \div 8$
16. $14 - n = 9$
17. $9 + 6 = n$
18. $7 \times n = 49$

19. $n \div 7 = 4$
20. $5 + 8 = n$
21. $13 - 7 = n$
22. $n = 5 \times 8$
23. $64 \div n = 8$
24. $7 + 5 = n$
25. $12 - n = 7$
26. $n \times 4 = 32$
27. $18 \div 2 = n$

28. $n + 9 = 12$
29. $13 - n = 10$
30. $6 \times 9 = n$
31. $n \div 5 = 6$
32. $7 + n = 19$
33. $n = 3 \times 3$
34. $n = 36 \div 9$
35. $n \times 9 = 81$
36. $15 + n = 19$

Watch the signs.

37. $\begin{array}{r} 9 \\ \times\ 8 \\ \hline \end{array}$

38. $\begin{array}{r} 13 \\ -\ 5 \\ \hline \end{array}$

39. $\begin{array}{r} 5 \\ +\ 7 \\ \hline \end{array}$

40. $5\overline{)35}$

41. $\begin{array}{r} 4 \\ \times\ 3 \\ \hline \end{array}$

42. $\begin{array}{r} 9 \\ +\ 3 \\ \hline \end{array}$

43. $\begin{array}{r} 18 \\ -\ 9 \\ \hline \end{array}$

44. $6\overline{)54}$

45. $\begin{array}{r} 7 \\ +\ 9 \\ \hline \end{array}$

46. $\begin{array}{r} 20 \\ -\ 12 \\ \hline \end{array}$

47. $\begin{array}{r} 12 \\ -\ 5 \\ \hline \end{array}$

48. $\begin{array}{r} 6 \\ +\ 5 \\ \hline \end{array}$

49. $\begin{array}{r} 9 \\ -\ 6 \\ \hline \end{array}$

50. $6\overline{)36}$

TIRES

15,000-Kilometer
guarantee
4 for $150
(any size)

30,000-Kilometer
guarantee
4 for $200
(any size)

60,000-Kilometer
guarantee
4 for $300
(any size)

BATTERIES

12-volt "HIGH CHARGE"
$30.00
2-year guarantee

12-volt "LONG LIFE"
$35.00
3-year guarantee

12-volt "OUR BEST"
$75.00
5-year guarantee

MUFFLERS

1-year guarantee
$30⁰⁰ installed

2-year guarantee
$40⁰⁰ installed

Guaranteed for as long
as you own your car
$70⁰⁰ installed

- Which of the batteries is the best buy? Why do you think so?
- Which of the tires is the best buy? Why do you think so?
- Which of the mufflers is the best buy? Why do you think so?

Remember, a **right angle** is an angle like the one in the figure. The corners of this page are right angles.

1. Look around you. Identify other right angles in the classroom. Make a list of at least 5 examples of right angles other than the corners of the page.

2. Look at the traffic signs below.
   a. Which of these traffic signs have at least 1 right angle?
   b. Try to name the shape of each sign.

Reprinted by permission of Rand McNally & Co.

Follow these steps to make a right angle.

A. Get a piece of paper. Imagine a line like this dotted one.

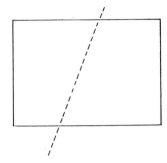

B. Fold along the line.

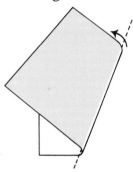

C. Your paper should look like this. Rub with your finger or a pencil to make a sharp crease.

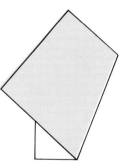

D. Imagine a line like the dotted one. Start to fold along the line.

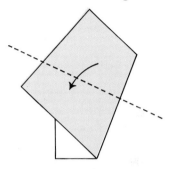

E. As you fold, make sure you line up the edges on the right.

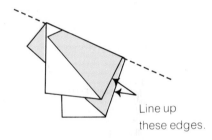

Line up these edges.

F. Your paper should look like this.

• Unfold your paper. How many right angles did you make?

Any 2 lines are **perpendicular** if the angles they make when they meet are right angles.

These lines are perpendicular.

1. Try to draw 2 lines that meet with 1 right angle and with the other 3 angles not right angles. The 2 lines must be straight and must continue straight through the point where they meet. Can you do it?
2. If 2 lines meet so that 1 angle formed is a right angle, what kind of angles will the other 3 angles be?
3. By folding paper, make 2 lines that are perpendicular. Draw the lines in 2 different colors.
4. Suppose you fold a piece of paper twice.
   a. What is the smallest number of right angles you can make?
   b. The greatest number?

In each case, tell whether the 2 lines are about perpendicular.

5.   6.   7.   8.

• Suppose you fold a piece of paper 3 times. What is the smallest number of right angles you can make? The greatest number?
• Suppose you fold a piece of paper 4 times. What is the smallest number of right angles you can make? The greatest number?

Parallel lines are lines that go in the same direction. The lines in this figure are parallel lines.

1. Do the 2 lines look as though they will ever meet each other?
2. Do the lines look as though they stay the same distance apart?

Parallel lines never meet. They remain the same distance apart no matter how far they are extended.

In each case, tell whether the 2 lines are parallel, perpendicular, or neither.

3.   4.   5.

6.   7.

8. Draw a line. Now draw 2 more lines, each perpendicular to the first. What do you think is true of these last 2 lines?

Remember: A square looks like this:

It has 4 right angles.
All its sides are equal.

Follow these steps to make a square.

A. Make a right angle by following the steps on page 171. Your paper should look like this.

B. Turn the paper around (like a knob) halfway so that it looks like this.

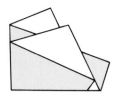

C. Imagine a line like the dotted one. Start to fold along the line.

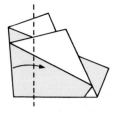

D. As you fold, make sure you line up the bottom edges.

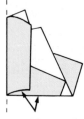

Line up these edges.

E. Your paper should now look like this.

F. Unfold your last fold so that your paper looks like this.

There should be a crease here.

G. Start to fold the corner up.

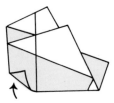

H. As you fold up the corner, make sure the edge is lined up with the crease.

Line up this edge with the crease.

I. Your paper should now look like this.

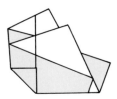

J. Imagine a line like the dotted one. Fold up along the line.

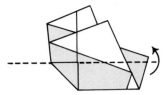

K. Your paper should look like this.

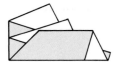

L. Unfold your paper all the way. Look for the big square formed by 4 little squares.

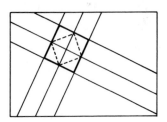

Cut out the big square and use it for page 176.

A **line of symmetry** in a figure cuts the figure into 2 parts that look the same.

If you fold a figure on a line of symmetry, the 2 sides will fall exactly on top of each other.

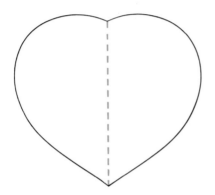

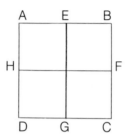

- In this heart-shaped figure, is the blue line a line of symmetry?
- *HF* is a line of symmetry. Fold a square along a line like *HF*. Do the 2 sides fall exactly on top of each other?
- Find another line of symmetry in your square. Is there a line like it in the square above?
- Try to find 2 more lines of symmetry in your square. Fold to make sure they are lines of symmetry.
- Are there any more lines of symmetry in your square? Check any line you think might be a line of symmetry by folding along it.
- How many lines of symmetry are there in your square?
- How many lines of symmetry do you think there are in other squares?

Trace the figures. Then find out how many lines of symmetry there are in each.

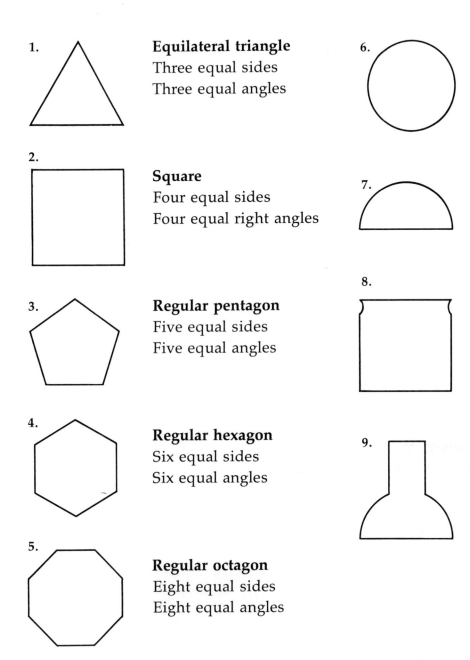

1. **Equilateral triangle**
Three equal sides
Three equal angles

6.

2. **Square**
Four equal sides
Four equal right angles

7.

8.

3. **Regular pentagon**
Five equal sides
Five equal angles

4. **Regular hexagon**
Six equal sides
Six equal angles

9.

5. **Regular octagon**
Eight equal sides
Eight equal angles

Trace the figures. Divide each figure into halves, using a line of symmetry. Shade $\frac{1}{2}$ of each figure.

1.

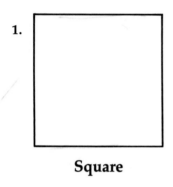

Square

3.

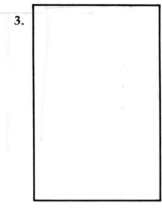

Rectangle

2.

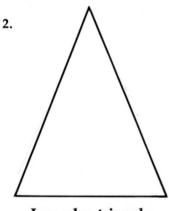

Isosceles triangle
2 equal sides
2 equal angles

4.

5. Trace each figure again. Try to shade $\frac{1}{2}$ the area of each figure in such a way that there is not a line of symmetry between the shaded and the unshaded parts. (This is hard for figures 3 and 4. Do the best you can.)

Parallel lines can be used to divide line segments into equal parts.

The 7 lines above are parallel, and the distances between them are the same.

Copy the line segment below on a sheet of tracing paper.

Place your paper with the line segment over the 7 parallel lines at the top of this page. Move the paper so that one end of the line segment just touches the top line and the other just touches the bottom line.

Mark the points where the line segment crosses each of the parallel lines.

- Into how many parts has your line segment been divided?
- Do the parts seem about equal in length?
- Is each part $\frac{1}{6}$ of the length of the segment?
- How many centimeters long is the segment?
- How many centimeters long is each small part of the segment?
- What is $\frac{1}{6}$ of 12?

Copy the line segment again. Divide the segment into 4 equal parts by placing it across 5 of the parallel lines.

- Measure to find how many centimeters there are in $\frac{1}{4}$ of the segment.
- What is $\frac{1}{4}$ of 12?

Look at the graph. What are the coordinates of these points?

1. A
2. B
3. C
4. D
5. E
6. F

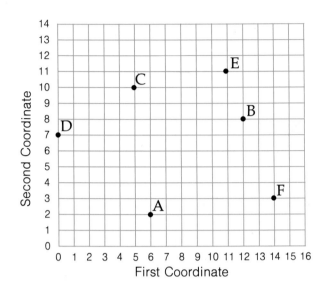

Second Coordinate / First Coordinate

Find the value of x or y.

7. $3 \longrightarrow \boxed{+5} \longrightarrow y$

8. $8 \longrightarrow \boxed{-2} \longrightarrow y$

9. $x \longrightarrow \boxed{\times 6} \longrightarrow 42$

10. $12 \longrightarrow \boxed{-5} \longrightarrow n \longrightarrow \boxed{\times 3} \longrightarrow y$

11. $4 \longrightarrow \boxed{\div 2} \longrightarrow n \longrightarrow \boxed{+9} \longrightarrow y$

12. $x \longrightarrow \boxed{\div 4} \longrightarrow n \longrightarrow \boxed{-6} \longrightarrow 2$

What is a possible function rule for each of these?

13. $x \longrightarrow \boxed{?} \longrightarrow y$

x	y
7	13
10	16
24	30
0	6

14. $x \longrightarrow \boxed{?} \longrightarrow y$

x	y
15	5
12	4
30	10
3	1

Solve for n.

15. $35 \div n = 7$
16. $6 \times n = 42$
17. $8 \times n = 64$
18. $n - 7 = 18$
19. $56 \div n = 7$
20. $63 \div 9 = n$

Add or subtract. Watch the signs.

21. 937
    + 793

22. 684
    − 96

23. 415,398
    − 22,501

24. 83,219
    + 19,882

25. Doug saves $3 a month. How long will it take him to save $24?

26. Heather lives 2 kilometers from her school. Laura lives 1 kilometer from the school. How far does Laura live from Heather?

27. Steve's tenth birthday was in 1979. In what year was his second birthday?

Tell whether each angle is a right angle.

28.

29.

For each pair of lines, tell whether the lines are parallel, perpendicular, or neither.

30.

31.

32.

How many lines of symmetry can be drawn in each figure?

33.

34.

Translate the messages by using the Code Graph to
translate ordered pairs to letters.

1. (12, 4), (9, 5), (28, 16), (8, 9), (24, 9)-
   (12, 4), (9, 5), (28, 16), (3, 11), (18, 0), (1, 6)
   (3, 11), (1, 6)   (20, 13), (20, 8), (9, 17).
2. (15, 15), (9, 5), (1, 6), (8, 9), (3, 11), (9, 17), (14, 9)-
   (28, 16), (17, 6), (9, 17)   (15, 15), (9, 5), (1, 6)
   (28, 16), (8, 9), (24, 9)   (20, 13), (3, 11), (3, 2), (1, 6), (28, 16)
   (26, 12), (3, 2), (24, 9), (1, 6), (3, 11)-
   (21, 3), (24, 9), (9, 17), (28, 16)
   (17, 6), (20, 13)   (28, 16), (8, 9), (24, 9)   (20, 8). (1, 6).
3. (15, 15), (9, 5), (1, 6), (8, 9), (3, 11), (9, 17), (14, 9)-
   (28, 16), (17, 6), (9, 17)
   (3, 11), (1, 6)   (28, 16), (8, 9), (24, 9)
   (18, 0), (9, 5), (26, 12), (3, 11), (28, 16), (9, 5), (6, 15)
   (17, 6), (20, 13)   (28, 16), (8, 9), (24, 9)   (20, 8). (1, 6).

Code Graph

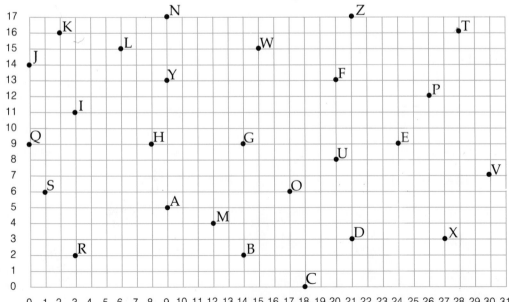

What is the value of *y*?

1. 24 —(+7)▸ *y*

2. 18 —(−3)▸ *y*

3. 7 —(×8)▸ *y*

4. 8 —(×0)▸ *y*

5. 36 —(−9)▸ *y*

6. 36 —(÷4)▸ *y*

7. 2956 —(+0)▸ *y*

8. 0 —(+2)▸ *y*

9. 3 —(×6)▸ *y*

10. 7 —(+98)▸ *y*

11. 63 —(÷7)▸ *y*

12. 82 —(−0)▸ *y*

What is the value of *x*?

13. *x* —(−8)▸ 0

14. *x* —(÷2)▸ 7

15. *x* —(+2)▸ 5

16. *x* —(÷4)▸ 7

17. *x* —(+5)▸ 26

18. *x* —(×1)▸ 179

19. *x* —(+0)▸ 0

20. *x* —(+3)▸ 56

21. *x* —(÷6)▸ 8

22. *x* —(−2)▸ 12

23. *x* —(×0)▸ 0

24. *x* —(+9)▸ 20

Give a possible function rule for each set of
ordered pairs.

1. $x \rightarrow (?) \rightarrow y$

x	y
1	7
8	14
5	11
0	6
10	16
9	15

4. $x \rightarrow (?) \rightarrow y$

x	y
12	3
18	9
30	21
54	45
63	54
36	27

7. $x \rightarrow (?) \rightarrow y$

x	y
7	7
18	18
171	171
5	5
63	63
45	45

2. $x \rightarrow (?) \rightarrow y$

x	y
0	0
6	2
15	5
30	10

5. $x \rightarrow (?) \rightarrow y$

x	y
5	2
34	31
52	49
8	5

8. $x \rightarrow (?) \rightarrow y$

x	y
8	56
9	63
7	49
6	42

3. $x \rightarrow (?) \rightarrow y$

x	y
0	0
1	8
7	56
10	80

6. $x \rightarrow (?) \rightarrow y$

x	y
9	13
1	5
6	10
12	16

9. $x \rightarrow (?) \rightarrow y$

x	y
8	72
9	81
6	54
7	63

Copy and complete each table of ordered pairs.
Then graph each set of points.

1. $x \rightarrow (\times 4) \rightarrow y$

x	y
0	■
3	■
■	8
1	■
■	16

4. $x \rightarrow (\times 4) \rightarrow n \rightarrow (+7) \rightarrow y$

x	y
0	■
3	■
■	15
1	■
■	23

7. $x \rightarrow (\times 3) \rightarrow n \rightarrow (-8) \rightarrow y$

x	y
3	■
■	7
■	4
10	■
■	19

2. $x \rightarrow (+7) \rightarrow y$

x	y
0	■
12	■
■	15
4	■
■	23

5. $x \rightarrow (-3) \rightarrow n \rightarrow (\times 2) \rightarrow y$

x	y
■	0
6	■
■	2
8	■
■	4

8. $x \rightarrow (+8) \rightarrow n \rightarrow (\div 3) \rightarrow y$

x	y
■	3
7	■
4	■
■	10
19	■

3. $x \rightarrow (\div 2) \rightarrow y$

x	y
6	■
■	6
■	5
16	■
■	10

6. $x \rightarrow (\div 2) \rightarrow n \rightarrow (-3) \rightarrow y$

x	y
6	■
12	■
■	2
16	■
■	7

9. $x \rightarrow (\div 5) \rightarrow n \rightarrow (+3) \rightarrow y$

x	y
5	■
25	■
■	7
■	4
■	5

Solve for *n*. Watch the signs.

1. $21 - n = 7$
2. $49 \div 7 = n$
3. $n = 8 \times 5$
4. $13 + 4 = n$
5. $4 = n \div 9$
6. $6 \times 7 = n$
7. $37 - 18 = n$

8. $n = 5 + 27$
9. $27 - 16 = n$
10. $n \times 4 = 16$
11. $n = 27 \div 3$
12. $21 + 39 = n$
13. $63 \div n = 9$
14. $n = 9 \times 9$

15. $7 + n = 36$
16. $42 - 24 = n$
17. $n \div 3 = 24$
18. $6 \times n = 36$
19. $n = 15 + 18$
20. $n - 28 = 13$

Add or subtract.

21. $312 - 154$
22. $782 + 429$
23. $294 - 123$
24. $781 + 317$

25. $238 + 513$
26. $508 - 274$
27. $3089 - 666$
28. $341 + 265$

29. $731 - 245$
30. $665 + 306$
31. $156 + 179$
32. $7376 - 6127$

Watch the signs.

33. $23 + 38$
34. $48 - 29$
35. $614 + 327$
36. $43.1 - 23.2$

37. $27.3 + 4.62$
38. $14.14 + 1.7$
39. $6.87 - 1.9$
40. $324.17 + 79.43$

1. Martin saves 10¢ each day. How long will it take him to save enough money to buy a box of crayons that costs 70¢?

2. Jackie is 6 years younger than her sister. They were both born in October. Jackie was born in 1970. In what year was her sister born?

3. Audrey had a stack of baseball cards. Then Harry gave her 20 cards and Lia gave her 35 cards. How many cards does Audrey have now?

4. Gail bought 6 pencils that cost 9¢ each. She gave the clerk a $1 bill. How much change should she get?

5. Norman had a package of 100 paper stars. He wanted to make a pattern of 6 rows with 8 stars in each row. Did he have enough stars to make 2 of these patterns?

6. Olivia runs 7 kilometers every day. How many days will it be before she has run at least 50 kilometers?

7. Victor bought 9 pieces of candy that cost 7¢ each. He gave the cashier 3 quarters. How much change should he get?

8. Freda collects bottle caps. Gary gave her 31 caps and Allen gave her 27.
   a. How many more bottle caps does Freda have now than before?
   b. How many bottle caps does Freda have?

1. Which of these angles are right angles?

a. b. c. d. e.

2. Draw a right angle.
3. Find 5 right angles in your classroom.

For each pair of lines, tell whether the lines are parallel, perpendicular, or neither.

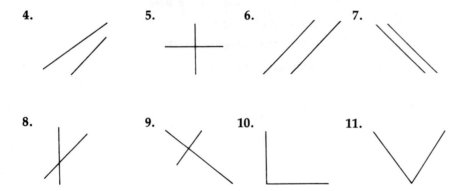

4. 5. 6. 7.

8. 9. 10. 11.

12. Find 3 pairs of perpendicular lines in your classroom.
13. Find 3 pairs of parallel lines in your classroom.

How many lines of symmetry can be drawn in each figure?

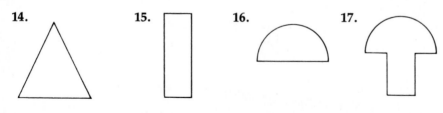

14. 15. 16. 17.

CUBO CHALLENGE

Using only the numbers 1, 2, 6, and 10, try to make each number from 0 to 20 by the rules of Cubo (page 119). Remember that you must use each number only once and may combine numbers using addition, subtraction, multiplication, and division. Keep track of **how** you make each number. You may use parentheses, if necessary.

Challenge problem: Following the rules of Cubo, what is the largest number you can make from 1, 2, 6, and 10?

Superchallenge problem: Try to make as many numbers as you can between 0 and 40 by the rules of Cubo, using 1, 2, 6, and 10. (All but 2 of the numbers from 0 to 40 are possible.)

Super-duper challenge problem: Try to make as many numbers as you can between 0 and 64. (All but 8 of the numbers from 0 to 64 are possible.)

Roll the 4 cubes until you find another set of 4 numbers that you think will work well. Then use those numbers in the challenge problems.

Use the same numbers as other people in the class and compare your results with theirs.

What are the coordinates of these points?

1. A
2. B
3. C
4. D
5. E

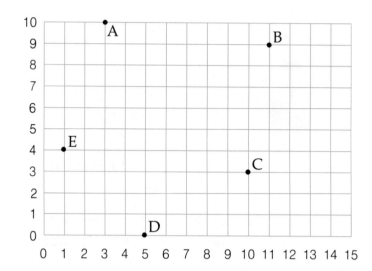

Find the value of x or y.

6. $8 \xrightarrow{\quad} (+9) \xrightarrow{\quad} y$

7. $42 \xrightarrow{\quad} (\div 7) \xrightarrow{\quad} y$

8. $x \xrightarrow{\quad} (\times 4) \xrightarrow{\quad} 24$

9. $17 \xrightarrow{\quad} (-7) \xrightarrow{\quad} n \xrightarrow{\quad} (\div 2) \xrightarrow{\quad} y$

10. $x \xrightarrow{\quad} (\div 3) \xrightarrow{\quad} n \xrightarrow{\quad} (-5) \xrightarrow{\quad} 2$

What is a possible function rule for each chart?

11. $x \to (?) \to y$

x	y
7	21
3	9
0	0
5	15

12. $x \to (?) \to y$

x	y
16	8
20	12
24	16
30	22

Solve for n.

13. $20 \div 4 = n$
14. $7 \times n = 42$
15. $n - 2 = 8$
16. $56 \div 7 = n$
17. $5 \times n = 45$
18. $n \times 3 = 18$

190

19. 67   20. 324   21. 706   22. 404
   + 49   − 98   + 214   − 187

23. Kim is saving to buy a baseball glove that costs $8. She saves $2 each week. How many weeks will it take her to save enough money to buy the glove?

24. Carl is reading a book about animals. This morning he was on page 39. By the end of the day he reached page 72. How many pages are in the book?

25. Bella was born in May of 1969. Her brother, Ken, was born in May of 1973. When Bella was 9 years old, how old was Ken?

26. Paul went to see his friend give a magic show. He noticed that there were 4 rows with 6 chairs in each row. There was also a row of 3 chairs. How many people could be seated for the show?

Tell whether each is a right angle.

27.

28.

For each pair of lines, tell whether the lines are parallel, perpendicular, or neither.

29. 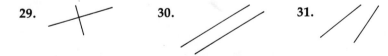   30.   31.

How many lines of symmetry can be drawn in each figure?

32.    33.

MULTIPLYING
WHOLE NUMBERS

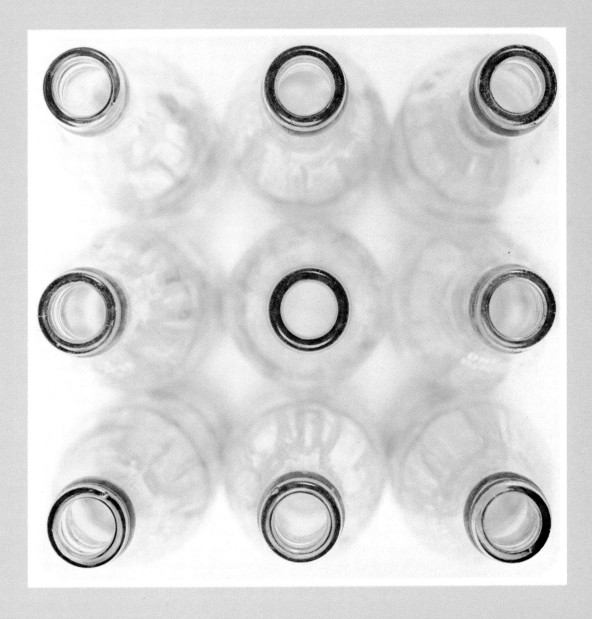

"I can add 0 to 3 and get 30," said Scott. "I just write 3 and then I add the 0 after it." He wrote 30 on the board.

"You aren't really adding 0," answered Carol. "You're multiplying by 10 when you write that 0 after the 3."

- When Scott writes 0 after 3, is he adding 0 to 3 or multiplying 3×10?
- How can you multiply 3 by 100?
- How can you multiply 3 by 1000?
- How can you multiply 3 by 10,000?
- State a general rule for multiplying by numbers like 10, 100, 1000, and so on. Discuss your rule with others. Why does your rule work?

Use your rule to solve for n.

1. $10 \times 7 = n$
2. $100 \times 7 = n$
3. $1000 \times 7 = n$
4. $1000 \times 6 = n$
5. $1000 \times 65 = n$
6. $100 \times 73 = n$
7. $10 \times 583 = n$
8. $583 \times 10 = n$
9. $68 \times 100 = n$
10. $10{,}000 \times 583 = n$
11. $657 \times 10 = n$
12. $100 \times 783 = n$
13. $594 \times 1000 = n$
14. $86 \times 100 = n$
15. $503 \times 10 = n$
16. $100 \times 10 = n$

- How many zeros are there in your answer to problem 16? Did you write 2 zeros after the 10 or did you write 1 zero after the 100? Does it make a difference in your answer?

Multiply.

17. 100×100
18. 1000×10
19. 1000×1000
20. 10×1000
21. $10{,}000 \times 100$
22. $10{,}000 \times 10{,}000$
23. 100×1000
24. $100{,}000 \times 10$
25. $1{,}000{,}000 \times 1000$
26. $100{,}000 \times 1000$

Multiply 400 × 800.

Think of a rectangle that is 800 units long and 400 units wide.

Now think of separating the rectangle into squares, so that each square is 100 units by 100 units.

- How many squares are there?
- What is the area of each square?
- What is the area of the entire rectangle?
- What is 400 × 800?

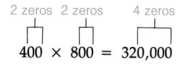

$$400 \times 800 = 320,000$$

Notice that the number of zeros in the answer is the sum of the numbers of zeros in the 2 factors.

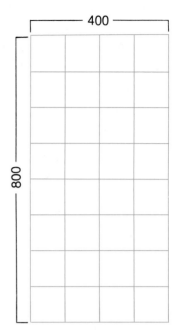

Multiply 300 × 60.

Look at another rectangle separated into rectangular sections.

- How many small rectangles are there?
- What is the area of each small rectangle?
- What is the area of the entire rectangle?
- What is 300 × 60?

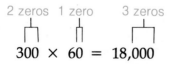

$$300 \times 60 = 18,000$$

Notice that the number of zeros in the answer is the sum of the numbers of zeros in the factors.

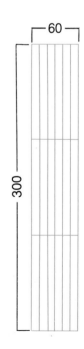

Multiply 90,000 × 2,000,000.
The answer is 9 × 2 with a lot of zeros after it. Here's
how to find out how many zeros.

Count the number of zeros in the 2 factors.
There are **4 zeros** in 90,000.
There are **6 zeros** in 2,000,000.
There are **10 zeros** in all in the 2 factors.

So the answer is 9 × 2 with 10 zeros after it.
The answer is 180,000,000,000.
(Read it "one hundred eighty billion.")

Multiply.

1.	30	2.	80	3.	600	4.	8000
	× 50		× 40		× 700		× 30

5. $900 \times 200 = n$

6. $5 \times 4 = n$

7. $50 \times 4 = n$

8. $5 \times 40 = n$

9. $500 \times 4 = n$

10. $5000 \times 4000 = n$

11. $60 \times 50 = n$

12. $20 \times 500 = n$

13. $600 \times 30 = n$

14. $900 \times 80 = n$

15. $8000 \times 7000 = n$

16. $1000 \times 4000 = n$

17. $10,000 \times 60 = n$

18. $200 \times 4000 = n$

19. $300 \times 40 = n$

20. $4 \times 7000 = n$

21. $30 \times 90 = n$

22. $800 \times 4000 = n$

23. $90 \times 5000 = n$

24. $80 \times 30 = n$

25. $3 \times 500 = n$

26. $4000 \times 7000 = n$

27. $90 \times 500 = n$

28. $600 \times 40 = n$

29. $8 \times 500 = n$

30. $90 \times 400 = n$

THE TREASURE OF MUGG ISLAND   Part 1

In this story, the children leave the island of Addonia.
Therefore numbers are now said in the usual way.

The queen of Addonia called Manolita, Mark,
Ferdie, and Portia to her castle. "I need your
help," she said. "Years ago pirates stole the
Royal Treasure. Now I have learned that it
is hidden on Mugg Island. Will you go there
with me to help find it?"

The children were happy to help. This
sounded like an adventure! Soon they were
flying over the sea in the Royal Helicopter.
The queen herself was the pilot.

"Where is Mugg Island?" Portia asked.

"I don't know," said the queen.
"We'll just have to fly around
until we see it."

"But how will we know which
island it is?" Portia asked.
"There are dozens and dozens
of islands out here."

"This should help," said the
queen.

She handed them a note.
It said: "Mugg Island.
The south shore of Mugg
Island is straight and
about 1 kilometer
long. On the

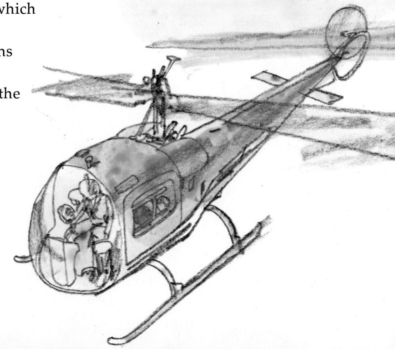

east side, the shore goes straight north for 2
kilometers. Then the shore goes west for 1
kilometer. Then the shore turns south for a short
distance. Then there is a large bulge of land,
about 1 kilometer across, sticking out toward
the west. After the bulge, the shore goes
straight south again until it meets the south
shore. In the middle of the bulge is a small
round lake. Out of the lake comes a stream,
which flows eastward to the sea. The
stream makes a line like a human face,
with a pointy nose pointing south."

"This is no help," said Ferdie.
"I can't tell what the island looks like
from reading this!"

"Try drawing a map," said
the queen.

1. Draw a map of Mugg Island. Try to use every fact that
   the story gives you. See which group can make the best
   map.

2. How would you describe the shape of Mugg Island?

Multiply.

1. 100 × 10
2. 100 × 1000
3. 10 × 1000
4. 1000 × 1000
5. 1,000,000 × 10

6. 10,000 × 1000
7. 1000 × 100
8. 10,000 × 100
9. 1000 × 10,000
10. 10 × 100,000

11. 300 × 400
12. 90 × 30
13. 4000 × 8000
14. 200 × 200
15. 300 × 50

16. 70 × 400
17. 8000 × 50
18. 50 × 400
19. 300,000 × 20
20. 6000 × 500

21. 100 × 40
22. 5000 × 900
23. 150 × 10
24. 3000 × 200
25. 309 × 10

26. 100 × 100
27. 603 × 100
28. 70,000 × 80
29. 45 × 100
30. 100 × 219

31. Miss Foster has 14 ten-dollar bills. Is that enough
money to pay for

a. the desk?   b. the sofa?   c. the chair?

• Which number in each pair is usually easier to work with?

   61 or 60?   214 or 200?   4971 or 5000?

Multiples of 10, 100, 1000, and so on are usually easier to work with than other numbers.

When we say, write, or use numbers, we often do not have to be exact. So we can replace a number by the nearest multiple of 10, or 100, or 1000, and so on. We call this rounding. How exact we need to be depends on what the numbers will be used for.

For each statement, choose the most appropriate answer. Use each answer only once.

1. a. The train will arrive
   b. Aunt Mary is coming for dinner
   c. The rocket will be launched

   (1) at 6:03 and 11 seconds.
   (2) at 6:03.
   (3) at about 6:00.

2. a. A map maker said the distance between those cities is
   b. Dad said that the trip to Wisconsin is
   c. The mechanic said to change the oil in the car at

   (1) about 2900 kilometers.
   (2) 2873 kilometers.
   (3) about 3000 kilometers.

Look at newspaper articles. Watch and listen to news reports. Can you find examples of rounded numbers?

Rounding is also useful when you do not need an exact answer to a calculation.

Alex wants to buy 7 packages of balsa wood for $1.97 (197 cents) each. He has $15. Does he have enough money for this balsa wood?

The answer is yes. You can figure that out without finding the exact cost.

The cost of each package of balsa wood is less than $2. So the cost for 7 packages is less than 7 × 2, or $14.

Since $15 is greater than $14, Alex has enough money to buy 7 packages of balsa wood.

Approximate. You don't need an exact answer to solve these problems.

1. Miss Laria wants to buy 25 books for $1.69 (169 cents) each. She has $50. Is that enough to buy the books?

2. Mr. Glass wants to buy 27 baseball shirts for his team. The shirts cost $7.98 (798 cents) each. He has $140 with him. Is that enough money to buy the shirts?

3. Phyllis wants to buy 18 bananas that cost 9¢ each. She has $2.00 (200 cents). Does she have enough to buy the bananas?

4. Chris wants to buy 30 pencils. The pencils cost 12¢ each. Chris has $3.00. Does he have enough money to buy the pencils?

5. Greta is 9 years old. She wants to know if she's more than 2500 days old. Is she?

6. Armando says there are more than 10 million seconds in a year. Is he right? (There are 60 seconds in 1 minute, 60 minutes in 1 hour, 24 hours in 1 day, and about 365 days in 1 year.)

7. The auditorium in Jan's school has 48 rows with 24 seats in each row. Can 750 people be seated for a school play?

8. Lindsey says that his school used more than 10,000 cans of soup last year for meals. A case of soup contains 24 cans. Lindsey's school used 831 cases last year. Is he right?

9. Margaret delivers 36 newspapers every day. Does she deliver more than 300 newspapers in a week (7 days)?

10. Suzy sells salted peanuts at football games for $0.95 a bag. If she sells 280 bags, will she take in $300?

11. Patrick collected 82 sea shells last summer. If he sells all of them for 35 cents each, will he earn enough money to buy a rubber raft that costs $23.99?

When you approximate an answer, you don't have to give just 1 number. You can give 2 numbers and say that the answer is between those 2 numbers.

A cutting board is 56 centimeters long and 27 centimeters wide. About how large is the cutting board?

The answer must be less than 60×30 square centimeters. So it must be less than 1800 square centimeters.

The answer must also be greater than 50×20 square centimeters. So it must be greater than 1000 square centimeters.

The answer must be between 1000 and 1800 square centimeters.

1. A garden is 28 meters long and 12 meters wide. Approximate the area by finding 2 numbers that it must be between.
   a. Can the area be 600 square meters?
   b. Suppose you calculated the area and got an answer of 278 square meters. How would you know that you had made a mistake?

2. A rug is 261 centimeters long and 194 centimeters wide. Approximate the area by finding 2 numbers that it must be between. (You may round to whole numbers of hundreds.) Which of these could be the actual area?
   a. 15,824 square centimeters
   b. 50,494 square centimeters
   c. 63,774 square centimeters

3. A playground is 92 meters long and 53 meters wide. Approximate the area by finding 2 numbers that it must be between. Which of these could be the actual area?

   a. 4266 square meters

   b. 6376 square meters

   c. 4906 square meters

In each problem, 2 of the answers are clearly wrong and 1 is correct. Choose the correct answer.

1. $32 \times 17 = $	a. 264	b. 544	c. 914
2. $46 \times 61 = $	a. 2806	b. 2316	c. 2026
3. $28 \times 195 = $	a. 5460	b. 6140	c. 7440
4. $206 \times 38 = $	a. 5828	b. 7828	c. 4828
5. $74 \times 803 = $	a. 59,422	b. 592,222	c. 5,942,222
6. $284 \times 579 = $	a. 13,896	b. 164,436	c. 187,296
7. $612 \times 559 = $	a. 342,108	b. 3,416,608	c. 3,402,108
8. $527 \times 312 = $	a. 1,826,394	b. 15,204	c. 164,424
9. $111 \times 8901 = $	a. 890,901	b. 89,011	c. 988,011
10. $72 \times 504 = $	a. 36,288	b. 3888	c. 396,288
11. $632 \times 59 = $	a. 373,588	b. 353,288	c. 37,288
12. $125 \times 8888 = $	a. 222,200	b. 111,000	c. 1,111,000
13. $574 \times 896 = $	a. 49,364	b. 794,644	c. 514,304
14. $994 \times 9735 = $	a. 9,676,590	b. 9,981,910	c. 9,872,540

THE CASE OF THE SODA BOTTLE CASES   Episode 1

Adam, Lenny, Murray, and Vernon want to earn some money. They can get money at the store for each soda bottle they return.

They collect lots of bottles and put them into cases like this one.

• How many bottles are in this case?

The boys filled 8 cases with bottles. Each case had 24 bottles. They wanted to know how many bottles they had altogether.

Lenny said, "If there were only 20 bottles in a case, we would have 160 bottles."

"How do you know?" asked Murray.

"Because 8 × 2 = 16, so 8 × 2 tens is 16 tens. And that's 160," answered Lenny.

"But you didn't count all the bottles," said Vernon. "You counted only 20 for each case."

"I left out only 4 from each case," Lenny said.

"But that means there are 32 bottles that you didn't count," said Vernon.

"I've got it!" said Adam. "If we add the 32 that Lenny didn't count to the 160 he did count, we would have the answer."

"That's it," said Murray. "We have 192 bottles."

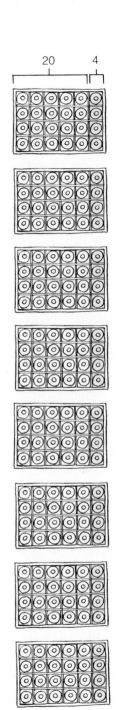

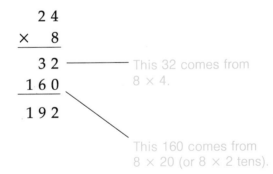

```
    2 4
  ×   8
  ───────
    3 2 ─────── This 32 comes from
  1 6 0          8 × 4.
  ───────
  1 9 2
              This 160 comes from
              8 × 20 (or 8 × 2 tens).
```

Here's a shorter way to multiply 8 × 24.

```
  2 4        Start at the right. Multiply the ones digit by 8.
×   8        8 × 4 = 32 (that's 3 tens and 2)
    2        Write the 2 and remember the 3 tens for the
             next column.
```

```
  2 4        Multiply the tens digit by 8.
×   8        8 × 2 = 16
1 9 2        16 tens plus the 3 tens you remembered is
             19 tens.
             Write 19.
```

   You may have trouble remembering the number that
you saved from the previous column. If you do, you may
use one of these methods to help:

a. Keep track of the number on your fingers. If the
   number is greater than 5, use both hands; you won't
   have to write until you've used that number.

b. You may write the number you are
   remembering in the place you will write
   the next part of the answer. Cross off
   the number as soon as you use it.

```
  2 4            2 4            2 4
×   8          ×   8          ×   8
          →        3      →       3̸
               2            1 9 2
```

c. Write the number above the next digit
   of the top number. Cross it off when
   you use it.

```
                  3              3̸
  2 4            2 4            2 4
×   8          ×   8          ×   8
          →              →
               2            1 9 2
```

Writing the numbers is messy and it may confuse you.
Avoid it if you can.

Multiply. Use shortcuts when you can.

1.	2.	3.	4.	5.
24	29	43	60	90
× 6	× 9	× 3	× 8	× 3

6.	7.	8.	9.	10.
24	46	65	19	78
× 8	× 7	× 4	× 4	× 9

11.	12.	13.	14.	15.
25	87	51	89	95
× 4	× 2	× 7	× 3	× 6

16. 68 × 3   20. 77 × 8   24. 99 × 8   28. 8 × 54
17. 37 × 5   21. 26 × 9   25. 40 × 3   29. 91 × 2
18. 4 × 70   22. 7 × 49   26. 6 × 39   30. 4 × 72
19. 29 × 3   23. 6 × 27   27. 68 × 5

Check to see that your answers make sense.

Example: The answer to problem 1 should be less than 6 × 30, which is 180.
The answer to problem 1 should be greater than 6 × 20, which is 120.
Is your answer to problem 1 less than 180 and greater than 120?
If so, the answer makes sense. (That does not tell you it is correct. But if it makes no sense, it must be wrong.)

THE CASE OF THE SODA BOTTLE CASES   Episode 2

Remember that Adam, Lenny, Murray, and Vernon collected 192 soda bottles. "I think we can get 9 cents at the store for each bottle we return," said Adam. "I wonder how much money we can get altogether."

"Let's see," said Murray, "192 is the same amount as 100 + 90 + 2. For 100 bottles we get 900 cents. For 90 bottles we get 810 cents. For 2 bottles we get 18 cents. How much is that altogether?"

"That's 1728 cents," said Vernon, "which is $17.28."

"Let's go get our money," they all said.

Look:

```
    1 9 2
  ×     9
  ─────────
      1 8  ──── This 18 comes from 9 × 2.
    8 1 0  ──── This 810 comes from 9 × 90 (or 9 × 9 tens).
    9 0 0  ──── This 900 comes from 9 × 100 (or 9 × 1 hundred).
  ─────────
  1 7 2 8  ──── This comes from 18 + 810 + 900.
```

210

Here's a shorter way to multiply 9 × 192.

$\begin{array}{r} 1\ 9\ 2 \\ \times\ \ \ \ 9 \\ \hline 8 \end{array}$	Start at the right. Multiply the ones digit by 9. 9 × 2 = 18 18 = 1 ten and 8 Write the 8 and remember the 1 ten.
$\begin{array}{r} 1\ 9\ 2 \\ \times\ \ \ \ 9 \\ \hline 2\ 8 \end{array}$	Multiply the tens digit by 9. 9 × 9 = 81 81 tens and 1 ten is 82 tens. 82 tens = 8 hundreds and 2 tens Write the 2 and remember the 8 hundreds.
$\begin{array}{r} 1\ 9\ 2 \\ \times\ \ \ \ 9 \\ \hline 1\ 7\ 2\ 8 \end{array}$	Multiply the hundreds digit by 9. 9 × 1 = 9 9 hundreds and 8 hundreds is 17 hundreds. 17 hundreds is 1 thousand and 7 hundreds. Write the 17.

Multiply. Use shortcuts when you can.

1. 352 × 8	**5.** 200 × 9	**9.** 453 × 4	**13.** 721 × 2
2. 684 × 7	**6.** 201 × 9	**10.** 795 × 5	**14.** 7 × 367
3. 47 × 6	**7.** 643 × 8	**11.** 497 × 2	**15.** 800 × 6
4. 308 × 7	**8.** 987 × 6	**12.** 4 × 606	**16.** 505 × 3

Check to see that your answers make sense.

Example: The answer to problem 1 should be less than
8 × 400, which is 3200.
It should be greater than 8 × 300, which is 2400.
Is your answer to problem 1 less than 3200
and greater than 2400?
If so, the answer makes sense.

CUBE 100 GAME

Players: 2
Materials: Two 0–5 cubes, two 5–10 cubes
Object: To score as close to 100 as possible without going over

Rules
1. Roll the cubes one at a time, adding the numbers as you roll.
2. After any roll, instead of adding that number you may multiply it by the sum of the previous numbers. But then your turn is over.
3. The player with the score closer to, but not over, 100 wins the round.

Sample Game

Wendy rolled **6** then **3**.

$$6 + 3 = 9$$

Then she rolled **9**.

$$9 \times 9 = 81$$

She stopped after 3 rolls.
Wendy's score was 81.

Todd rolled **5** then **5**.

$$5 + 5 = 10$$

Then he rolled **6**.

$$10 + 6 = 16$$

He rolled **6** again.

$$16 \times 6 = 96$$

Todd's score was 96.
Todd won the round.

Can you think of any other ways to play this game?

Multiply.

1.	64	**2.**	308	**3.**	99	**4.**	726	**5.**	394
	× 7		× 4		× 5		× 8		× 2

6.	501	**7.**	663	**8.**	48	**9.**	90	**10.**	307
	× 8		× 7		× 3		× 9		× 9

11. 56 × 7   **14.** 840 × 9   **17.** 82 × 5   **19.** 28 × 6
12. 434 × 3   **15.** 107 × 5   **18.** 19 × 8   **20.** 730 × 4
13. 72 × 6   **16.** 321 × 4

21. Jamie rides her bike 3 kilometers every day. How far does she ride in 15 days?

22. Judy gets 8 baseball cards in every pack of gum she buys. How many cards will she get in 9 packs?

23. Anthony is packing supplies for a camping trip. He will bake biscuits 5 times. He will use 4 packages of biscuit mix each time he bakes biscuits. How many packages of biscuit mix should he pack?

THE TREASURE OF MUGG ISLAND   Part 2

Soon the Royal Helicopter came to an island that had the shape of a coffee mug. "This is it," said Manolita. "Mugg Island."

The island was rocky and full of trees. At first they could not find anyplace to land. Then they found a place where the land was flat and there were no trees. So they landed there.

They all climbed out of the Royal Helicopter. "Now," said the queen, "we must find the hollow tree. The dotted line on the map shows the trail to follow." Here is the map she showed them:

"This can't be the whole map," said Mark.

"It's all I have," said the queen. "That's why I need your help. If I had the whole map, I could find the hollow tree myself."

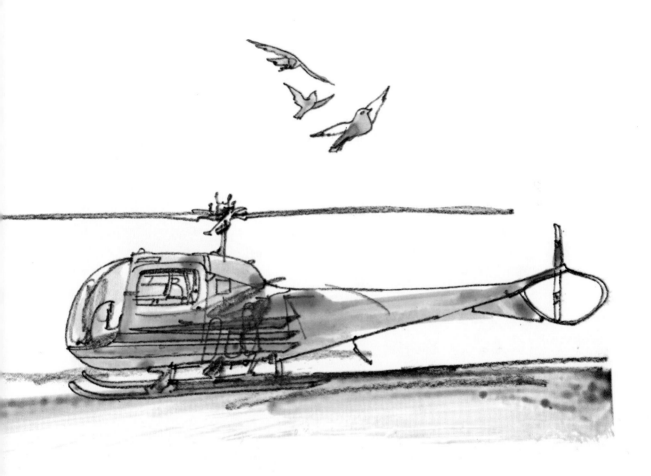

1. How could Mark tell that this was only part of the map showing how to find the hollow tree?

2. Why might the trail show up in 2 different places on the map?

3. Where is the hollow tree on the island? Use the map of the whole island to help you.

CUTTING A PROBLEM DOWN TO SIZE

Emiko, Beth, Don, and Tak are working in Mr. Ogata's garden.

Don said, "We need enough fertilizer to cover the garden. How many bags of fertilizer is that?"

"The garden is 57 meters long," said Beth.

"And it's 36 meters wide," added Tak.

Emiko said, "Each bag of fertilizer covers 100 square meters."

"First we need to find the area of the garden," said Beth.

So the children drew a picture of the garden. It didn't seem to help.

"We don't know how to multiply 57 × 36," they said.

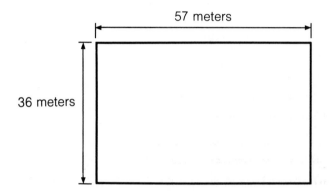

"I have an idea," Emiko said suddenly. "Let's draw lines to make a few sections, like this."

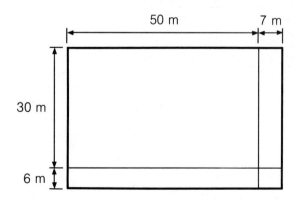

"Then we can figure out the area of each section and add them up."

"I know the area of the small section," said Don. "It's 7 meters long and 6 meters wide. So its area is 6 × 7, or 42, square meters."

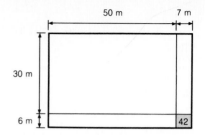

"And I know the area of the section on the bottom," said Tak. "It's 50 meters long and 6 meters wide. So its area is 50 × 6, or 300, square meters."

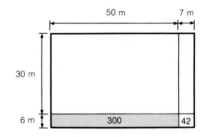

"And I know the area of the section on the side," said Beth. "It's 30 meters long and 7 meters wide. So its area is 30 × 7, or 210, square meters."

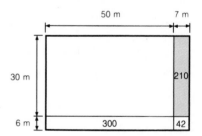

"And I know the area of the large section," said Emiko. "It's 50 meters long and 30 meters wide. So its area is 1500 square meters."

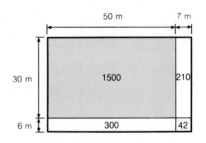

"Now we can add up the areas of the 4 sections to find the area of the garden," said Don. "42 + 300 + 210 + 1500 is 2052. So the area is 2052 square meters."

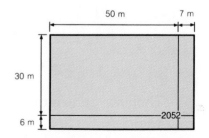

218

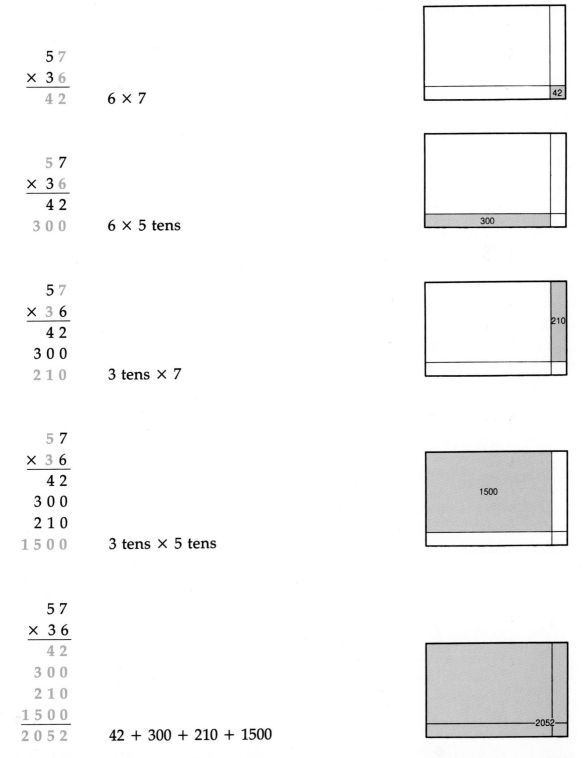

$$
\begin{array}{r}
5\,7 \\
\times\;3\,6 \\
\hline
4\,2
\end{array}
$$
6 × 7

$$
\begin{array}{r}
5\,7 \\
\times\;3\,6 \\
\hline
4\,2 \\
3\,0\,0
\end{array}
$$
6 × 5 tens

$$
\begin{array}{r}
5\,7 \\
\times\;3\,6 \\
\hline
4\,2 \\
3\,0\,0 \\
2\,1\,0
\end{array}
$$
3 tens × 7

$$
\begin{array}{r}
5\,7 \\
\times\;3\,6 \\
\hline
4\,2 \\
3\,0\,0 \\
2\,1\,0 \\
1\,5\,0\,0
\end{array}
$$
3 tens × 5 tens

$$
\begin{array}{r}
5\,7 \\
\times\;3\,6 \\
\hline
4\,2 \\
3\,0\,0 \\
2\,1\,0 \\
1\,5\,0\,0 \\
\hline
2\,0\,5\,2
\end{array}
$$
42 + 300 + 210 + 1500

219

Here's a shorter way to multiply 36 × 57.

```
    5 7        Start at the right. Multiply the top number by the ones digit.
  × 3 6        6 × 57 = 342
    3 4 2      Write 342 so that the digit on the right (2)
               is in the ones column.
```

```
    5 7        Multiply the top number by the tens digit.
  × 3 6        3 × 57 = 171   There are 171 tens.
    3 4 2      Write 171 so that the digit on the right (1)
  1 7 1        is in the tens column.
```

```
    5 7        Add to get final answer.
  × 3 6
    3 4 2
  1 7 1
  2 0 5 2
```

Check to see that the answer makes sense.

The answer should be less than 40 × 60, which is 2400.

The answer should be greater than 30 × 50, which is 1500.

2052 is less than 2400 and greater than 1500, so the answer makes sense.

The area of the garden is 2052 square meters. Remember that each bag of fertilizer covers 100 square meters. So the children need 21 bags of fertilizer.

Multiply. Use shortcuts when you can.

1.	43 × 54	2.	96 × 27	3.	18 × 67	4.	420 × 20	5.	86 × 59
6.	47 × 35	7.	53 × 8	8.	64 × 9	9.	58 × 5	10.	21 × 20
11.	39 × 9	12.	75 × 8	13.	67 × 51	14.	64 × 39	15.	58 × 50
16.	39 × 90	17.	21 × 21	18.	13 × 29	19.	84 × 84	20.	68 × 56
21.	50 × 50	22.	54 × 79	23.	29 × 75	24.	21 × 38	25.	50 × 51

Check to see that your answers make sense.

26. Students from the West Park School are going on a field trip. 525 people are going. Each bus can seat 45 people. It costs $55 to rent each bus for a day.
   a. Will 12 buses be too few, just enough, or too many?
   b. How many extra seats will there be?
   c. How much will it cost to rent 12 buses for a day?

1. A rectangle is 63 meters long and 42 meters wide.
   a. What is the area of the rectangle?
   b. What is the perimeter of the rectangle?

2. A rectangle is 63 centimeters long and 42 centimeters wide.
   a. What is its area?
   b. What is the perimeter of the rectangle?

3. Yusef bought 6 containers of milk. They cost 97¢ each. How many cents did he pay for the 6 containers? How much is that in dollars and cents?

4. Tara bought 5 loaves of bread. Each loaf cost 72¢. How much did she pay for the 5 loaves? Give your answer in cents and then in dollars and cents.

5. Barry owns 6 dogs. Each dog weighs about 32 kilograms. Do they weigh more than 240 kilograms altogether?

6. Each of Barry's 6 dogs can jump a stream that is 350 centimeters wide without getting wet. About how wide a stream can they jump together?

7. There are 12 eggs in a carton. How many eggs are there in 6 cartons?

8. There are 100 centimeters in a meter. How many centimeters are there in 7 meters?

9. A carton of canned peas has 6 rows with 8 cans in each row. How many cans are there in 15 cartons?

A bottle of soda costs 25 cents at Terwilliger's Drugstore. You must also pay 10 cents deposit on the bottle. If you return the bottle, you get back the 10 cents. At the One-Stop Grocery Store you can buy a case of 24 bottles of soda for $6.96, including the 10-cent deposit on each bottle.

1. Bryan wants to buy 48 bottles of soda. How much will he have to pay, including the deposit, at Terwilliger's Drugstore?

2. How much will 48 bottles cost at the One-Stop Grocery Store?

3. How much would Bryan save by buying his soda at the One-Stop Grocery Store instead of at Terwilliger's?

4. How much money would Bryan get back when he returned the 48 bottles?

5. Boyd and Niki have found 13 empty soda bottles from Terwilliger's Drugstore. When they return them to Terwilliger's, will they get enough money to buy 3 bottles of soda?

FOUR CUBE MULTIPLICATION GAME

Players: 2 or more
Materials: Two 0–5 cubes, two 5–10 cubes
Object: To get the greatest product

Rules

1. Take turns rolling all 4 cubes. If a 🔟 is rolled, roll that cube again.
2. Combine the numbers you rolled to make a 2-digit by 2-digit or a 3-digit by 1-digit multiplication problem.

If you rolled: These are some problems you could make:

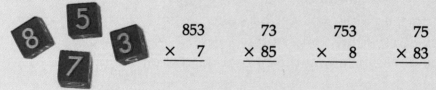

853	73	753	75
× 7	× 85	× 8	× 83

3. The player with the greatest product wins. (Find the exact products only if you need to.)

Sample Game

Terri rolled: 4 2 7 8   Earl rolled: 3 0 6 5

She made this problem: He made this problem:

    82   53
  × 74   × 60

   Terri won the round. (Terri and Earl did not have to find the exact products to see that Terri's product was greater.)

Multiply. Use shortcuts when you can.

1. 26	2. 68	3. 96	4. 32	5. 55
× 35	× 49	× 17	× 90	× 25

6. 38	7. 72	8. 87	9. 17	10. 63
× 43	× 95	× 70	× 36	× 91

11. 18	12. 30	13. 66	14. 76	15. 57
× 22	× 31	× 36	× 41	× 43

16. 70 × 70   19. 82 × 91   22. 71 × 70   24. 67 × 24

17. 53 × 53   20. 17 × 71   23. 77 × 11   25. 90 × 90

18. 27 × 58   21. 39 × 46

26. The ice-cube maker in Zack's refrigerator makes 14 ice cubes every hour. How many ice cubes can it produce in 12 hours?

27. Yuki's soccer team is selling magazine subscriptions to raise money. They can keep $0.35 for each subscription they sell. If the 14 members sell 1 subscription each, how much money will they raise?

28. Barney's father plans to plant 12 rows of blue spruce trees. Each row will contain 21 trees. How many trees will Barney's father plant?

Check to see that your answers make sense.

THE TREASURE OF MUGG ISLAND   Part 3

When they found the hollow tree, the children all ran up to it. They looked inside. "No treasure here," said Manolita. "Just a piece of paper."

"Let me see," said the queen.

Here is the piece of paper they found in the hollow tree:

From tree go NW 13
to spider rock.
From spider rock go
23 paces to peg.

"Dear me," said the queen. "It seems that some animal has eaten part of the note. Now we'll never find the treasure."

226

1. What would the missing parts of the note tell you? (Be careful. Try to think of all that is missing.)

2. How far might the spider rock be from the tree? What are some possible distances?

3. Which of these makes sense for the distance from the tree to the spider rock: (a) 13 centimeters, (b) 132 kilometers, or (c) 132 paces? Why or why not?

4. **NW** means northwest—a direction halfway between north and west. Knowing this, how could you find the spider rock?

5. What don't you know about where the peg is?

6. How could you find the peg anyway?

Multiply: 49 × 376

```
    3 7 6        Start at the right. Multiply the top
×     4 9        number by the ones digit.
  3 3 8 4        9 × 376 = 3384
```
Write 3384 so that the digit on the right
(4) is in the **ones** column.

```
    3 7 6        Multiply by the tens digit.
×     4 9        4 × 376 = 1504
  3 3 8 4        There are 1504 tens.
1 5 0 4
```
Write 1504 so that the digit on the right
(4) is in the **tens** column.

```
    3 7 6        Add to get the final answer.
×     4 9
  3 3 8 4
1 5 0 4
1 8,4 2 4
```

Check to see that the answer makes sense.

The answer should be less than 50 × 400, which is 20,000.
The answer should be greater than 40 × 300, which is 12,000.
18,424 is less than 20,000 and greater than 12,000. So the answer makes sense.

Multiply: 30 × 312

Here's how you would multiply using the way shown on page 228.

        3 1 2   Multiply the top number by the **ones** digit.
    ×   3 0   0 × 312 = 0
              0   Write 0 in the **ones** column.

        3 1 2   Multiply by the **tens** digit.
    ×   3 0   3 × 312 = 936   There are 936 tens.
              0   Write 936 so that the digit on the right (6)
    9 3 6   is in the **tens** column.

        3 1 2   Add.
    ×   3 0
              0
    9 3 6
    9 3 6 0

Here's a shorter way to multiply 30 × 312.

        3 1 2   Multiply the top number by the **ones** digit.
    ×   3 0   0 × 312 = 0
              0   Write 0 in the **ones** column.

        3 1 2   Multiply by the **tens** digit.
    ×   3 0   3 × 312 = 936   There are 936 tens.
    9 3 6 0   Write the 936 next to the 0.

Remember

$$\begin{array}{r} 387 \\ \times\ \ 46 \\ \hline \end{array} \rightarrow \begin{array}{r} 387 \\ \times\ \ 46 \\ \hline 2322 \end{array} \rightarrow \begin{array}{r} 387 \\ \times\ \ 46 \\ \hline 2322 \\ 1548 \end{array} \rightarrow \begin{array}{r} 387 \\ \times\ \ 46 \\ \hline 2322 \\ 1548 \\ \hline 17{,}802 \end{array}$$

Multiply. Use shortcuts when you can.

1. $\begin{array}{r}247 \\ \times\ 26 \\ \hline\end{array}$	**2.** $\begin{array}{r}813 \\ \times\ 59 \\ \hline\end{array}$	**3.** $\begin{array}{r}512 \\ \times\ 64 \\ \hline\end{array}$	**4.** $\begin{array}{r}256 \\ \times\ 32 \\ \hline\end{array}$	**5.** $\begin{array}{r}243 \\ \times\ 27 \\ \hline\end{array}$
6. $\begin{array}{r}806 \\ \times\ 37 \\ \hline\end{array}$	**7.** $\begin{array}{r}281 \\ \times\ 7 \\ \hline\end{array}$	**8.** $\begin{array}{r}281 \\ \times\ 70 \\ \hline\end{array}$	**9.** $\begin{array}{r}394 \\ \times\ 8 \\ \hline\end{array}$	**10.** $\begin{array}{r}394 \\ \times\ 80 \\ \hline\end{array}$
11. $\begin{array}{r}38 \\ \times\ 27 \\ \hline\end{array}$	**12.** $\begin{array}{r}380 \\ \times\ 27 \\ \hline\end{array}$	**13.** $\begin{array}{r}7 \\ \times\ 8 \\ \hline\end{array}$	**14.** $\begin{array}{r}70 \\ \times\ 8 \\ \hline\end{array}$	**15.** $\begin{array}{r}700 \\ \times\ 8 \\ \hline\end{array}$
16. $\begin{array}{r}70 \\ \times\ 80 \\ \hline\end{array}$	**17.** $\begin{array}{r}700 \\ \times\ 80 \\ \hline\end{array}$	**18.** $\begin{array}{r}6 \\ \times\ 7 \\ \hline\end{array}$	**19.** $\begin{array}{r}60 \\ \times\ 70 \\ \hline\end{array}$	**20.** $\begin{array}{r}600 \\ \times\ 70 \\ \hline\end{array}$

Check to see that your answers make sense.

1. Chuck earns $5.00 per hour as a short-order cook. He works 27 hours a week. How much does he earn in a week?

2. Elliott's dog Pudgy eats about 275 grams of dog food per day. About how many grams will Pudgy eat in April (30 days)?

3. The chart shows how much time Carlos spends eating each day. Copy and complete the chart. There are 365 days in a year.

Meal	Time Carlos Spends Eating	
	Daily	Yearly
Breakfast	15 minutes	
Lunch	25 minutes	
Dinner	45 minutes	
Total		

4. Marsha has gone to school for 4 years (including kindergarten). She has spent about 180 days in school each year. About how many days has she gone to school?

5. Oleta is 9 years old today.
   a. Assuming 365 days in a year, how many days old is she?
   b. If there have been 2 leap years (366 days) since she was born, how many days old is she?

6. Figure out your age in days in this way:
   a. Find how many days old you were on your last birthday. Don't forget to include leap years.
   b. Find how many days ago your last birthday was.
   c. Add to find how many days old you are today.

Esther's class is publishing a magazine for the school. The magazine will have 24 pages. The students will print 650 copies, enough for everyone in the school to get one. They have to buy paper, which comes in packages of 500 sheets. Each package costs $3.

1. How many sheets of paper will they need for each copy of the magazine? They will print on both sides of each sheet.

2. About how many sheets of paper will they need altogether?

3. Will 10 packages of paper be enough?   15 packages? 16 packages?

4. How much will the paper cost?

5. If the students charge 5¢ for a copy of the magazine, and if they sell all 650 copies, will they make a profit?

6. The students decide to sell advertising space in the magazine to make extra money. They sell 23 advertisements at 75 cents each. How much is that in cents? In dollars and cents?

7. How much money will the students make if they charge 5¢ for a copy of the magazine and also sell advertising space? If paper is their only cost, will the class make a profit?

8. If the school charges $5 for the use of the mimeograph machine for printing the magazine, will the class make a profit?

Multiply: 749 × 583

```
    5 8 3
  × 7 4 9
  5 2 4 7
```
Multiply the top number by the **ones** digit.
9 × 583 = 5247
Write 5247 so that the digit on the
right (7) is in the **ones** column.

```
    5 8 3
  × 7 4 9
  5 2 4 7
  2 3 3 2
```
Multiply by the **tens** digit.
4 × 583 = 2332   There are 2332 tens.
Write 2332 so that the digit on the
right (2) is in the **tens** column.

```
    5 8 3
  × 7 4 9
  5 2 4 7
  2 3 3 2
4 0 8 1
```
Multiply by the **hundreds** digit.
7 × 583 = 4081   There are 4081
hundreds.
Write 4081 so that the digit on the
right (1) is in the **hundreds** column.

```
    5 8 3
  × 7 4 9
  5 2 4 7
  2 3 3 2
4 0 8 1
4 3 6,6 6 7
```
Add to get the final answer.

Check to see that the answer makes sense.

The answer should be less than 800 × 600, which is
480,000.

The answer should be greater than 700 × 500, which is
350,000.

436,667 is less than 480,000 and greater than 350,000.
So the answer makes sense.

When there is a 0 in the multiplier, you can save time by using a shorter way. Look at these 2 examples.

```
    6 2 4
  × 3 7 0
        0
```
Multiply by the **ones** digit.
$0 × 624 = 0$
Write the 0 in the **ones** column.

```
    6 2 4
  × 3 7 0
  4 3 6 8 0
```
Multiply by the **tens** digit.
$7 × 624 = 4368$ There are 4368 tens.
Write 4368 next to the 0.

```
      6 2 4
    × 3 7 0
    4 3 6 8 0
  1 8 7 2
  2 3 0,8 8 0
```
Multiply by the **hundreds** digit.
$3 × 624 = 1872$ There are 1872 hundreds.
Write 1872 so that the digit on the
right (2) is in the **hundreds** column.
Add.

```
    6 2 4
  × 3 0 7
    4 3 6 8
```
Multiply by the **ones** digit.
$7 × 624 = 4368$
Write 4368 so that the digit on the
right (8) is in the **ones** column.

```
    6 2 4
  × 3 0 7
    4 3 6 8
      0
```
Multiply by the **tens** digit.
$0 × 624 = 0$ There are 0 tens.
Write the 0 in the **tens** column.

```
      6 2 4
    × 3 0 7
      4 3 6 8
  1 8 7 2 0
  1 9 1,5 6 8
```
Multiply by the **hundreds** digit.
$3 × 624 = 1872$ There are 1872
hundreds.
Write the 1872 next to the 0.
Add.

235

Remember

```
  7 2 1        7 2 1          7 2 1          7 2 1          7 2 1
× 3 6 5   →  × 3 6 5   →   × 3 6 5   →   × 3 6 5   →   × 3 6 5
             3 6 0 5        3 6 0 5        3 6 0 5        3 6 0 5
                           4 3 2 6        4 3 2 6        4 3 2 6
                                         2 1 6 3        2 1 6 3
                                                      2 6 3,1 6 5
```

```
  4 9 8        4 9 8          4 9 8          4 9 8          4 9 8
× 6 0 3   →  × 6 0 3   →   × 6 0 3   →   × 6 0 3   →   × 6 0 3
             1 4 9 4        1 4 9 4        1 4 9 4        1 4 9 4
                               0         2 9 8 8 0      2 9 8 8 0
                                                      3 0 0,2 9 4
```

Multiply. Use shortcuts when you can.

1. 287 × 596	**2.** 831 × 609	**3.** 434 × 292	**4.** 816 × 333	**5.** 417 × 28
6. 604 × 17	**7.** 604 × 170	**8.** 365 × 108	**9.** 9 × 6	**10.** 90 × 6
11. 900 × 6	**12.** 9 × 60	**13.** 9 × 600	**14.** 90 × 60	**15.** 900 × 60
16. 90 × 600	**17.** 900 × 600	**18.** 901 × 599	**19.** 902 × 598	**20.** 903 × 507

Check to see that your answers make sense.

Marco's class is making and selling leather pencil cases. Each case requires a rectangular piece of leather 20 centimeters long and 15 centimeters wide. The students in the class buy the leather in large sheets that are 80 centimeters long and 60 centimeters wide.

1. Draw a picture to find out how many pencil cases they can make from 1 sheet of leather.

2. Marco's class buys 5 sheets of leather. How many pencil cases can the students make?

3. Each sheet of leather cost $5.29 (529 cents), including tax. How much did the students pay for the 5 sheets they bought?

4. The students sold each pencil case for 98 cents, and they sold every one. How much money did the class take in?

5. The class also paid for other supplies besides the leather. The other supplies cost $4.37 altogether. How much profit did the class make?

ROLL A PROBLEM GAME (MULTIPLICATION)

Players: 2 or more
Materials: One 0–5 cube
Object: To get the greatest product

Rules

1. Use blanks to outline a multiplication problem on your paper, like this:

$$\begin{array}{r} \underline{}\;\underline{} \\ \times\;\underline{}\;\underline{} \\ \hline \end{array}$$

2. The first player rolls the cube 4 times.
3. Each time the cube is rolled, write that number in one of the blanks in your outline.
4. When all the blanks have been filled in, find the product of the 2 numbers.
5. The player with the greatest product wins the round.

Other Ways to Play This Game

1. Try to get the smallest product.
2. Multiply a 1-digit number and a 3-digit number.
3. Multiply two 3-digit numbers.
4. Use a 5–10 cube. If you roll a 10, roll again.

Can you think of other ways to play this game?

Copy and complete these function machine charts.

1. $x \rightarrow (+6) \rightarrow y$

x	y
0	
12	
	14
	20
	13

2. $x \rightarrow (-7) \rightarrow y$

x	y
35	
	9
42	
70	
	0

3. $x \rightarrow (\times 26) \rightarrow y$

x	y
13	
10	
0	
6	
1	

Solve for n.

4. $n = 9 + 6$
5. $7 + n = 22$
6. $9 \times 6 = n$
7. $n = 63 \div 7$

8. $n = 9 \times 7$
9. $27 \div n = 9$
10. $n \div 8 = 8$
11. $n - 8 = 8$

12. $7 \times n = 56$
13. $36 \div 4 = n$
14. $n \div 10 = 60$
15. $n - 9 = 47$

Watch the signs.

16. $49 + 13 = n$
17. $419 - 394 = n$
18. $10 \times 25 = n$
19. $1000 \times 99 = n$
20. $5 \times 10,000 = n$

21. $49 - 13 = n$
22. $519 \times 304 = n$
23. $256 \times 100 = n$
24. $100 \times 15 = n$
25. $51 \times 1000 = n$

26. $49 \times 13 = n$
27. $439 + 396 = n$
28. $367 \times 1000 = n$
29. $5 \times 100 = n$
30. $100 \times 969 = n$

31.
```
  47
  39
+ 56
```

32.
```
  512
   39
  414
+ 602
```

33.
```
  1007
   962
+  419
```

34.
```
  17
  29
  34
  18
+ 29
```

35.
```
  39
  40
  60
+ 14
```

THE TREASURE OF MUGG ISLAND   Part 4

Remember the note in the hollow tree!

> From tree go NW 13
> to spider rock.
>   From spider rock go
> 23 paces to peg.

Manolita had a good idea. She said, "Let's all walk northwest and count our steps. Maybe one of us will find the spider rock."

The queen had a compass. They used it to find northwest. Then they all started walking in the same direction. Soon they found a rock that had marks on it like a spider web.

"This must be it," said Manolita. "And I walked 134 steps."

"That's funny," said Portia. "I walked 172 steps to get here."

Mark walked 105 giant steps, the queen walked 324 dainty steps, and Ferdie forgot to count.

"Now," said Mark, "I have an idea. The peg is 23 paces from the spider rock. But we don't know in what direction. So let's walk all around the rock, 23 paces away from it."

Everyone did that. The queen walked 23 dainty steps away from the rock and then went around it in a circle. Mark walked 23 giant steps from the rock and then went around it in a circle. Manolita and Portia, each in her own way, walked 23 steps away from the rock and then went around it in a circle. Ferdie went away from the rock, but he forgot how many paces. Then he went around it in a circle. Finally one of them said, "I found it! Here is the peg in the ground."

1. What size steps did the different people take in getting to the spider rock? Explain.

2. How could Mark's idea work for finding the peg?

3. If all the treasure hunters took the same size steps as they did before, who do you think would find the peg? Why do you think so?

Both Ray and Clara have gardens in their yards. They wanted to know whose garden was bigger. They measured and got the following results:

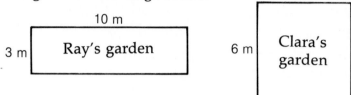

"My garden is longer!" Ray shouted.
"But mine is wider," said Clara.
"Let's measure the distance around them," said Ray.

- What is the perimeter of Ray's garden?
- What is the perimeter of Clara's garden?

"My garden is bigger," bragged Ray.
"Let's find the areas," said Clara.
"Why?" asked Ray. "Yours can't have more area if it's smaller around."

- What is the area of Ray's garden?
- What is the area of Clara's garden?
- Can a garden with a smaller perimeter than another garden have a larger area?

"You see," said Clara, "my garden is bigger."
"I still say mine is bigger," Ray insisted.

- Who is right? What does "bigger" mean?
- Whose garden is bigger if you're talking about how much fertilizer you need?
- Whose garden is bigger if you're talking about how much fencing you need?
- Try to draw 2 rectangles so that one has a larger area and the other has a larger perimeter.

Bob lives in Weston. The public swimming pool there is 30 meters long and 20 meters wide. Josh lives in Easton. The pool there is 40 meters long and 15 meters wide.

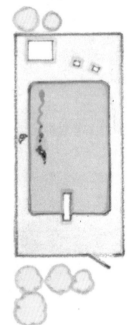

1. Each boy has agreed to paint the bottom of the pool in his town before the pool is filled with water for the summer. Who has the bigger job?

2. When someone swims up and down the length of a pool, we say they have swum 1 lap of the pool. Bob swims 24 laps of the Weston pool every day. How many meters does he swim each day?

3. Josh swims in the Easton pool. But he doesn't swim up and down the length of the pool. He swims around the pool 12 times every day. How many meters does he swim each day?

4. When Josh visits Bob, the boys go to the Weston pool for their daily swim.
   a. Suppose Josh swims 12 times around the Weston pool. Will he swim more or less than the distance he usually swims?
   b. About how many times do you think Josh should swim around the Weston pool?

Easton
Public Pool

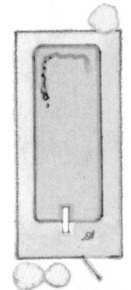

The field where Haruko plants beans is 157 meters long and 53 meters wide. Leo's bean field is a square, 98 meters on a side.

5. Both Haruko and Leo buy fertilizer for their beans. Each package of fertilizer covers 1000 square meters. Who has to buy more fertilizer?

6. Both Haruko and Leo plan to put fencing around their fields. Who will need more fencing?

You can multiply any 2 whole numbers. Use the same
procedures you have been using.

Multiply: 5306 × 8924

```
    8 9 2 4
  × 5 3 0 6
  5 3 5 4 4
```
Start at the right. Multiply by the
ones digit.
Write the answer so that the digit on
the right is in the **ones** column.

```
    8 9 2 4
  × 5 3 0 6
  5 3 5 4 4
          0
```
Multiply by the **tens** digit.
If it happens to be a 0, write a 0 in
the **tens** column.

```
    8 9 2 4
  × 5 3 0 6
  5 3 5 4 4
2 6 7 7 2 0
```
Multiply by the **hundreds** digit.
Write the answer so that the digit on
the right is in the **hundreds** column.
Continue in the same way.

```
      8 9 2 4
    × 5 3 0 6
    5 3 5 4 4
  2 6 7 7 2 0
4 4 6 2 0
```
The next digit is in the **thousands**
column. So multiply by the **thousands**
digit. Write the answer so that the
digit on the right is in the **thousands**
place.

```
    8 9 2 4
  × 5 3 0 6
    5 3 5 4 4
  2 6 7 7 2 0
4 4 6 2 0
4 7,3 5 0,7 4 4
```

When you have gone through every
digit in the multiplier, add to get the
final answer.

Check to see that the answer makes sense.

The answer should be less than 9000 × 6000, which is
54,000,000.
The answer should be greater than 5000 × 8000, which is
40,000,000.
47,350,744 is less than 54,000,000 and greater than
40,000,000. So the answer makes sense.

Multiply. Use shortcuts when you can.

1.	160	**2.**	8134	**3.**	2132	**4.**	5139
	× 18		× 305		× 4422		× 2041

5.	16	**6.**	5432	**7.**	1600	**8.**	1600
	× 18		× 678		× 18		× 1800

9.	24	**10.**	2400	**11.**	864	**12.**	86,400
	× 26		× 2006		× 365		× 365

Check to see that your answers make sense.

THE TREASURE OF MUGG ISLAND   Part 5

When the children found the peg in the ground,
they thought the treasure was there. But it
wasn't. On the peg was another note.
The note was burned into the wood.
Here is what the note said:

"This is hard," they all said.
Then they started off walking,
first north, then east, then north,
then west, then north, and so on.
But Ferdie didn't do that.

"I know how to get to the flat rock
a shorter way," he said. He started
walking straight north.

In a little while Ferdie called, "Hey, come
quick!" Everyone came running. "I found out
why you have to go in such a funny zigzag way,"
Ferdie said.

"Why is that?" the queen asked.

"First pull me out of this quicksand and then I'll tell
you," said Ferdie.

1. Draw a map showing the way from the peg to the flat rock.

2. What shorter way could Ferdie have gone? How far would he have to go by that way? How far would the others have to go, if they followed all the directions of the note?

3. What could be a reason for going the way the note said, instead of going by Ferdie's shorter way?

Are You Shiny or Rusty?

Very shiny	45 or more right
Shiny	40–44 right
A bit rusty	35–39 right
Rusty	Less than 35 right

Solve for n. Watch the signs.

1. $7 + 6 = n$
2. $14 - 5 = n$
3. $n = 6 + 3$
4. $n = 7 \times 5$
5. $n = 6 \times 8$
6. $5 \times 9 = n$
7. $4 \div 1 = n$
8. $27 - 3 = n$

9. $10 \times 5 = n$
10. $n = 6 \times 8$
11. $14 + 3 = n$
12. $17 - 9 = n$
13. $n = 6 \times 3$
14. $n = 30 \div 6$
15. $n = 7 \times 7$
16. $n = 5 + 5$

17. $6 \times 6 = n$
18. $6 + 6 = n$
19. $6 \div 6 = n$
20. $6 - 6 = n$
21. $n - 7 = 12$
22. $12 + 19 = n$
23. $11 = n + 7$

24. $n = 3 \times 7$
25. $n + 6 = 20$
26. $5 + n = 13$
27. $28 \div 4 = n$
28. $n = 10 \times 6$
29. $7 + 9 = n$
30. $n = 2 \times 9$

Solve. Watch the signs.

31. 742 $+ 243$	32. 742 $- 243$	33. 65 $\times\ 7$	34. 89 $\times 25$	35. 314 $\times\ 5$
36. 36 $+ 92$	37. 47 $- 39$	38. 362 $+ 279$	39. 87 $\times 87$	40. 341 $\times 265$
41. 877 $- 392$	42. 52 $+ 99$	43. 73 $\times\ 6$	44. 901 $- 723$	45. 327 $\times\ 18$
46. 597 $+ 623$	47. 382 $+ 469$	48. 777 $- 209$	49. 73 $\times\ 8$	50. 563 $- 384$

On the highway, Hank travels about 75 kilometers in 1 hour. His car can go about 13 kilometers on 1 liter of gasoline. The tank holds 45 liters.

1. About how far can Hank travel on 1 tankful of gasoline?

2. About how far does he travel in 3 hours on the highway?

3. At the speed Hank drives, it's about 14 hours of driving time from his home to his cousin's house in Pharoff City. About how many kilometers long is the trip?

4. Can Hank make it there on 2 tankfuls of gasoline?

Hank's neighbor, Isabel, has the same kind of car as Hank. But Isabel drives faster. She goes about 85 kilometers in 1 hour. But, because she goes faster, her car gets only about 11 kilometers to 1 liter of gasoline.

5. About how far does Isabel travel on 1 tank of gasoline?

6. Who travels farther on 1 tankful, Hank or Isabel? About how much farther?

7. Who travels farther in 1 hour, Hank or Isabel? About how much farther?

8. Can Isabel make the 1050-kilometer trip to Pharoff City on 2 tankfuls of gasoline?

MORE OR LESS GAME

Players: 2
Materials: Two 0–5 cubes, two 5–10 cubes
Object: To make a product larger or smaller than the product
          made by the other player

Rules
1. Make a game form like this one: _____ < _____
2. Roll the 4 cubes and use the numbers rolled to make
   two 2-digit numbers.
3. Write the two 2-digit numbers with a multiplication
   sign on the game form on either side of the < sign.
4. The other player rolls the 4 cubes, makes two 2-digit
   numbers, and writes them with a multiplication sign
   on the game form on the other side of the < sign.
5. If the number sentence made by the other player is not
   true, you win the round. If it is true, the other player
   wins the round.
6. You don't have to multiply unless the products are too
   close to approximate.
7. Take turns being the first player.

Sample Game

Keiko rolled: **1** **4** **7** **9**   Lawrence rolled: **3** **2** **6** **7**

She wrote 91 × 74.   He wrote 72 × 63.

91 × 74 < _____   91 × 74 < 72 × 63

Keiko and Lawrence agreed that this number sentence is
not true (they didn't need to multiply to know that). So
Keiko won this round.

Ink has spilled on this page. Choose the correct answer in each case.

Example: 307
                  × 5

       a. 14,10
       b. 179,902
       c. 15,108,507

The answer must be greater than 500 × 300, which is 150,000.
The answer must be less than 600 × 400, which is 240,000.

---

1.   8,7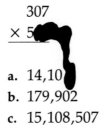
         × 6,

       a. 247,508
       b. 4,821,643
       c. 56,995,947

2.   50,
         ×   86

       a. 3,089,666
       b. 4,333,884
       c. 5,402,220

3.   238
         × 5

       a. 41,
       b. 12,
       c. 3,

4. 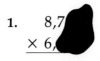 0
       ×

       a.   43
       b.   370
       c.   ,595

5.   00
       ×   0

       a.   ,650
       b.   ,000
       c. 53,100

6.   36
         × 2

       a. 720
       b. 5,648
       c. 8,760

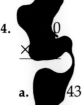

THE TREASURE OF MUGG ISLAND   Part 6

Finally, after going back and forth many paces, the children found the flat rock. Under the rock they found a bottle. In it was another note. It read:

To find the treasure, go 300 paces north and 400 paces west.

"At last we're near my treasure," said the queen. But it was not so easy. They could go 300 paces north, all right. But then they came to a huge pile of rocks. There had been a landslide. The side of a mountain had fallen down. They could not walk west at all.

They went back to the flat rock. "I have an idea," said Portia. "Let's draw a map. Let's try to figure out how to go straight to the treasure instead of going first north and then west."

Ferdie had a ruler. They used his ruler
to draw the lines on a map. Then they used his
ruler to figure out how far it was to the treasure,
if they went in a straight line. But Manolita didn't
help. She started off walking straight west. A little
while later she called to them. "You can stop
figuring. I found the treasure! It's right here,
where the note said it would be!"

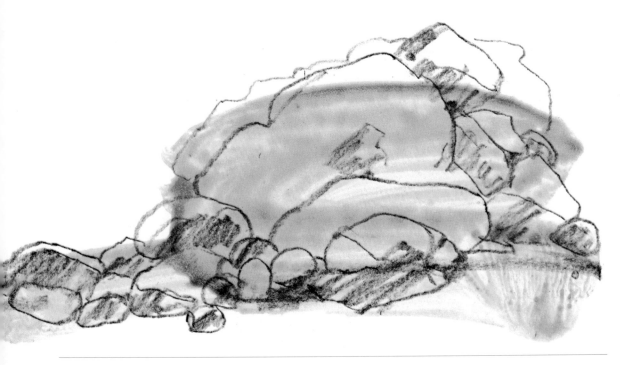

1. Draw lines. Use a ruler. Try to figure out how far it is
   from the flat rock to the treasure, if you go in a straight
   line.

2. After you know how far it is, what else do you have to
   know to find the treasure?

3. How could Manolita find the treasure by starting off
   walking straight west? What way would she go? Why
   would it work?

Multiply to solve for n.

1. $n = 6 \times 8$	5. $8 \times 7 = n$	9. $n = 6 \times 6$	13. $n = 7 \times 6$
2. $5 \times 7 = n$	6. $5 \times 8 = n$	10. $9 \times 6 = n$	14. $7 \times 9 = n$
3. $4 \times 9 = n$	7. $9 \times 8 = n$	11. $n = 8 \times 5$	15. $n = 8 \times 8$
4. $n = 3 \times 6$	8. $7 \times 7 = n$	12. $9 \times 9 = n$	

Multiply. Use shortcuts when you can.

16. 20×7	20. 600×8	24. 91×89	28. $34,805 \times 7$
17. 14×3	21. 504×7	25. 60×80	29. $20,711 \times 38$
18. 11×6	22. 90×90	26. 213×31	30. 8000×700
19. 243×6	23. 38×43	27. 127×58	

Watch the signs.

31. $\begin{array}{r} 57 \\ + 14 \\ \hline \end{array}$	32. $\begin{array}{r} 57 \\ - 14 \\ \hline \end{array}$	33. $\begin{array}{r} 57 \\ \times 14 \\ \hline \end{array}$	34. $\begin{array}{r} 834 \\ \times 555 \\ \hline \end{array}$	35. $\begin{array}{r} 834 \\ + 555 \\ \hline \end{array}$	36. $\begin{array}{r} 834 \\ - 555 \\ \hline \end{array}$

In each problem, 2 of the answers are clearly wrong and 1 is correct. Choose the correct answer.

37. $\begin{array}{r} 367 \\ \times \quad 93 \\ \hline \end{array}$ a. 34,131   b. 47,281   c. 26,911

39. $\begin{array}{r} 8121 \\ \times \quad 375 \\ \hline \end{array}$ a. 286,575   b. 3,045,375   c. 2,319,875

38. $\begin{array}{r} 702 \\ \times 311 \\ \hline \end{array}$ a. 207,152   b. 249,982   c. 218,322

40. $\begin{array}{r} 7903 \\ \times \quad 614 \\ \hline \end{array}$ a. 5,628,442   b. 496,372   c. 4,852,442

Solve for n. Watch the signs.

41. $n \div 8 = 4$	44. $n + 15 = 41$	47. $87 + n = 93$	49. $6 \times n = 42$
42. $9 \times n = 27$	45. $n \times 7 = 63$	48. $n - 16 = 57$	50. $81 \div 9 = n$
43. $27 - 6 = n$	46. $49 \div 7 = n$		

51. 1 loaf of bread costs 52¢. Ike buys 2 loaves of bread each day.

  a. How many cents does Ike spend on bread each day?

  b. How much will he spend on bread in 6 days?

52. A rectangle is 23 centimeters wide and 47 centimeters long.

  a. What is the area of the rectangle, in square centimeters?

  b. What is the perimeter of the rectangle?

53. An auditorium has 36 rows with 36 seats in each row. Can 2000 people be seated?

54. There are 100 centimeters in 1 meter.

  a. How many centimeters are there in 100 meters?

  b. How many are there in 1000 meters?

55. Cinder is an Irish setter. She eats about 850 grams of dog food every day. About how many grams of dog food will she eat in June (30 days)?

56. Georgia plays the piano 45 minutes each day. About how many minutes will she play the piano in a year (365 days)?

57. In a certain book there are about 350 words per page. The book has 512 pages. About how many words are in the book?

58. A bag of dried peas costs 37¢. Ramón uses 7 bags to make a kettle of pea soup.

  a. How much do the dried peas cost for 1 kettle of soup?

  b. Ramón cooks a kettle of pea soup twice a month. How much do the dried peas cost for a year?

Multiply to solve for n.

1. $3 \times 7 = n$
2. $n = 9 \times 4$
3. $n = 4 \times 8$
4. $3 \times 8 = n$
5. $0 \times 7 = n$
6. $n = 6 \times 5$
7. $n = 10 \times 9$
8. $8 \times 7 = n$

9. $2 \times 6 = n$
10. $1 \times 7 = n$
11. $n = 5 \times 8$
12. $10 \times 5 = n$
13. $6 \times 4 = n$
14. $n = 9 \times 8$
15. $2 \times 7 = n$
16. $n = 3 \times 5$

17. $7 \times 8 = n$
18. $10 \times 6 = n$
19. $n = 4 \times 4$
20. $7 \times 4 = n$
21. $n = 3 \times 9$
22. $9 \times 7 = n$
23. $5 \times 9 = n$
24. $n = 9 \times 9$

25. $8 \times 1 = n$
26. $n = 2 \times 5$
27. $9 \times 10 = n$
28. $6 \times 0 = n$
29. $n = 4 \times 5$
30. $9 \times 2 = n$

Solve for n. Watch the signs.

31. $n \div 5 = 7$
32. $8 \times n = 40$
33. $35 + 62 = n$
34. $n - 19 = 21$
35. $n \times 8 = 56$

36. $85 - 39 = n$
37. $28 \div n = 7$
38. $n + 78 = 97$
39. $97 - 49 = n$
40. $n \times 6 = 36$

41. $8 \times 9 = n$
42. $27 \div n = 9$
43. $n + 37 = 72$
44. $71 - n = 54$
45. $n \times 9 = 18$

46. $47 + 29 = n$
47. $n \div 7 = 28$
48. $n = 53 + 45$
49. $7 \times 5 = n$
50. $n - 23 = 58$

51.
$$\begin{array}{r} 1203 \\ \times\ \ 114 \\ \hline \end{array}$$

52.
$$\begin{array}{r} 376 \\ \times\ 204 \\ \hline \end{array}$$

53.
$$\begin{array}{r} 2013 \\ \times\ \ \ 68 \\ \hline \end{array}$$

54.
$$\begin{array}{r} 4135 \\ \times\ \ \ 77 \\ \hline \end{array}$$

55.
$$\begin{array}{r} 98{,}765 \\ \times\ \ \ \ \ \ 7 \\ \hline \end{array}$$

56.
$$\begin{array}{r} 12 \\ \times\ 9 \\ \hline \end{array}$$

57.
$$\begin{array}{r} 123 \\ \times\ \ 9 \\ \hline \end{array}$$

58.
$$\begin{array}{r} 1234 \\ \times\ \ \ \ 9 \\ \hline \end{array}$$

59.
$$\begin{array}{r} 12{,}345 \\ \times\ \ \ \ \ \ 9 \\ \hline \end{array}$$

60.
$$\begin{array}{r} 123{,}456 \\ \times\ \ \ \ \ \ \ \ 9 \\ \hline \end{array}$$

61.
$$\begin{array}{r} 142{,}857 \\ \times\ \ \ \ \ \ \ \ 7 \\ \hline \end{array}$$

62.
$$\begin{array}{r} 2079 \\ \times\ \ 481 \\ \hline \end{array}$$

Watch the signs.

| 1. | 90 $\times$ 80 | 2. | 1221 $-$ 819 | 3. | 2457 $+$ 407 | 4. | 4906 $-$ 997 |

| 5. | 30 $\times$ 40 | 6. | 4906 $+$ 997 | 7. | 87 $\times$ 39 | 8. | 87 $+$ 39 |

| 9. | 87 $-$ 39 | 10. | 101 $+$ 99 | 11. | 7024 $-$ 889 | 12. | 65 $\times$ 65 |

In each problem, 2 of the answers are clearly wrong and 1 is correct. Choose the correct answer.

13. 27
$\times$ 89
a. 2753
b. 1093
c. 2403

14. 37
$\times$ 89
a. 3293
b. 36,593
c. 1803

15. 45
$\times$ 99
a. 4455
b. 34,555
c. 2425

16. 53
$\times$ 18
a. 7824
b. 954
c. 434

17. 43
$\times$ 81
a. 32,863
b. 3193
c. 3483

18. 121
$\times$ 47
a. 3887
b. 5687
c. 54,767

19. 709
$\times$ 374
a. 26,526
b. 2,651,666
c. 265,166

20. 507
$\times$ 92
a. 46,644
b. 44,874
c. 448,794

21. 407
$\times$ 29
a. 11,803
b. 7143
c. 23,003

22. 457
$\times$ 91
a. 34,927
b. 41,587
c. 46,587

1. A 2-liter container of milk costs 89¢.
   a. How much do 7 containers cost?
   b. When the containers are full, how much milk do they contain altogether?
   c. Ava buys 3 containers of milk each day for a week (7 days). How much does this cost?

2. A rectangle is 89 meters wide and 97 meters long.
   a. What is the area of the rectangle, in square meters?
   b. What is the perimeter of the rectangle?

3. 1 container of paint will cover about 50 square meters. Mrs. Andrews is going to paint the side of a building (without windows) that is 57 meters long and 13 meters high. Will 10 containers of paint be enough?

4. There are 1000 grams in a kilogram. There are 1000 kilograms in a metric ton. How many grams are there in a metric ton?

5. A shrew weighs about 3 grams. It eats about 8 times its own weight every day. About how many grams of food would a shrew eat in a year (365 days)?

6. Some baby whales drink about 200 liters of milk each day for about 7 months. About how many liters of milk is this? (Assume 1 month is 30 days.)

7. Cliff has a string 67 centimeters long that he used to measure a room. The room is just about 14 strings long. About how many centimeters long is the room?

About how much is 4,962,100 × 37,942,614?

An approximate answer is 5,000,000 × 40,000,000. That is, 5 × 4 followed by the number of zeros in the 2 factors.

So an approximate answer is 20 followed by 13 zeros: 200,000,000,000,000.

Solve these problems by approximating.

1. Light travels 299,792,500 meters in 1 second. There are 31,556,926 seconds in 1 year. About how many meters does light travel in 1 year? (That is, about how many meters are there in 1 light-year?)

2. The sun is about 150,000,000,000 meters from the earth. Suppose you read that it takes light about 8 minutes (or 480 seconds) to reach the earth from the sun. Would that figure make sense?

3. Our galaxy is about 80,000 light-years across.
   a. About how many meters is that?
   b. How many years would it take light to travel across our galaxy?

Multiply to solve for n.

1. $8 \times 7 = n$ 5. $9 \times 9 = n$ 9. $9 \times 7 = n$ 13. $n = 4 \times 4$

2. $n = 7 \times 6$ 6. $3 \times 8 = n$ 10. $n = 8 \times 5$ 14. $5 \times 4 = n$

3. $6 \times 8 = n$ 7. $n = 7 \times 4$ 11. $7 \times 7 = n$ 15. $6 \times 4 = n$

4. $9 \times 5 = n$ 8. $6 \times 6 = n$ 12. $n = 8 \times 8$

Multiply. Use shortcuts when you can.

16.	17.	18.	19.	20.
52	43	31	60	203
× 56	× 29	× 24	× 25	× 54

21.	22.	23.	24.	25.
876	28	500	142,857	346
× 9	× 431	× 700	× 7	× 210

Watch the signs.

26.	27.	28.	29.	30.
35	35	35	407	407
− 25	+ 25	× 25	− 209	+ 209

In each problem, 2 of the answers are clearly wrong and 1 is correct. Choose the correct answer.

31. 76   a. 6763   33. 407   a. 85,063
    × 67   b. 6776   × 209   b. 8563
             c. 5092   c. 65,630

32. 305   a. 318   34. 595   a. 140,755
    × 13   b. 1305   × 129   b. 40,755
             c. 3965   c. 76,755

Solve for n. Watch the signs.

35. $n + 16 = 53$ 37. $36 \div 4 = n$ 39. $n = 42 + 21$ 41. $7 \times n = 56$

36. $7 \times n = 49$ 38. $89 - n = 52$ 40. $n \div 3 = 6$ 42. $93 - 56 = n$

43. A high-speed train travels 160 kilometers in 1 hour. At that rate, how far can it go in 15 hours?

44. What is the area of a playground that is 85 meters long and 47 meters wide?

45. One large bottle of cola costs 59¢. How many cents would you have to pay for 12 bottles?

46. A liter of milk costs 51¢ and a liter of cola costs 68¢. Which costs more? How much more?

47. A liter of milk costs 51¢ and a loaf of bread costs 72¢. How much do they cost together?

48. 1 can of beans costs 53¢. How much will 16 cans of beans cost? Give your answer in cents. Also give your answer in dollars and cents.

49. Cans of beans are packed in cartons that have 8 rows with 12 cans in each row. How many cans are there in 10 cartons?

50. Liam wants to put his baseball card collection in a scrapbook. Each page of the scrapbook will hold 12 cards. There are 33 pages. How many cards will the scrapbook hold?

UNIT V   DIVIDING
        WHOLE NUMBERS

THE 7-WAY SPLIT

Rosa and 6 of her friends were out playing one day when they found an envelope.

Inside the envelope was money. There were eight $1000 bills, nine $100 bills, three $10 bills, and six $1 bills.

- How much money is that altogether?
- What would you do if you found that much money?

The 7 children took the money to the police station and gave it to the person at the lost-and-found department.

After 30 days, nobody had claimed the money. So the police gave the $8936 back to the children.

"How shall we divide the money?" asked Marvin.

"Let's each take a $1000 bill," replied Louis.

Each of the 7 children took one $1000 bill.

The children decided to keep a record of what they were doing. Because they wanted the $8936 to be divided into 7 equal amounts of money, they wrote the problem this way:

$$7\overline{)8936}$$

Each child took $1000. They kept track of this on the top of the record.

$$\begin{array}{r} 1000 \\ 7\overline{)8936} \end{array}$$ —— This is how much each child has taken so far.

Now they had used up $7000, leaving $1936. They kept track of this at the bottom of the record.

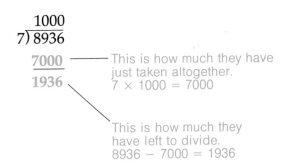

$$\begin{array}{r} 1000 \\ 7\overline{)8936} \\ \underline{7000} \\ 1936 \end{array}$$

This is how much they have just taken altogether.
7 × 1000 = 7000

This is how much they have left to divide.
8936 − 7000 = 1936

Each child has taken a $1000 bill.

Now the 7 children have one $1000 bill, nine $100 bills, three $10 bills, and six $1 bills. "How shall we divide the rest of the money?" asked Kelli.

"We could each take a $100 bill," said Leonard.

"But what will we do with the $1000 bill?" asked Nora.

• What would you do?

Kelli suggested they take the extra $1000 bill to the bank and change it for ten $100 bills.

• How many $100 bills will they have if they do this?

At the bank, they changed the $1000 bill for ten $100 bills. Now they had nineteen $100 bills.

"We can each take two $100 bills," said Elaine.

"Yes, but we're going to have some left over," Rosa said.

• How many $100 bills will be left after each child has taken two of them?

The children each took two $100 bills. Then they put that
on their record.

$$
\begin{array}{r}
200 \\
1000 \\
7\overline{)8936} \\
7000 \\
\hline
1936
\end{array}
$$

- How much money does each child have now?
- How many $100 bills are left in the pile?
- How much money is left in the pile altogether?

The children also put on their record that they took
fourteen $100 bills altogether, leaving $536 in the pile.

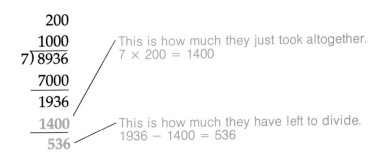

$$
\begin{array}{r}
200 \\
1000 \\
7\overline{)8936} \\
7000 \\
\hline
1936 \\
1400 \\
\hline
536
\end{array}
$$

This is how much they just took altogether.
7 × 200 = 1400

This is how much they have left to divide.
1936 − 1400 = 536

They decided that the way to divide up the remaining
five $100 bills was to exchange them for $10 bills.

- How many $10 bills should they get for five $100 bills?
- How many $10 bills will they have altogether?
- How many $10 bills should each child get?
- How many $10 bills will be left?

Each child took seven $10 bills. Now their record looked like this:

```
      70 ——— Each child took seven $10 bills (or $70).
     200
    1000
7)  8936
    7000
    1936
    1400
     536
     490 ——— 7 × 70 = 490
      46 ——— There was $46 left in the pile to be divided.
```

They traded the four $10 bills for forty $1 bills, so they had forty-six $1 bills in the pile.

- How many $1 bills can each child take?
- How many $1 bills will be left?
- What would you do with the extra $4?

Now their record looked like this:

```
         6 ———— Each child took six $1 bills (or $6).
        70
       200
      1000
   7) 8936
      7000
      1936
      1400
       536
       490
        46
        42 ———— 7 × 6 = 42
         4 ———— There was $4 left.
```

Marvin suggested they change the remaining $4 for 40 dimes and divide those among them. Elaine suggested they have a party with the extra $4. They had a vote. Then they had a party.

Before the party, Kelli wanted to be sure she got the right amount of money.

- How much money should Kelli have?
- How much money should Nora have?
- How much money should each child have?
- What is 7 × $1276?
  Why is that $4 less than the total they found, $8936?

All the children decided to put their money in the bank and save it for their education.

The steps the children took looked like this:

Step 1

```
 1000
7) 8936
```

Step 2

```
 1000
7) 8936
 7000
```

Step 3

```
 1000
7) 8936
 7000
 1936
```

Step 7

```
   70
  200
 1000
7) 8936
 7000
 1936
 1400
  536
```

Step 8

```
   70
  200
 1000
7) 8936
 7000
 1936
 1400
  536
  490
```

Step 9

```
   70
  200
 1000
7) 8936
 7000
 1936
 1400
  536
  490
   46
```

Step 4

```
  200
 1000
7) 8936
 7000
 1936
```

Step 5

```
  200
 1000
7) 8936
 7000
 1936
 1400
```

Step 6

```
  200
 1000
7) 8936
 7000
 1936
 1400
  536
```

Step 10

```
    6
   70
  200
 1000
7) 8936
 7000
 1936
 1400
  536
  490
   46
```

Step 11

```
    6
   70
  200
 1000
7) 8936
 7000
 1936
 1400
  536
  490
   46
   42
```

Step 12

```
    6
   70
  200
 1000
7) 8936
 7000
 1936
 1400
  536
  490
   46
   42
    4
```

The answer is 1276, remainder 4.

Using play money, work in groups to solve these problems. One person in each group should be the banker to exchange bills. One person should keep the record. Everyone should help solve the problems. Everyone should see that each record is right.

1. 6 children want to divide $948 equally. How much should each child get? Will any money be left over?

2. 7 people want to divide $364 equally. How much should each person get? Will any money be left over?

3. 4 people want to divide $7433 equally. How much should each person get? How many dollars will be left over? What might they do with it?

4. 5 people want to divide $2707 equally. How much should each person get? How many dollars will be left over? What might they do with it?

5. 9 people want to divide $4536 equally. How much should each person get? How many dollars will be left over? What might they do with it?

Here are the names for the parts of a division problem:

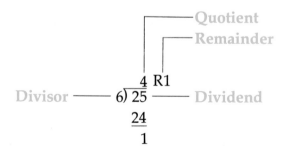

If you wish, you may keep your records in a shorter form.

For example

Long Form	Shorter Form	
	With Zeros	**Without Zeros**
1276 Remainder 4 6 70 200 1000 7)8936 7000 1936 1400 536 490 46 42 4	Be careful to put the answers in the correct column. 1276 R4 7)8936 7000 1936 1400 536 490 46 42 4	Subtract and "bring down" only the next digit. Be careful to put the answers in the correct column. 1276 R4 7)8936 7 19 14 53 49 46 42 4

Divide. Keep your records in any of the ways shown on this page. Use money if you like.

1. 5)100
2. 3)46
3. 7)91
4. 6)91
5. 5)745
6. 8)416
7. 3)513
8. 4)804
9. 2)7046
10. 2)41,312
11. 9)729
12. 5)52,365

Divide. Use money if you need to. Keep records in the way you like best. When there is a remainder, show it.

1. $3\overline{)591}$ 2. $4\overline{)6128}$ 3. $6\overline{)144}$ 4. $7\overline{)574}$

5. $8\overline{)232}$ 6. $9\overline{)241}$ 7. $5\overline{)125}$ 8. $6\overline{)216}$

9. $4\overline{)64}$ 10. $3\overline{)62}$ 11. $2\overline{)90}$ 12. $5\overline{)0}$

Check your answers.

A. Multiply divisor × quotient.
B. Add the remainder.
C. You should get the dividend.

Examples: $7\overline{)97}^{\,13\ R6}$ Check: 13
                                                         × 7
                                                         91   91 + 6 = 97

$3\overline{)861}^{\,287}$ Check: 287
                                         × 3
                                         861

$7\overline{)439}^{\,62\ R5}$ Check: 62
                                            × 7
                                            434   434 + 5 = 439

Find the missing digit.

1.
```
    2 9
5)1 4 5
  1 0
   ■5
   4 5
```

2.
```
   1 0 3  R1
9)9 2 8
  9
   2 8
   2 ■
     1
```

3.
```
   1 ■ 3  R2
9)9 2 9
  9
   2 9
   2 7
     2
```

4.
```
     4 ■  R1
7)3 0 9
   2 8
   2 9
   2 8
     1
```

5.
```
    1 0 4
■)6 2 4
  6
   2 4
   2 4
```

6.
```
   1 8 ■  R1
4)7 2 1
  4
   3 2
   3 2
     1
```

7.
```
     8 4  R6
8)6 7 ■
   6 4
     3 8
     3 2
       6
```

8.
```
   1 0 ■  R7
9)9 0 7
  9
     7
```

9.
```
   1 ■ 1  R6
8)9 7 4
  8
  1 7
  1 6
    1 4
       8
       6
```

10.
```
    2 8 7  R1
■)8 6 2
  6
  2 6
  2 4
    2 2
    2 1
      1
```

11.
```
   1 1 5  R■
8)9 2 3
  8
  1 2
     8
     4 3
     4 0
       3
```

12.
```
   2 6 ■  R2
3)8 0 0
  6
  2 0
  1 8
    2 0
    1 8
      2
```

13.
```
   ■ 0 8
5)5 4 0
  5
   4 0
   4 0
```

14.
```
   1 ■ 0
5)7 5 0
  5
  2 5
  2 5
```

15.
```
   1 3 0
7)9 ■ 0
  7
  2 1
  2 1
```

16.
```
   2 ■ 7  R1
4)8 2 9
  8
   2 9
   2 8
     1
```

ESTIMATING IS ROUGH Part 1

"I found a job you might try for," said Mrs. Breezy. "It's a job as chief estimator."

"I'll take it," said Mr. Sleeby. "What does an estimator do?"

"An estimator tries to make good guesses about amounts. I'll show you. See that girl out in the hall? How old would you say she is?"

"I don't know," said Mr. Sleeby.

"You don't have to say exactly. Just **about** or **approximately** how old is she?"

"About 6 years old," said Mr. Sleeby.

"What made you say 6 years old?"

"Six was the first number that came into my head," Mr. Sleeby said.

"That's not the way to estimate," said Mrs. Breezy. "I'll show you how. The girl is reading a book.

276

That means she is probably older than 6. She is about the same size as my son, Mark. He is 10. So I estimate she is 10 years old. Let's ask her."

Mr. Sleeby opened the door. He asked the girl in the hall if she was about 6 years old.

"I am **exactly** 9 years old," the girl said.

"Happy birthday!" said Mrs. Breezy. Then she said, "You see, my estimate is better. It's closer to 9."

"No, my answer is better," said Mr. Sleeby. "If you turn my 6 upside down, you'll get her exact age—which is 9!"

1. In what ways is estimating the same as guessing?

2. In what ways is estimating different from guessing?

3. When Mrs. Breezy was estimating the girl's age, why did she talk about the fact that the girl was reading and about the girl's size?

4. What are some clues you would use to estimate a person's age?

5. Which estimate was better, Mr. Sleeby's estimate or Mrs. Breezy's estimate? Why?

6. A detective question: Why do you think Mrs. Breezy said "Happy birthday" to the girl?

7. A superdetective question: About how old is Mrs. Breezy?

DIVISO GAME

Players: 2 or more
Materials: Two 0–5 cubes, two 5–10 cubes
Object: To get a quotient with no remainder

Rules
1. Roll any 2 cubes.
2. Make a division problem in this way: Use the product of the numbers rolled as the dividend. Choose another number as the divisor, but do not use either of the numbers rolled, their product, or the number 1.
3. Find the quotient.
4. The player who makes a problem with no remainder wins the round.

Sample Game

Round One

Tess rolls:
$3 \times 2 = 6$
She cannot use 3, 2, 6, or
1 as a divisor.
Tess does not score.

Kate rolls:
$0 \times 8 = 0$
She chooses 7 as the divisor.

$$7)\overline{0} \quad \begin{array}{c} 0 \end{array}$$ Kate wins 1 point.
Kate wins this round.

Round Two

Tess rolls:
$7 \times 10 = 70$
She chooses 2 as the divisor.

$$2)\overline{70} \quad \begin{array}{c} 35 \end{array}$$ Tess wins 1 point.

Kate rolls:
$5 \times 4 = 20$
She chooses 2 as the divisor.

$$2)\overline{20} \quad \begin{array}{c} 10 \end{array}$$ Kate wins 1 point.
This round is a tie.

Find the missing digits.

1.
```
      1 ■ 5  R1
   5) 6 7 6
      5
      1 7
      1 5
        2 6
        2 5
          1
```

2.
```
      1 ■ 7  R2
   6) 8 2 4
      6
      2 2
      1 8
        4 4
        4 2
          2
```

3.
```
      1 3 4  R1
   4) 5 3 7
      4
      1 3
      1 ■
        1 7
        1 6
          1
```

4.
```
      2 6 9  R2
   3) 8 ■ 9
      6
      2 0
      1 8
        2 9
        2 7
          2
```

5.
```
      ■ 4  R1
   9) 3 0 7
      2 7
      3 7
      3 6
        1
```

6.
```
      1 ■ 9  R6
   8) 8 7 8
      8
      7 8
      7 2
        6
```

7.
```
      2 0 ■  R3
   4) 8 0 7
      8
        7
        4
        3
```

8.
```
      1 ■ 3  R1
   2) 2 0 7
      2
        7
        6
        1
```

9.
```
      1 0 9
   7) 7 6 3
      ■
      6 3
      6 3
```

10.
```
      5 0
   9) 4 5 0
      4 ■
```

11.
```
      2 0 9
   3) 6 2 7
      6
      ■ 7
      2 7
```

12.
```
      1 0 0  R3
   7) 7 0 3
      7
        ■
```

13.
```
      5 ■  R6
   7) 4 0 5
      3 5
      5 5
      4 9
        6
```

14.
```
      6 7  R ■
   4) 2 7 0
      2 4
      3 0
      2 8
        2
```

15.
```
      ■ 7
   5) 4 3 5
      4 0
      3 5
      3 5
```

16.
```
      7 ■  R1
   5) 3 7 6
      3 5
      2 6
      2 5
        1
```

279

Annette wants to buy soup. The store offers 3 cans of soup for 72¢ or 4 cans of the same kind of soup for 92¢.

How much does soup cost per can if you buy it in groups of 3 cans?

Per means "for each." We can find the cost for each can by dividing 72 by 3.

$$\begin{array}{r} 24 \\ 3\overline{)72} \\ \underline{6} \\ 12 \\ \underline{12} \end{array}$$

The soup costs 24¢ per can when you buy it in groups of 3 cans.

How much does soup cost per can if you buy it in groups of 4 cans? We can find the cost per can by dividing 92 by 4.

$$\begin{array}{r} 23 \\ 4\overline{)92} \\ \underline{8} \\ 12 \\ \underline{12} \end{array}$$

The soup costs 23¢ per can when you buy it in groups of 4.

• Which do you think is the better buy? Why?

Luis wants to buy milk. A 4-liter container costs $1.48 (148¢). An 8-liter container of the same kind of milk at a different store costs $3.04 (304¢).

1. How much does milk cost per liter in a 4-liter container?
2. How much does milk cost per liter in an 8-liter container?
3. Which do you think is the better buy? Why?

• Could you have found the better buy without dividing?

280

Rosalinda wants to buy a bag of potatoes. A 2-kilogram bag costs 90¢. A 5-kilogram bag costs $1.50 (150¢).

4. How much do potatoes cost per kilogram in 2-kilogram bags?

5. How much do potatoes cost per kilogram in 5-kilogram bags?

6. Which do you think is the better buy? Why?

Solve.

7. 3 cans of soup cost 75¢. How much is 1 can of soup?

8. 7 pencils cost 91¢. How much is that per pencil?

9. 3 liters of milk cost $1.23. How much is that per liter?

10. 4 apples cost 52¢. How much is that per apple?

11. 6 oranges cost 72¢. How much is that per orange?

12. A 5-kilogram turkey costs $7.50 (750¢). A 6-kilogram turkey costs $9.00 (900¢). Which turkey is the better buy? Why?

13. 3 boxes of tissue cost $1.38 (138¢). How much is that per box?

14. An 8-bottle carton of soda costs $1.76 (176¢). How much is that per bottle?

15. A box of 9 doughnuts costs 81¢. How much is that per doughnut?

Some people like to use a still shorter method of keeping records in a division problem. It's the shortest.

Shorter Form   **Shortest Form**

$$
\begin{array}{r}
1 \\
7\overline{)8936} \\
7 \\
\hline
19
\end{array}
$$

$$
7\overline{)8\,{}^{1}9\ 3\ 6}
$$
$$
1
$$

There is one whole 7 in 8 (write 1 in the answer above the 8). The remainder is 1 (write a small 1 in front of the 9).

$$
\begin{array}{r}
12 \\
7\overline{)8936} \\
7 \\
\hline
19 \\
14 \\
\hline
53
\end{array}
$$

$$
1\ \ 2
$$
$$
7\overline{)8\,{}^{1}9\,{}^{5}3\ 6}
$$

There are two 7s in 19 (write 2 in the answer above the 9). The remainder is 5 (write a 5 in front of the 3).

$$
\begin{array}{r}
127 \\
7\overline{)8936} \\
7 \\
\hline
19 \\
14 \\
\hline
53 \\
49 \\
\hline
46
\end{array}
$$

$$
1\ \ 2\ \ 7
$$
$$
7\overline{)8\,{}^{1}9\,{}^{5}3\,{}^{4}6}
$$

There are seven 7s in 53 (write a 7 in the answer above the 3). The remainder is 4 (write a 4 in front of the 6).

$$
\begin{array}{r}
1276\ \text{R4} \\
7\overline{)8936} \\
7 \\
\hline
19 \\
14 \\
\hline
53 \\
49 \\
\hline
46 \\
42 \\
\hline
4
\end{array}
$$

$$
1\ \ 2\ \ 7\ \ 6\ \text{R4}
$$
$$
7\overline{)8\,{}^{1}9\,{}^{5}3\,{}^{4}6}
$$

There are six 7s in 46 (write a 6 in the answer above the 6). The remainder is 4 (write R4 in the answer).

Divide. Use whichever method you prefer. Check your answers to the first 5 problems by multiplying.

1. $7\overline{)343}$ Check: Does 7 × quotient = 343?

2. $6\overline{)174}$ Check: Does 6 × quotient = 174?

3. $2\overline{)317}$ Check: Does (2 × quotient) **+ remainder** = 317?

4. $5\overline{)812}$ Check: Does (5 × quotient) **+ remainder** = 812?

5. $9\overline{)342}$ Check: Does 9 × quotient = 342?

Divide. Use shortcuts when you can.

6. $3\overline{)876}$ 7. $4\overline{)512}$ 8. $4\overline{)1000}$ 9. $8\overline{)54}$

10. $1\overline{)42,506}$ 11. $6\overline{)372}$ 12. $3\overline{)10}$ 13. $0\overline{)15}$

- Did you get an answer to problem 13?
- Is there any answer that would work?
- Can it ever be that 0 × number = 15?

There is no number you can multiply by 0 to get 15. So no answer could check, unless you decided the remainder is 15. But the remainder is not supposed to be bigger than the divisor. Even if we said the remainder is 15, then any number could be the quotient. But that is not useful. So we make this rule:

Division by 0 is not allowed.

ESTIMATING IS ROUGH Part 2

Mr. Sleeby went to try for the job of chief estimator. First he had to fill in a card. It asked for his address. He lived at 577 12th Street. But he wrote:

Approximately 600 Tenth Street

The card asked for his telephone number. It was 554-5550, so he wrote:

Approximately 6 million

The card asked how long he worked in his last job. He wrote: *1 year, 2 months, 17 days, 6 hours, and approximately 30 minutes*

After he filled out the card, Mr. Sleeby went to talk to the woman who was the boss. Another woman was also trying for the job. "I will give you both a problem," said the boss. "The one who gives the better estimate gets the job. Here is the problem. How many elephants will fit in this room?"

"Let me see," said the woman. "An elephant is about 3 meters high and 3 meters long. It is a bit less than 2 meters wide. This room is about 3 meters high, 6 meters long, and 5 meters wide. So I estimate that 5 elephants could fit in this room."

"Are we talking about canned elephants or whole elephants?" Mr. Sleeby asked.

"Whole elephants."

"Then my estimate is 0."

1. What is silly about each of the answers Mr. Sleeby wrote on the card?

2. How could 5 elephants fit in the room? Draw a picture of the room to show where they would be. (Hint: Draw the room like this, so that each square stands for 1 square meter.)

3. What could make Mr. Sleeby think that no elephants would fit in the room? (Hint: About how many cars could you get into your classroom?)

4. A superchallenge question: Can you think of a time when giving an approximate address might be good enough?

285

FOUR CUBE DIVISION GAME

Players: 2 or more
Materials: Two 0–5 cubes, two 5–10 cubes
Object: To get the smallest quotient

Rules

1. Roll all 4 cubes. If you roll a **10**, roll that cube again.
2. Make a division problem using 3 of the numbers rolled as a 3-digit dividend and the other number as the divisor. 0 may not be used as the first number of the dividend and, of course, it cannot be used as the divisor.
3. Find the quotient.
4. The player with the smallest quotient wins the round. If 2 players have the same quotient, then the player with the smaller remainder is the winner.

Sample Round

Matthew rolled: 3 4 9 8   He made: $9\overline{)348}$ 38 R6

Cathy rolled: 2 8 3 5   She made: $8\overline{)235}$ 29 R3

Max rolled: 1 0 9 5   He made: $9\overline{)105}$ 11 R6   Max won the round.

Other Ways to Play This Game

1. The smallest remainder wins.
2. The smallest quotient wins, but the remainder must be greater than 5.

1. Mrs. Quincy paid $1.05 (105¢) for 7 apples. How much did each apple cost?

2. Antonio bought 9 doughnuts for 72¢. How much should 10 doughnuts cost?

3. The grocery store has 2 cans of cat food on sale for 37¢. How much do you think 1 can of cat food would cost? (Think about this. What would you do if you owned the store?)

4. Greg drove for 7 hours. He traveled about 85 kilometers each hour. About how many kilometers did he drive?

5. Christy has 27 apples. She wants to divide the apples equally among 5 children.
   a. How many apples should she give each child?
   b. Will there be any apples left over?
   c. What should she do with them?

6. Miss Zim needs 45 balloons for a party. Balloons come in packages of 8.
   a. How many packages should she buy?
   b. How many extra balloons will she have?

Divide. Use shortcuts when you can.

7. $6\overline{)480}$ 10. $7\overline{)523}$ 13. $5\overline{)35}$ 16. $8\overline{)326}$

8. $9\overline{)720}$ 11. $9\overline{)722}$ 14. $3\overline{)426}$ 17. $8\overline{)223}$

9. $8\overline{)222}$ 12. $8\overline{)56}$ 15. $3\overline{)471}$ 18. $3\overline{)472}$

These 7 children went out to pick apples. This chart shows how many apples each child picked.

Name	Number of Apples Picked
Marcia	37
Erin	62
Fred	35
Rita	34
Douglas	58
Charles	26
Edgar	14

Edgar said, "I wish I had as many apples as everybody else."

Rita suggested that they put all their apples together and then take an equal share.

- How many apples do the 7 children have altogether?
- How many would each child get if they put all their apples together and then each took an equal number?
- Do you think any of the children might object to Rita's suggestion? Which children?
- Which children picked an above-average number of apples?
- Which children picked a below-average number of apples?
- Which children picked exactly the average number of apples?

The number 38 is the **average,** or **mean,** of the numbers 37, 62, 35, 34, 58, 26, and 14.

What do you think about each statement? Some people may not agree about some of them.

1. Kenny used to live at 600 Elm Street. Now he lives at 200 Elm Street. So on the average he has lived at 400 Elm Street.

2. Adela and Vincent were in the running for the spelling award. Adela's test scores were 96, 94, 98, and 96. Vincent's scores were 92, 94, 100, and 90. Adela won the award because she had the higher average, even though Vincent had the highest single score.

3. Hana is 14 years old. She used to be 6 years old. So her average age is 10.

4. In the United States, the average number of people in a family is about $3\frac{1}{2}$.

5. 100 years ago, the average number of children in a family was about 3. Now the average number of children in a family is about $1\frac{1}{2}$. So families are smaller now than they were 100 years ago.

6. Billy Gene was 140 centimeters tall on his 10th birthday. On his 14th birthday he was 180 centimeters tall. He grew an average of 10 centimeters a year from age 10 to age 14.

7. The corn in Miss Anaya's corn field was 9 centimeters tall at the end of June. It was 73 centimeters tall at the end of July. So Miss Anaya said her corn was 41 centimeters tall in the middle of July.

8. Alan's average bowling score for his first 9 games is 100. He bowls a 200 on his 10th game, so his average score for the 10 games is 150.

Example: Find the average of 10, 7, 9, 4, and 10.

Add the numbers. $10 + 7 + 9 + 4 + 10 = 40$

How many numbers were added?   5

Divide the sum by how many numbers were added. $5\overline{)40}^{\,8}$

The average of 10, 7, 9, 4, and 10 is 8.

Find the average of each set of numbers. Use shortcuts
when you can.

1. 3, 4, 5, 6, 7
2. 13, 14, 15, 16, 17
3. 30, 40, 50, 60, 70
4. 7, 12, 63, 15, 28
5. 82, 57, 49, 63, 85, 42

6. 4, 2, 8, 16, 0, 5, 12, 17, 25, 11
7. 44, 44, 44, 44, 44, 44, 44, 44
8. 27, 103, 59, 68, 112, 96, 84, 11
9. 125, 39, 247, 362, 189, 154
10. 2843, 2844, 2845, 2846, 2847

11. Neal bowled 3 games. His scores were 143, 129, and 151. What was his average score for the 3 games?

12. Alma bowled 3 games. Her scores were 187, 202, and 192. About what was her average score for the 3 games?

13. Debbie drove 595 kilometers in 7 hours. What was the average number of kilometers she drove each hour? (We call this the average speed.)

14. Carolyn sells hot dogs at the ball park. She sold 192 on Monday, 160 on Tuesday, 233 on Friday, 220 on Saturday, and 260 on Sunday. There were no games on Wednesday and Thursday. For this week, what was the average number of hot dogs Carolyn sold during a day's work?

Divide.

Look for patterns that will help you find answers quickly.

1. $3\overline{)10}$	12. $6\overline{)1000}$	23. $4\overline{)1256}$	34. $9\overline{)2520}$
2. $3\overline{)100}$	13. $6\overline{)100}$	24. $5\overline{)847}$	35. $2\overline{)210}$
3. $3\overline{)1000}$	14. $5\overline{)10}$	25. $7\overline{)9482}$	36. $3\overline{)210}$
4. $2\overline{)10}$	15. $1\overline{)873}$	26. $1\overline{)2520}$	37. $5\overline{)210}$
5. $2\overline{)100}$	16. $8\overline{)1000}$	27. $2\overline{)2520}$	38. $7\overline{)210}$
6. $2\overline{)1000}$	17. $8\overline{)2000}$	28. $3\overline{)2520}$	39. $8\overline{)210}$
7. $4\overline{)100}$	18. $9\overline{)1000}$	29. $4\overline{)2520}$	40. $7\overline{)1,000,000}$
8. $4\overline{)1000}$	19. $9\overline{)2000}$	30. $5\overline{)2520}$	41. $7\overline{)2,000,000}$
9. $4\overline{)10,000}$	20. $9\overline{)3000}$	31. $6\overline{)2520}$	42. $7\overline{)3,000,000}$
10. $5\overline{)100}$	21. $2\overline{)246}$	32. $7\overline{)2520}$	43. $7\overline{)4,000,000}$
11. $5\overline{)1000}$	22. $3\overline{)785}$	33. $8\overline{)2520}$	44. $9\overline{)1,000,000}$

Divide to solve for n.

45. $900 \div 9 = n$	50. $210 \div 7 = n$	55. $200 \div 8 = n$
46. $100 \div 4 = n$	51. $72 \div 9 = n$	56. $360 \div 6 = n$
47. $360 \div 4 = n$	52. $360 \div 9 = n$	57. $360 \div 8 = n$
48. $360 \div 5 = n$	53. $350 \div 7 = n$	58. $80 \div 5 = n$
49. $900 \div 6 = n$	54. $2871 \div 9 = n$	59. $1024 \div 8 = n$

60. Michelle wants to give a pen to each of the 28 people
    coming to her party. The pens she wants come in
    packages of 8.
    a. How many packages does she need to buy?
    b. How many extra pens will she have?

1. 9 people took a 40-word spelling test. Their scores were 39, 38, 30, 39, 26, 31, 35, 7, and 34.
   a. What was the average score?
   b. How many people had above-average scores?
   c. How many people had below-average scores?
   d. How many people had exactly average scores?

2. 7 people took a 30-problem arithmetic quiz. Their scores were 21, 29, 30, 20, 17, 14, and 11.
   a. About what was the average score?
   b. How many people had above-average scores?
   c. How many people had below-average scores?
   d. How many people scored within 1 point of the average score?

3. Mr. Epstein knows that his living room rug is rectangular and that its area is 42 square meters.
   a. He knows it is 6 meters wide, but he cannot remember how long it is. How long is the rug?
   b. If the local cleaner charges $1.53 (153¢) for each square meter of rug cleaned, how much will it cost Mr. Epstein to have his rug cleaned?

4. Miss McConnell was told that cabbages at her favorite store weigh about 1 kilogram (1000 grams). She bought 9 cabbages and weighed them to see if they weighed 1 kilogram each. Their weights were 932 grams, 961 grams, 982 grams, 989 grams, 994 grams, 996 grams, 1008 grams, 1087 grams, and 1096 grams.

  a. How many of the 9 cabbages weighed more than 1 kilogram?
  b. What was the average weight of the 9 cabbages?
  c. Would it have cost Miss McConnell less to buy the cabbages for 65¢ a cabbage or for 65¢ a kilogram?

When Roland bowls, he bowls a series of 3 games. The last 7 times he bowled, his total scores for 3 games were 561, 570, 572, 568, 430, 564, and 571.

  • For the last 7 times he bowled, could Roland's average score for a series of 3 games be 400?
  • Could it be 430?
  • Could it be 600?
  • Could it be 572?
  • Make your best guess of Roland's average score. Then calculate the average to see how close you were.
  • About what do you think Roland's score will be the next time he bowls?
  a. About 450   b. About 570   c. About 510

The temperature has varied greatly over the past 15 days. The high temperatures for each day were 36°C, 24°C, 21°C, 37°C, 23°C, 27°C, 17°C, 21°C, 20°C, 21°C, 26°C, 25°C, 26°C, 26°C, and 25°C.

  • What was the average high temperature in this 15-day period?
  • During the past 100 years, the average daily high temperature for this 15-day period was 23°C. Would you say that this period this year is warmer than usual, cooler than usual, or about average?

Solve for n.

1. $36 + 9 = n$

2. $36 - 9 = n$

3. $36 \times 9 = n$

4. $36 \div 9 = n$

5. $36 + 6 = n$

6. $36 - 6 = n$

7. $36 \times 6 = n$

8. $36 \div 6 = n$

9. $n = 42 \times 7$

10. $n = 42 - 7$

11. $n = 42 \div 7$

12. $n = 42 + 7$

13. $n = 243 + 512$

14. $n = 648 - 471$

15. $286 \times 8 = n$

16. $n = 512 \div 4$

17. $407 \times 58 = n$

18. $n = 63 \times 57$

19. $n = 1000 \div 8$

20. $73 \times 89 = n$

21. $2 \times 2 = n$

22. $2 + 2 = n$

23. $0 \times 5783 = n$

24. $n = 5783 + 0$

25. $0 \times 5 = n$

26. $n = 0 \div 5$

27. $n = 5 \div 0$ — Is this allowed?

28. $0 \div 9 = n$

29. $9 \times 0 = n$

30. $9 \div 0 = n$

31. $7 \times 8 = n$

32. $56 \div 7 = n$

33. $n = 42 \div 6$

34. $n = 83 + 249$

35. $n = 1000 - 783$

36. $n = 426 + 574$

Solve. Watch the signs.

37.
$$\begin{array}{r} 8562 \\ + 9408 \\ \hline \end{array}$$

38.
$$\begin{array}{r} 52{,}071 \\ - 3{,}468 \\ \hline \end{array}$$

39.
$$\begin{array}{r} 832 \\ \times 706 \\ \hline \end{array}$$

40.
$$\begin{array}{r} 647 \\ + 352 \\ \hline \end{array}$$

41.
$$\begin{array}{r} 5407 \\ + 4593 \\ \hline \end{array}$$

42.
$$\begin{array}{r} 10{,}000 \\ - 7{,}654 \\ \hline \end{array}$$

43.
$$\begin{array}{r} 10{,}000 \\ - 3{,}819 \\ \hline \end{array}$$

44.
$$\begin{array}{r} 301 \\ \times 299 \\ \hline \end{array}$$

45.
$$\begin{array}{r} 250 \\ + 250 \\ \hline \end{array}$$

46.
$$\begin{array}{r} 70 \\ \times 30 \\ \hline \end{array}$$

47.
$$\begin{array}{r} 1000 \\ - 998 \\ \hline \end{array}$$

48.
$$\begin{array}{r} 600 \\ \times 40 \\ \hline \end{array}$$

Divide.

49. $9\overline{)54}$

50. $7\overline{)497}$

51. $6\overline{)2844}$

52. $8\overline{)26{,}648}$

Find the missing digits.

1.
```
      1 ■ 8  R3
   5) 5 4 3
      5
      ─
      4 3
      4 0
      ───
        3
```

2.
```
        6 2  R3
   7) 4 3 7
      4 2
      ───
      ■ 7
      1 4
      ───
        3
```

3.
```
        7 4  R■
   8) 5 9 9
      5 6
      ───
        3 9
        3 2
        ───
          7
```

4.
```
        2 3  R2
   9) 2 0 9
      1 8
      ───
        2 9
        2 7
        ───
          ■
```

5.
```
        4 0  R■
   8) 3 2 2
      3 2
      ───
          2
```

6.
```
        1 0 ■  R5
   8) 8 0 5
      8
      ─
          5
```

7.
```
        ■ 8
   8) 6 2 4
      5 6
      ───
        6 4
        6 4
```

8.
```
        1 ■ 6
   6) 6 3 6
      6
      ─
        3 6
        3 6
```

9.
```
      1 1 9
   8) 9 5 2
      8
      ─
      1 ■
        8
      ───
        7 2
        7 2
```

10.
```
      4 ■ 2
   2) 9 6 4
      8
      ─
      1 6
      1 6
      ───
          4
          4
```

11.
```
      1 ■ 3
   4) 7 3 2
      4
      ─
      3 3
      3 2
      ───
        1 2
        1 2
```

12.
```
      2 ■ 9
   3) 8 0 7
      6
      ─
      2 0
      1 8
      ───
        2 7
        2 7
```

13.
```
      1 6 7
   3) 5 0 1
      3
      ─
      2 0
      1 ■
      ───
        2 1
        2 1
```

14.
```
      1 2 7
   6) ■ 6 2
      6
      ─
      1 6
      1 2
      ───
        4 2
        4 2
```

15.
```
      1 1 8
   7) 8 2 6
      ■
      ─
      1 2
        7
      ───
        5 6
        5 6
```

16.
```
        1 6 3
   ■) 3 2 6
      2
      ─
      1 2
      1 2
      ───
          6
          6
```

ESTIMATING IS ROUGH

Mr. Sleeby began his new job in a new office.

One day his boss took him down to the port and showed him 2 ships. "These are my ships," she said. "The S.S. *Chubby* and the S.S. *Slim*."

"The S.S. *Slim* is much bigger and dirtier than the other one," said Mr. Sleeby.

"The ships are really about the same size," said the boss. "They are just different shapes. The *Slim* looks dirtier because the *Chubby* has a new coat of paint. See, the painters are just finishing."

The boss said the painters were going to paint the *Slim* next. Mr. Sleeby's job was to estimate how many cans of paint they would need. "I hope you make a good estimate," said the boss. "Our last estimator did a poor job. He had us buy far too much paint for the *Chubby*."

"Don't worry," said Mr. Sleeby. "Sleeby is never wrong—by much. Now let me see . . . If you stack up 50 cans of paint, they should be as high as the ship. So 50 cans of paint is my estimate."

"But what about how long the ship is?" said the boss.

OTTO SLEEBY
CHIEF ESTIMATOR
Sleeby is never
wrong by much

"I forgot about that," said Mr. Sleeby. "But after all, it's only an estimate."

Just then the painters came by. "We finished painting the *Chubby*," said one. "We used only half the paint. What shall we do with the 50 cans that are left?"

"Go paint the S.S. *Slim* with it," Mr. Sleeby said. "Fifty cans was my first estimate for the job. And my first estimates are always as good as my last ones."

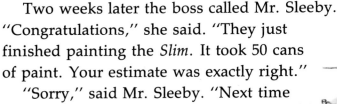

Two weeks later the boss called Mr. Sleeby. "Congratulations," she said. "They just finished painting the *Slim*. It took 50 cans of paint. Your estimate was exactly right."

"Sorry," said Mr. Sleeby. "Next time I'll try to be just almost right."

1. What was wrong with Mr. Sleeby's way of estimating how much paint would be needed? Draw pictures of ships to show why his way could give bad estimates sometimes.

2. Mr. Sleeby said his first estimates are always as good as his last ones. If that is true, does that prove his first estimates are good? Why or why not?

3. What was Mr. Sleeby sorry about at the end of the story?

4. A detective question: How could you figure out that 50 cans of paint would be about right for the S.S. *Slim*?

OODLES OF GOOPLES

Mickey dreamed about a trip to Lotsamonia. He went there with his friends Mindy, Charlie, Sally, Tony, and Leslie.

They landed near a hamburger stand, which reminded them how hungry they were.

"How much are your hamburgers?" Mickey asked the man behind the counter.

"23 gooples," he said.

"Gooples!" said Mickey. "What are those?"

"Gooples are our unit of money in Lotsamonia," the man explained.

"We have dollars and cents," said Mickey.

"Well, then," said the man, "go exchange them for gooples."

Off they went to the bank of Lotsamonia, where they found out that 23 gooples were worth exactly 1 dollar.

"How many gooples can I get for $3?" Leslie asked the teller.

• Do you know the answer to that question?

"I gave the teller $27," said Sally, "and he gave me 621 gooples. Does that make sense?"

"I have an idea," said Tony. "Let's make a graph so we can check whether we are getting about the right number of gooples for our dollars."

"OK," they all agreed.

First they made a chart using some numbers that were easy to multiply.

Dollars	Gooples
0	0
100	2300

298

Next, Mickey and his friends made a graph of the ordered pairs on the chart: (0, 0) and (100, 2300). They drew a straight line through the points.

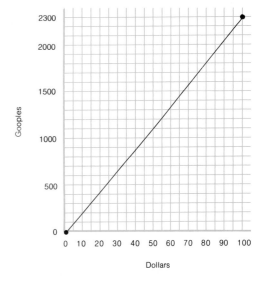

"I have $65," said Leslie. "About how many gooples will I get?"

"Simple," said Tony, "find 65 on the sideways axis, go straight up to the line, then go across to the up-and-down axis."

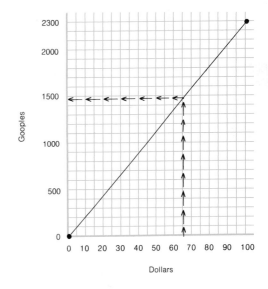

Leslie watched Tony put his finger on 65 and then move it up and over. "I see," he said, "my 65 dollars are worth about 1500 gooples."

They all exchanged their dollars for gooples and used the graph to check their amounts.

"Now we can get some hamburgers and then go shopping," said Mickey. And off they went.

299

Charlie saw a radio that he wanted to buy. Then he saw the price.

"It costs 1000 gooples," he said. "That's too much money."

"It's not as much as it sounds," Tony said. "You have to divide 1000 by 23 to find out how much that is in dollars."

"But we don't know how to divide by big numbers like 23," said Charlie.

"We can use our graph to get an approximate answer," said Tony. "Remember, dividing is the opposite, or inverse, of multiplication. So, if we can use the graph to multiply, we can just do the opposite to divide. Look."

"I see," said Charlie. "1000 gooples are worth a little less than $45."

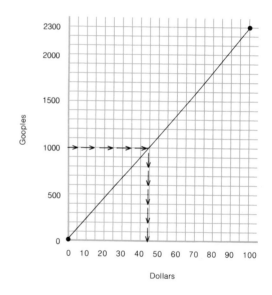

Use the graph to approximate how many dollars each of these items costs.

1. Running suit—649 gooples
2. Baseball glove—415 gooples
3. Shirt—110 gooples
4. Bicycle—1820 gooples
5. Calculator—225 gooples
6. Tape recorder—803 gooples

Remember

If you put 35 into a ×23 machine, 805 will come out.

A ÷23 machine does the opposite. If you put in 805, then 35 will come out.

   35 ——(×23)——→ 805

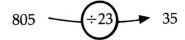   805 ——(÷23)——→ 35

In each problem, find the value of x or y. The answers to the problems on the left will help you do the problems on the right.

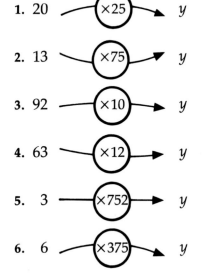
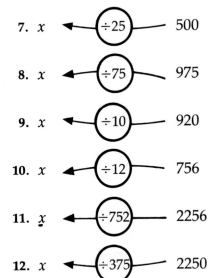

1. 20 ——(×25)——→ y

2. 13 ——(×75)——→ y

3. 92 ——(×10)——→ y

4. 63 ——(×12)——→ y

5. 3 ——(×752)——→ y

6. 6 ——(×375)——→ y

7. x ←——(÷25)—— 500

8. x ←——(÷75)—— 975

9. x ←——(÷10)—— 920

10. x ←——(÷12)—— 756

11. x ←——(÷752)—— 2256

12. x ←——(÷375)—— 2250

Remember

Multiplication is the inverse of division. So if you multiply by 7 and then divide by 7, you get back the number you started with.

Example A: Start with 8 and multiply by 7.

$7 \times 8 = 56$

$56 \div 7 = 8$

Example B:

$$\begin{array}{r} 283 \\ \times\ \ 28 \\ \hline 2264 \\ 566\ \ \\ \hline 7924 \end{array}$$

Start with 283 and multiply by 28.

$28 \times 283 = 7924$

$$\begin{array}{r} 283 \\ 28)\overline{7924} \end{array}$$

$7924 \div 28 = 283$

Solve these problems without dividing or subtracting.
Use the information at the bottom of the page.

1. $25)\overline{625}$ 5. $250)\overline{1000}$ 9. $843)\overline{22{,}761}$

2. $125)\overline{1000}$ 6. $52)\overline{2496}$ 10. $48)\overline{2496}$

3. $4)\overline{1000}$ 7. $79)\overline{6399}$ 11. $81)\overline{6399}$

4. $8)\overline{1000}$

8. $\begin{array}{r} 13{,}129 \\ -\ \ 7{,}846 \\ \hline \end{array}$ 12. $\begin{array}{r} 13{,}129 \\ -\ \ 5{,}283 \\ \hline \end{array}$

$25 \times 25 = 625$ $843 \times 27 = 22{,}761$ $5283 + 7846 = 13{,}129$

$81 \times 79 = 6399$ $4 \times 250 = 1000$ $8 \times 125 = 1000$

$52 \times 48 = 2496$

302

For each problem, several answers are given but only 1 is correct. Choose the correct answer without dividing.

Example: $25)\overline{175}$ a. 4   b. 6   c. 7   d. 10   e. 11

$$\begin{array}{r} 25 \\ \times\ \ 4 \\ \hline 100 \end{array} \qquad \begin{array}{r} 25 \\ \times\ \ 6 \\ \hline 150 \end{array} \qquad \begin{array}{r} 25 \\ \times\ \ 7 \\ \hline 175 \end{array} \qquad \begin{array}{l} 7 \times 25 = 175 \\ \text{So } 175 \div 25 \text{ must be 7.} \\ \text{The correct answer is \textbf{c}.} \end{array}$$

1. $12)\overline{96}$ a. 7   b. 8   c. 9   d. 10   e. 11

2. $15)\overline{225}$ a. 5   b. 8   c. 10   d. 13   e. 15

3. $24)\overline{96}$ a. 4   b. 5   c. 6   d. 7   e. 8

4. $250)\overline{1000}$ a. 3   b. 4   c. 5   d. 6   e. 7

5. $12)\overline{144}$ a. 8   b. 9   c. 10   d. 12   e. 14

6. $15)\overline{75}$ a. 5   b. 6   c. 7   d. 8   e. 10

7. $11)\overline{154}$ a. 12   b. 14   c. 16   d. 20   e. 24

8. $17)\overline{357}$ a. 19   b. 20   c. 21   d. 22   e. 23

9. $22)\overline{242}$ a. 9   b. 11   c. 13   d. 15   e. 17

10. $16)\overline{96}$ a. 5   b. 6   c. 8   d. 14   e. 16

11. $13)\overline{169}$ a. 2   b. 5   c. 7   d. 9   e. 13

12. $150)\overline{600}$ a. 4   b. 5   c. 6   d. 7   e. 8

13. $12)\overline{108}$ a. 7   b. 8   c. 9   d. 10   e. 11

14. $14)\overline{182}$ a. 11   b. 12   c. 13   d. 14   e. 15

15. $19)\overline{247}$ a. 2   b. 3   c. 5   d. 13   e. 17

This flag was the United States flag longer than any other flag.

From 1818 to 1836 the United States flag had 20 stars.

1912–1960

• How do you think the stars were arranged?

For many numbers of stars it is possible to arrange them in different rectangles. For some numbers, the only possible rectangles would have 1 row (or 1 column). All the possible rectangles that can be made with 36 stars are:

1 by 36	3 by 12	6 by 6	12 by 3	36 by 1
2 by 18	4 by 9	9 by 4	18 by 2	

Solve these problems.

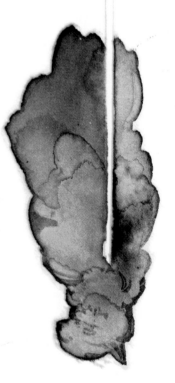

1. List all possible rectangles that could be made with
   a. 1 star   c. 3 stars   e. 5 stars
   b. 2 stars   d. 4 stars   f. 6 stars

2. How many rectangles did you list for 1 star? Do you think there are any other numbers besides 1 for which there is only 1 rectangle?

3. How many rectangles did you list for 2, 3, and 5 stars? Do you think there are other numbers for which there are only 2 rectangles?

4. List 3 other numbers for which there are only 2 rectangles.

5. How many rectangles did you list for 4 stars? Can you think of 3 other numbers for which there are exactly 3 rectangles?

304

6. List 5 numbers for which there are more than 3 rectangles.

Prime numbers have exactly 2 rectangles.
Composite numbers have more than 2 rectangles.

7. List 5 prime numbers.
8. List 5 composite numbers.
9. Is the number 1 prime or composite?

A factor of a number is any number that divides it without a remainder. For example, the factors of 36 are 1, 2, 3, 4, 6, 9, 12, 18, and 36. You can divide 36 by any of these numbers and there will be no remainder.

10. What are the factors of
    a. 1?   b. 2?   c. 3?   d. 4?   e. 5?   f. 6?

11. How many factors does 1 have?

12. How many factors
    a. does 2 have?   b. does 3 have?   c. does 5 have?

13. How many factors does 4 have?

14. List all numbers that you think have just 1 factor.

15. List 4 numbers that have exactly 2 factors.

16. List 6 numbers that have more than 2 factors.

17. How many factors do prime numbers have?

18. How many factors do composite numbers have?

19. Why might $(6 \times 5) + (5 \times 4)$ remind someone of the flag of the United States?

Challenge problem
List all the prime numbers less than 100.

ESTIMATING IS ROUGH

Part 4

"I need your help, Mr. Sleeby," said the grocer. "Could you help me figure out how many turkeys to order for Christmas?"

"Is your store open on Christmas Day?"

"No," said the grocer.

"Then my estimate is 1," said Mr. Sleeby. "Unless you have a very large family."

"I have a small family," said the grocer. "But I have lots of customers. Some of them buy turkeys for Christmas. I'd like you to estimate how many."

Mr. Sleeby stopped a shopper. "Pardon me, sir. Do you plan to buy a turkey for Christmas?"

"I don't think so," said the shopper. "We don't have a big roasting pan."

Mr. Sleeby asked more shoppers. But he changed the question. He found that 41 had big roasting pans and 42 didn't. Then he asked the grocer, "How many customers do you have altogether?"

"About 2000."

"Then I estimate you will need 1000 turkeys."

"But . . . but I've never sold that many! I sold only 600 at Thanksgiving."

"I forgot Thanksgiving," said Mr. Sleeby. "You have 1000 people buying turkeys. You sold 600 turkeys at Thanksgiving. That means you will sell 400 at Christmas. Order 400 turkeys—and 600 ducks. That way everyone with a roasting pan will have something to roast."

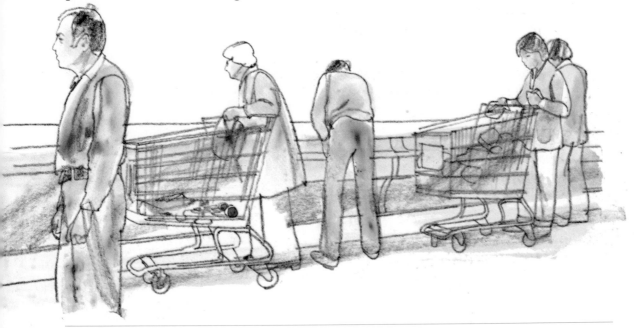

1. How did Mr. Sleeby get his first estimate of 1000 turkeys?

2. Were his reasons for saying 1000 very good reasons? Why or why not?

3. How did Mr. Sleeby get his second estimate of 400?

4. Were his reasons for saying 400 turkeys very good reasons? Why or why not?

5. A superchallenge question: If you were asking the questions instead of Mr. Sleeby, what questions would you have asked to figure out how many turkeys to order?

Lori earns $2.00 an hour washing cars. The bar graph shows the total amount of money she earned each day during a typical week.

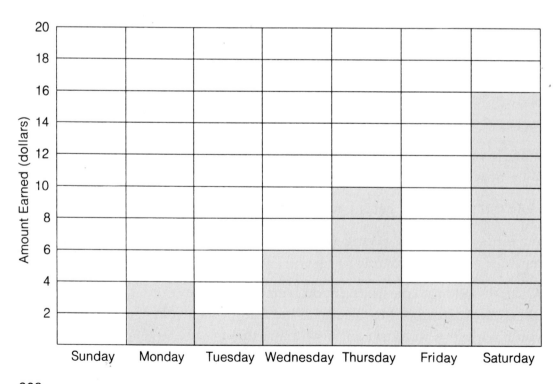

Use the graph to answer these questions.

1. How much money did Lori earn on Monday?

2. How much money did she earn on Tuesday?

3. How much money did she earn on Friday?

4. How many hours did Lori work on Wednesday? (Remember, she earns $2 an hour.)

5. How many hours did she work on Saturday?

6. How many hours did Lori work on Tuesday?

7. On which day did she earn the most money?

8. How much money did Lori earn during the entire week?

9. What was the average amount of money she made per day for the 6 days she worked?

10. If she had earned $3 an hour, how much would Lori have earned during the entire week?

Divide.

11. $8\overline{)410}$	17. $6\overline{)236}$	23. $5\overline{)500}$	29. $3\overline{)271}$	35. $9\overline{)810}$
12. $4\overline{)237}$	18. $3\overline{)229}$	24. $4\overline{)804}$	30. $6\overline{)732}$	36. $7\overline{)210}$
13. $9\overline{)63}$	19. $8\overline{)539}$	25. $2\overline{)107}$	31. $7\overline{)622}$	37. $8\overline{)48}$
14. $3\overline{)408}$	20. $4\overline{)792}$	26. $6\overline{)360}$	32. $9\overline{)72}$	38. $6\overline{)201}$
15. $3\overline{)273}$	21. $8\overline{)32}$	27. $9\overline{)706}$	33. $6\overline{)240}$	39. $8\overline{)324}$
16. $2\overline{)970}$	22. $6\overline{)437}$	28. $8\overline{)342}$	34. $9\overline{)108}$	40. $4\overline{)960}$

Study Mr. Cooper's telephone bill. Then answer the questions.

The Dingletown Telephone Company   James Cooper
577 12th St.
Monthly Statement   Dingletown
October   Telephone Number   554-5505

Date	Calls to	Number of minutes	Price
Oct. 10	Middledorf	5	$1.25
Oct. 13	Middledorf	10	$2.50
Oct. 24	Shortport	10	$ .80
Oct. 25	Ringville	3	$6.00
Oct. 27	Longway	2	$8.30
Oct. 29	Dingles Ferry	15	$1.50
Oct. 30	Middledorf	8	$3.00

Dingletown Telephone Company rate information:
All calls to other cities are charged by the minute.
The farther a city is from Dingletown, the higher is the rate.

1. How much per minute does it cost to call
   a. Middledorf?   c. Ringville?   e. Dingles Ferry?
   b. Shortport?   d. Longway?

2. Which city is farther from Dingletown—Shortport or Middledorf?

3. There is an error in one of the charges on Mr. Cooper's telephone bill. Help him find the error. How much will Mr. Cooper save if he finds the error?

4. Order the cities Mr. Cooper called, from the nearest to the farthest from Dingletown.

5. For how many minutes did Mr. Cooper use the telephone in October on calls that he made to other cities?

Divide. Watch for remainders.

1. 3)‾42‾   6. 5)‾125‾   11. 1)‾100‾   16. 4)‾100‾   21. 10)‾100‾

2. 3)‾20‾   7. 4)‾1298‾   12. 7)‾507‾   17. 5)‾75‾   22. 5)‾63,407‾

3. 8)‾16‾   8. 2)‾100‾   13. 7)‾8575‾   18. 6)‾44‾   23. 1)‾73,596‾

4. 9)‾9‾   9. 8)‾1000‾   14. 7)‾98‾   19. 9)‾0‾   24. 6)‾35,172‾

5. 9)‾18‾   10. 9)‾80‾   15. 2)‾84‾   20. 6)‾6‾   25. 8)‾500‾

26. Last week Kirsten jogged every day. She didn't jog
the same amount each day. These are the distances
she jogged during the week: 14 kilometers, 18
kilometers, 20 kilometers, 15 kilometers, 17 kilometers,
20 kilometers, 8 kilometers.
   a. What is the average distance Kirsten jogged
      each day?
   b. Did she jog the average distance on any day?
   c. On how many days did she run more than the
      average distance?
   d. On how many days did Kirsten run less than the
      average distance?

1. Mr. Nolan drove 510 kilometers in 6 hours. What was his average speed?

2. Miss Lin drove 250 kilometers in 3 hours. About what was her average speed?

3. Mrs. Vega drove for 7 hours. She drove 90 kilometers the first hour, 85 kilometers the second hour, 50 kilometers the third hour, 50 kilometers the fourth hour, 85 kilometers the fifth hour, 85 kilometers the sixth hour, and 80 kilometers the seventh hour. About what was her average speed?

4. Sita can buy 6 bottles of cola for $1.44. What is the cost for each bottle of cola?

5. Gregory can buy 8 bottles of cola for $1.68 (or 168¢). What is the cost for each bottle of cola if he buys it in sets of 8?

6. Janet and her 3 friends wanted to share 36 peaches equally. How many should each child get?

7. Hari bought 9 melons that cost 72¢ each. The tax was 39¢. He gave the storekeeper a $10 bill. How much change should he get back?

8. Judith bought 9 cans of orange juice. The storekeeper charged her $5.85 (585¢) for the 9 cans. How much did each can of juice cost?

9. Kimberly and Jonathan left Tinytown at the same time. Kimberly drove 532 kilometers and Jonathan drove 510 kilometers. How far apart were they?

10. Mr. Ortiz drove 530 kilometers one day and 610 kilometers the next. His total trip was to be about 1500 kilometers. About how far did he still have to go?

For each problem, several answers are given but only 1 is correct. Choose the correct answer without dividing.

1. $1\overline{)350}$ **a.** 27   **b.** 35   **c.** 270   **d.** 350   **e.** 400

2. $10\overline{)350}$ **a.** 27   **b.** 35   **c.** 270   **d.** 350   **e.** 400

3. $15\overline{)60}$ **a.** 2   **b.** 3   **c.** 4   **d.** 5   **e.** 6

4. $2\overline{)10}$ **a.** 2   **b.** 3   **c.** 4   **d.** 5   **e.** 6

5. $20\overline{)100}$ **a.** 2   **b.** 3   **c.** 4   **d.** 5   **e.** 6

6. $3\overline{)100}$ **a.** 3 R1   **b.** 30 R1   **c.** 33 R1   **d.** 3 R2   **e.** 33 R2

7. $33\overline{)100}$ **a.** 3 R1   **b.** 30 R1   **c.** 33 R1   **d.** 3 R2   **e.** 33 R2

8. $10\overline{)2300}$ **a.** 2300   **b.** 4600   **c.** 46   **d.** 230   **e.** 23

9. $100\overline{)2300}$ **a.** 2300   **b.** 4600   **c.** 46   **d.** 230   **e.** 23

10. $100\overline{)23,000}$ **a.** 2300   **b.** 4600   **c.** 46   **d.** 230   **e.** 23

11. $7\overline{)67}$ **a.** 9 R2   **b.** 9 R3   **c.** 9 R4   **d.** 8 R5   **e.** 7 R6

12. $18\overline{)90}$ **a.** 3   **b.** 4   **c.** 5   **d.** 6   **e.** 7

13. $11\overline{)132}$ **a.** 12   **b.** 14   **c.** 16   **d.** 18   **e.** 20

14. $5\overline{)75}$ **a.** 13   **b.** 14   **c.** 15   **d.** 16   **e.** 17

15. $50\overline{)750}$ **a.** 15   **b.** 150   **c.** 30   **d.** 35   **e.** 50

16. $50\overline{)75,000}$ **a.** 150   **b.** 175   **c.** 600   **d.** 1500   **e.** 3000

17. $13\overline{)195}$ **a.** 14   **b.** 15   **c.** 17   **d.** 19   **e.** 23

18. $4\overline{)84}$ **a.** 17   **b.** 18   **c.** 20   **d.** 21   **e.** 22

19. $40\overline{)8400}$ **a.** 210   **b.** 220   **c.** 420   **d.** 620   **e.** 820

20. $40\overline{)84,000}$ **a.** 420   **b.** 21,000   **c.** 187   **d.** 210   **e.** 2100

ESTIMATING IS ROUGH Part 5

The grocer and some other people went to see Mr. Sleeby's boss. "We don't think Mr. Sleeby knows how to estimate," said the grocer. "He comes up with answers in nutty ways."

"But his estimates are good," said the boss. "He was exactly right about how many cans of paint we would need to paint the S.S. *Slim*."

"He must be lucky, then," said the grocer. "I'll bet he can't even estimate how many eggs are in a dozen."

"We'll see about that," said the boss. She called in Mr. Sleeby and told him to estimate how many eggs are in a dozen.

"That will take some work," said Mr. Sleeby. "I'll try to have the estimate for you by tomorrow."

Mr. Sleeby thought about how he would make the estimate. "Let's see," he said. "Most people buy a dozen eggs at a time. I'll find out how many eggs most people have on hand. That should give me a good estimate."

Mr. Sleeby went from house to house. He asked people how many eggs they had. These are the numbers he got: 21, 11, 8, 0, 7, 9, 0, 12. He added up the numbers and divided by 6. "The answer is 11 and some left over," he said. "So I guess the average number of eggs people have is about $11\frac{1}{2}$."

The next day Mr. Sleeby told his boss, "I have my estimate. A dozen is about $11\frac{1}{2}$ eggs."

"That is close," said the boss. "But I thought you would know exactly how many eggs are in a dozen."

"Please," said Mr. Sleeby. "I am an estimator. If you wanted the exact answer, you should have asked a chicken."

1. Does it make sense to estimate how many eggs are in a dozen? Why or why not?

2. What do you think Mr. Sleeby was trying to do when he added the numbers and divided them by 6?

3. How would you find the average of the numbers Mr. Sleeby got?

4. A challenge question: Mr. Sleeby is right that most people buy a dozen eggs at a time. Why, then, did Mr. Sleeby find that the average number of eggs people have is not 12?

Find the missing digits.

1.
```
     1 ■ 5
  6) 6 3 0
     6
     3 0
     3 0
```

2.
```
     1 1 0
  5) 5 5 0
     ■
       5
       5
```

3.
```
     2 ■ 8
  3) 6 2 4
     6
     2 4
     2 4
```

4.
```
     1 2 0
  7) 8 4 ■
     7
     1 4
     1 4
```

5.
```
     8 0  R2
  8) ■ 4 2
     6 4
       2
```

6.
```
     7 0
  7) 4 ■ 0
     4 9
```

7.
```
     9 0
  9) 8 1 0
     ■ 1
```

8.
```
     ■ 0
  9) 8 1 0
     8 1
```

9.
```
     1 2 ■  R4
  6) 7 6 6
     6
     1 6
     1 2
       4 6
       4 2
         4
```

10.
```
     2 3 1  R2
  4) 9 2 6
     8
     ■ 2
     1 2
         6
         4
         2
```

11.
```
     1 1 5 R■
  8) 9 2 3
     8
     1 2
       8
       4 3
       4 0
         3
```

12.
```
     1 1 3  R3
  8) 9 0 7
     8
     1 0
       ■
       2 7
       2 4
         3
```

13.
```
     7 ■  R1
  5) 3 9 1
     3 5
     4 1
     4 0
       1
```

14.
```
     7 8 R■
  8) 6 2 7
     5 6
     6 7
     6 4
       3
```

15.
```
     4 7  R3
  8) 3 7 9
     3 2
     ■ 9
     5 6
       3
```

16.
```
     1 3 3 R■
  5) 6 6 6
     5
     1 6
     1 5
       1 6
       1 5
         1
```

Solve for n. Watch the signs.

1. $n = 16 \div 8$
2. $16 + 8 = n$
3. $n = 5 \times 9$
4. $49 \div n = 7$
5. $37 - 19 = n$

6. $19 + n = 58$
7. $9 \times 7 = n$
8. $36 - n = 27$
9. $n \div 7 = 5$
10. $6 \times 9 = n$

11. $n = 81 \div 9$
12. $n + 28 = 77$
13. $33 = 41 - n$
14. $7 \times 8 = n$
15. $27 \div n = 9$

Multiply.

16. 9×100
17. 10×23
18. $100 \times 10,000$
19. $100 \times 10,001$
20. 90×100

21. 14×1000
22. $10,000 \times 37$
23. $10,000 \times 370$
24. $10,001 \times 370$
25. 900×100

Add, subtract, multiply, or divide. Watch the signs. Use shortcuts when you can.

26. 3×9
27. $90 \div 2$
28. $16 + 7$
29. $33 - 15$
30. $28 \div 7$

31. $81 + 17$
32. 9×7
33. $35 - 29$
34. 12×13
35. $16 + 17$

36. $91 \div 7$
37. $39 + 22$
38. $87 - 69$
39. 7×6
40. $47 + 74$

Divide. Use shortcuts when you can.

41. $8 \overline{)\, 56}$
42. $3 \overline{)\, 120}$
43. $7 \overline{)\, 4900}$
44. $9 \overline{)\, 63}$
45. $2 \overline{)\, 8006}$

46. $4 \overline{)\, 404}$
47. $5 \overline{)\, 450}$
48. $6 \overline{)\, 4200}$
49. $4 \overline{)\, 3200}$
50. $7 \overline{)\, 6300}$

51. $3 \overline{)\, 30,000}$
52. $4 \overline{)\, 40,000}$
53. $4 \overline{)\, 80,000}$
54. $4 \overline{)\, 160,000}$
55. $1 \overline{)\, 3,987,263}$

Divide. Watch for remainders.

1. $3\overline{)62}$ 3. $9\overline{)999}$ 5. $7\overline{)287}$ 7. $6\overline{)2964}$

2. $8\overline{)300}$ 4. $4\overline{)10,000}$ 6. $5\overline{)386}$ 8. $3\overline{)2721}$

Choose the correct answers.
(1 answer is correct in each case.)

9. $17\overline{)51}$ a. 2   b. 3   c. 4   d. 5   e. 6

10. $39\overline{)468}$ a. 2   b. 4   c. 12   d. 50   e. 100

11. $25\overline{)625}$ a. 10   b. 15   c. 17   d. 20   e. 25

12. $11\overline{)1342}$ a. 12   b. 120   c. 121   d. 122   e. 1202

13. $37\overline{)518}$ a. 11   b. 12   c. 14   d. 24   e. 34

14. $13\overline{)351}$ a. 17   b. 18   c. 27   d. 37   e. 47

Solve for n.

15. $n = 13 - 7$ 18. $n + 18 = 25$ 21. $32 \div 8 = n$
16. $7 + 13 = n$ 19. $37 - n = 16$ 22. $4 \times 80 = n$
17. $7 \times 13 = n$ 20. $n \div 6 = 6$ 23. $4 = n \div 80$

Find the average of each set of numbers.

24. 7, 10, 5, 0, 8

25. 70, 100, 50, 0, 80

26. 1000, 2000, 3000, 4000, 5000, 6000

27. Harriet took 5 spelling tests this month. Her scores
were 91, 82, 100, 85, and 92. What was her average
score for the 5 tests?

28. Mr. Mora drove 792 kilometers in 9 hours. What was his average speed?

29. Daniel mows lawns and gets paid $1 for each hour he works. He worked 4 hours on Saturday and 3 hours on Sunday. How much did he earn for the 2 days?

30. Shannon has $3. Does she have enough money to buy 6 notebooks that cost 79¢ each?

31. Robbie wants to jog 50 kilometers this week. He jogged 7 kilometers each day from Monday to Saturday. How many kilometers must he jog on Sunday to reach his goal?

32. Lola is setting up chairs for a show. She sets up 9 rows with 7 chairs in each row and 1 row of 8 chairs. How many people can be seated for the show?

33. Terry is growing a bean plant. On Monday the plant was 8 centimeters tall. On Friday the plant was 16 centimeters tall. How much did the plant grow between Monday and Friday?

34. Janelle works part time at a grocery store. The total hours she worked for the past 7 weeks were 18, 23, 11, 16, 25, 17, and 16 hours. About what is the average number of hours she works in a week?

Hal takes care of a dolphin named Finny at an aquarium. He feeds Finny 3 kilograms of fish a day.

35. How much fish does Finny eat in a week?

36. A kilogram of fish costs $5.71. How much does Finny's fish cost the aquarium each week?

Divide. If there is a remainder, write **R** and the remainder after the quotient.

1. $3\overline{)72}$	**5.** $4\overline{)62}$	**9.** $8\overline{)735}$	**13.** $9\overline{)263}$	**17.** $4\overline{)280}$
2. $5\overline{)75}$	**6.** $6\overline{)922}$	**10.** $2\overline{)1063}$	**14.** $5\overline{)211}$	**18.** $3\overline{)725}$
3. $5\overline{)325}$	**7.** $2\overline{)713}$	**11.** $3\overline{)805}$	**15.** $2\overline{)603}$	**19.** $6\overline{)2345}$
4. $3\overline{)72}$	**8.** $7\overline{)600}$	**12.** $4\overline{)209}$	**16.** $7\overline{)625}$	**20.** $6\overline{)1005}$

Choose the correct answer.

21. $10\overline{)400}$ **a.** 4   **b.** 20   **c.** 30   **d.** 40   **e.** 50

22. $100\overline{)6000}$ **a.** 6   **b.** 30   **c.** 60   **d.** 300   **e.** 600

23. $12\overline{)63}$ **a.** 5 R2   **b.** 5   **c.** 5 R3   **d.** 5 R4   **e.** 5 R1

24. $18\overline{)108}$ **a.** 5   **b.** 6   **c.** 7   **d.** 8   **e.** 9

25. $12\overline{)104}$ **a.** 10   **b.** 10 R4   **c.** 8   **d.** 8 R4   **e.** 8 R8

Find the missing digits.

26.
```
      ■4 R15
27)2 0 1 3
  1 8 9
  1 2 3
  1 0 8
    1 5
```

27.
```
        3 ■ R8
31)1 2 1 7
   9 3
   2 8 7
   2 7 9
       8
```

Solve for n. Watch the signs.

28. $n + 5 = 8$ **31.** $5 \times n = 35$ **34.** $3 \times n = 9$

29. $16 \div n = 8$ **32.** $n \div 4 = 6$ **35.** $243 \div 9 = n$

30. $47 - n = 28$ **33.** $2 \times 2 = n$ **36.** $n = 64 \times 32$

1. Bud drove 850 kilometers in 10 hours.
   Arlene drove 595 kilometers in 7 hours.
   a. What was Bud's average speed?
   b. What was Arlene's average speed?
   c. How much farther did Bud drive than Arlene?

Find the average for each set of numbers.

2. 10, 10, 10, 10, 10
3. 8, 9, 10, 11, 12
4. 18, 19, 20, 21, 22
5. 10, 20, 30, 40, 50, 60
6. 6, 8, 9, 8, 14
7. 8, 10, 11, 10, 16

Solve.

8. Mr. Angelo weighed 70 kilograms at the beginning of
   September. He gained 3 kilograms during September.
   Then he lost 5 kilograms during October. How much
   did Mr. Angelo weigh at the end of October?

9. When Juli was 2 years old, she was 75 centimeters tall.
   During the next 18 years, her height doubled. How tall
   was she at the age of 20?

10. Penny bought 2 pads of paper that cost 38¢ each. She
    was charged 80¢ for the 2 pads, including tax.
    a. How much was the tax?
    b. If Penny paid with a $1 bill, how much change
       should she get?

Carmen wants to earn money to buy a bicycle that costs $92. She made a chart to show how many hours she would have to work to earn the money. Help Carmen complete the chart. Then answer the questions.

1. Copy the chart and complete it.

If I Make This Much per Hour	In 40 Hours I Will Make	In 60 Hours I Will Make	In 100 Hours I Will Make
50¢	$20.00		
75¢	$30.00		
$1.00 (100¢)	$40.00		
$1.25 (125¢)	$50.00		

2. Will Carmen earn enough money for the bicycle if she works for 60 hours at 75¢ per hour?

3. Will she earn enough if she works for 60 hours at $1.25 per hour?

4. Will she earn enough if she works for 100 hours at $1.25 per hour?

5. Challenge questions: Exactly how many hours must Carmen work to buy the bicycle if she earns
   a. 50¢ per hour?   **c.** $1.00 per hour?
   b. 75¢ per hour?   **d.** $1.25 per hour?

Mrs. Ortega has a solid fence that is 100 meters long and 2 meters high. She wants to paint both sides of the fence. She has the following recipe for making her own whitewash.

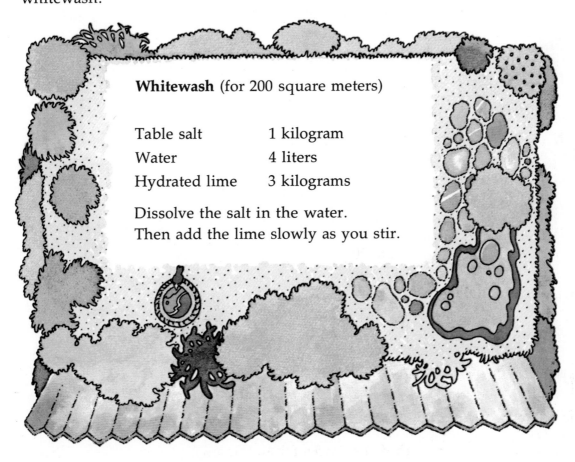

Whitewash (for 200 square meters)

Table salt	1 kilogram
Water	4 liters
Hydrated lime	3 kilograms

Dissolve the salt in the water.
Then add the lime slowly as you stir.

1. How much of each will Mrs. Ortega need?
   a. Table salt   **b.** Water   **c.** Hydrated lime

2. Mrs. Ortega went to the store and found out that table salt costs 40¢ per kilogram and hydrated lime costs 60¢ per kilogram. How much money will she have to spend for both of these items to make enough whitewash for her fence?

Divide. If there is a remainder, write **R** and the remainder after the quotient.

1. $7\overline{)42}$ 4. $3\overline{)82}$ 7. $8\overline{)100}$

2. $5\overline{)317}$ 5. $9\overline{)99}$ 8. $4\overline{)13,476}$

3. $6\overline{)312}$ 6. $2\overline{)76}$ 9. $7\overline{)147}$

Choose the correct answer for each problem.

10. $12\overline{)36}$ a. 3   b. 4   c. 5   d. 6   e. 7

11. $15\overline{)105}$ a. 3   b. 4   c. 5   d. 6   e. 7

12. $24\overline{)144}$ a. 3   b. 4   c. 5   d. 6   e. 7

Solve for n.

13. $n = 15 + 3$ 16. $42 + 7 = n$ 19. $13 + n = 17$
14. $n = 15 - 3$ 17. $24 = n \times 8$ 20. $n - 7 = 15$
15. $42 \div 7 = n$ 18. $24 = n \div 8$ 21. $6 \times 7 = n$

Find the average of each set of numbers.

22. 8, 9, 10, 11, 12
23. 80, 90, 100, 110, 120
24. 5, 23, 12, 11, 15, 16, 9
25. 7, 9, 11, 124, 15

Solve these problems.

26. Lois bowled 3 games and got scores of 145, 132, and 129. Could her average score be 129?

27. Danielle got these scores on 4 mathematics tests: 92, 84, 79, and 89. What was her average score for the 4 tests?

28. Annie has $1 and wants to buy 4 rulers that cost 18¢ each. Does she have enough money?

29. Reggie gets paid a certain amount for each hour he works. Today he worked 6 hours and earned $18. How much money does he earn in an hour?

30. Mr. Byrd needs 45 hamburger rolls for a cookout. The rolls come in packages of 8. How many packages does he need?

31. Ethel bought a pencil case for 39¢ and a notebook for 49¢. The storekeeper charged her 93¢ for the 2 items, including tax. How much was the tax?

32. Cheryl's puppy weighed 4 kilograms last month and 5 kilograms today. How much weight did the puppy gain during the month?

33. Cal wants to paint the bottom of his sailboat. The bottom is 43 square meters. One can of bottom paint covers 8 square meters. How many cans of paint does Cal need to buy to paint the bottom?

UNIT VI

DECIMALS AND MEASUREMENT
FRACTIONS AND PROBABILITY

FRACTIONS AND MEASUREMENT

"I just made up a game," said June. "What's the smallest number greater than 0 that you can make?"

"I know," shouted Alia. "It's 1."

"I can do better than that," said Mel. "I say one-half."

"That's not fair," said Alia. "We can't use that kind of number."

"It's my game," said June. "Any kind of number is all right. And I'm going to say one-tenth."

"Well," said Alia, "I can make a number that's still smaller."

• Can you make a smaller number?

If you divide a whole into 10 equal parts,
each part is one-tenth of the whole.

We can write one-tenth in 2 ways:

As a fraction: $\frac{1}{10}$

As a decimal: 0.1

When you read 0.1, you say, "one-tenth"
or "zero point one."

$\frac{1}{10} = 0.1$

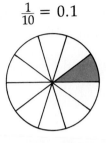

If you divide a whole into 100 equal parts,
each part is one-hundredth of the whole.

We can write one-hundredth in two ways:

As a fraction: $\frac{1}{100}$

As a decimal: 0.01

When you read 0.01, you say, "one-hundredth"
or "zero point zero one."

$\frac{1}{100} = 0.01$

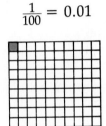

1. Suppose you divide something into 1000 equal parts.
   What would each part be? Write it in 2 ways.
2. Suppose you divide something into 10,000 equal parts.
   Show 2 ways to write what each part would be.
3. Suppose you divide something into 100,000 equal
   parts. Show 2 ways to write what each part would be.
4. Suppose you divide something into 1,000,000 equal
   parts. Show 2 ways to write what each part would be.
5. Which is greater, $\frac{1}{10}$ or $\frac{1}{100}$?
6. Which is greater, 0.1 or 0.01?
7. Which is greater, 0.1 or 0.001?

Remember, if a whole is divided into 10 equal parts, 1 part would be $\frac{1}{10}$, or 0.1.

3 parts would be $\frac{3}{10}$, or 0.3.

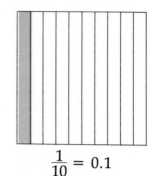

$$\frac{1}{10} = 0.1$$

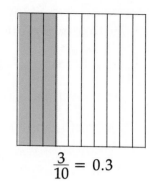

$$\frac{3}{10} = 0.3$$

If a whole is divided into 100 equal parts, 1 part would be $\frac{1}{100}$, or 0.01.

3 parts would be $\frac{3}{100}$, or 0.03.

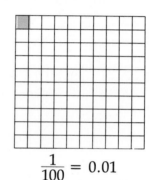

$$\frac{1}{100} = 0.01$$

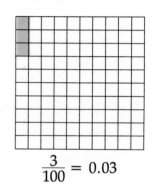

$$\frac{3}{100} = 0.03$$

Suppose you divided a whole into 1000 equal parts.
- What would 1 part be?
- What would 3 parts be?
- What would 7 parts be?

Remember, a dime is $\frac{1}{10}$ dollar and a cent is $\frac{1}{100}$ dollar. 10 cents is the same as 1 dime. So 1 dime is greater than 9 cents and 3 cents is less than 1 dime.

Replace ● with >, <, or =.

1. 0.1 ● 0.3
2. 0.01 ● 0.03
3. 0.01 ● 0.07
4. 0.07 ● 0.03
5. 0.1 ● 0.01

6. 0.03 ● 0.1
7. 0.7 ● 0.08
8. 0.1 ● 0.001
9. 0.01 ● 0.001
10. 0.001 ● 0.003

11. 0.007 ● 0.03
12. 0.2 ● 0.09
13. 0.3 ● 0.03
14. 0.04 ● 0.04
15. 0.04 ● 0.004

- Which is greater, 0.1 or 0.10?

$$\frac{1}{10} = 0.1$$

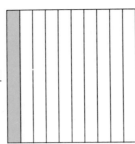

$$\frac{10}{100} = 0.10$$

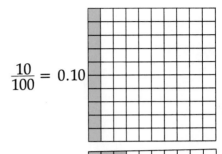

- Which is greater, 0.3 or 0.30?

$$\frac{3}{10} = 0.3$$

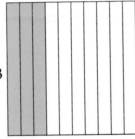

$$\frac{30}{100} = 0.30$$

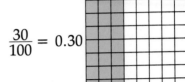
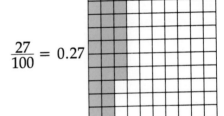

- Which is greater, 0.2 or 0.27?

$$\frac{2}{10} = 0.2$$

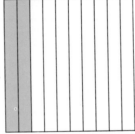

$$\frac{27}{100} = 0.27$$

In each case, tell which is more money (or whether they are the same amount).

1. 3 dimes or 33 cents?
2. 8 dimes or 80 cents?
3. 6 cents or 1 dime?
4. 10 cents or 1 dime?
5. 11 cents or 1 dime?
6. 7 dimes or 8 cents?

Write each amount as a decimal.

7. 3 dimes and 7 cents = $0.37
8. 6 dimes and 4 cents = ▨
9. 0 dimes and 8 cents = ▨
10. 2 dimes and 9 cents = ▨
11. 8 dimes and 0 cents = ▨
12. 8 cents = ▨
13. 64 cents = ▨
14. 3 dimes = ▨
15. 6 cents = ▨
16. 90 cents = ▨

331

For each figure, show what portion is shaded by writing a fraction and a decimal. The first one has been done for you.

1.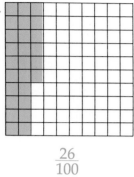

$$\frac{26}{100}$$

0.26

2.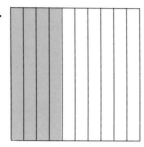

3.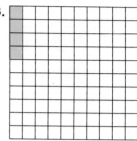

4.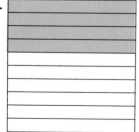

5.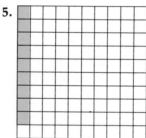

6.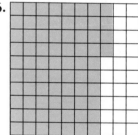

7.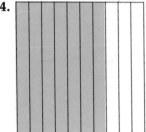

8.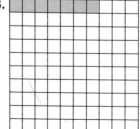

9.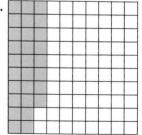

10.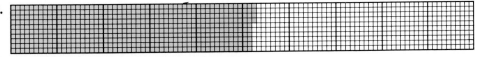

11.

Write each of these fractions as a decimal.

Examples: $\dfrac{3}{100} = 0.03$ $\dfrac{7}{10,000} = 0.0007$

12. $\dfrac{5}{100} = $ ▩   **16.** $\dfrac{6}{10} = $ ▩   **20.** $\dfrac{7}{1000} = $ ▩   **24.** $\dfrac{843}{1000} = $ ▩

13. $\dfrac{8}{100} = $ ▩   **17.** $\dfrac{1}{10} = $ ▩   **21.** $\dfrac{70}{1000} = $ ▩   **25.** $\dfrac{6,286}{10,000} = $ ▩

14. $\dfrac{10}{100} = $ ▩   **18.** $\dfrac{8}{10} = $ ▩   **22.** $\dfrac{700}{1000} = $ ▩   **26.** $\dfrac{66}{100} = $ ▩

15. $\dfrac{11}{100} = $ ▩   **19.** $\dfrac{9}{10} = $ ▩   **23.** $\dfrac{78}{1000} = $ ▩   **27.** $\dfrac{543}{1000} = $ ▩

Copy each pair of numbers, but replace ⬤ with
<, >, or =.

28. 0.02 ⬤ 0.3   **33.** 0.47 ⬤ 0.53   **38.** 0.406 ⬤ 0.407

29. 0.83 ⬤ 0.80   **34.** 0.8 ⬤ 0.80   **39.** 0.8 ⬤ 0.83

30. 0.62 ⬤ 0.90   **35.** 0.9 ⬤ 0.90   **40.** 0.62 ⬤ 0.9

31. 0.48 ⬤ 0.70   **36.** 0.48 ⬤ 0.7   **41.** 0.100 ⬤ 0.1

32. 0.230 ⬤ 0.23   **37.** 0.230 ⬤ 0.023   **42.** 0.010 ⬤ 0.1

Our system of writing numbers is based on 10. Look at
the number 3333.

thousands	hundreds	tens	ones
3	3	3	3

The red 3 stands for 3 ones.

What does the orange 3 stand for?

What does the green 3 stand for?

What does the blue 3 stand for?

As we move to the left, each place is worth 10 times as much.
A 3 in the tens place is 10 times the value of a 3 in the ones place.
A 3 in the hundreds place is 10 times a 3 in the tens place.
And so on.

If you move to the right, it's just the opposite. Each place is worth
one-tenth as much.
A 3 in the tens place is one-tenth of a 3 in the
hundreds place.
A 3 in the ones place is one-tenth of a 3 in the tens place.

Thousands	Hundreds	Tens	Ones

• What happens if you keep going to the right?

The next place is one-tenth of 1. That's the tenths place.

Thousands	Hundreds	Tens	Ones	Tenths	?

• What happens if you keep going?

The next place is one-tenth of one-tenth. That's the hundredths place.

Thousands	Hundreds	Tens	Ones	Tenths	Hundredths

- How do you know what place you are in?

Use a dot between the ones place and the tenths place.
The dot is called a decimal point.

Suppose you want to write 4 tens, 3 ones, 5 tenths, and
4 hundredths.
You would write it like this: 43.54
When you read it, you would say "forty-three and
fifty-four hundredths" or "forty-three point five-four."

What does the blue digit stand for?

Example: 27.61   6 tenths

1. 0.05   3. 1.63   5. 20.37   7. 62.76   9. 74.35
2. 0.57   4. 2.59   6. 91.35   8. 53.47   10. 22.22

Write in standard form.

11. 5 ones, 2 tenths, 4 hundredths
12. 7 hundreds, 2 tens, 6 ones, 3 tenths
13. 3 tens, 3 ones, 3 tenths, 3 hundredths
14. 9 hundreds, 0 tens, 3 ones, 4 tenths, 5 hundredths
15. 4 tens, 9 ones, 0 tenths, 7 hundredths

Write in standard form.

16. 30 + 4 + 0.6 + 0.04   34.64   18. 60 + 0 + 0.7 + 0.03
17. 50 + 9 + 0.3 + 0.07   19. 10 + 3 + 0.9 + 0.06

ROLL A DECIMAL GAME

Players: 2
Materials: One 0–5 cube, one 5–10 cube
Object: To make the greater decimal

Rules
1. Roll the 0–5 cube. If you roll **0** , roll again.
2. Write a decimal point followed by as many blanks as the number rolled. If you rolled a **3** , you would write:

   .____ ____ ____

3. Roll the 5–10 cube as many times as there are blanks in your decimal. If you roll **10**, roll again.
4. Each time you roll the cube, write that number in one of your blanks.
5. The player with the greater decimal is the winner.

Sample Game

Sara rolled:	Sara wrote:	David rolled:	David wrote:

Sara rolled:	Sara wrote:	David rolled:	David wrote:
0 — rolled again		3	.____ ____ ____
2	.____ ____	6	.____ 6 ____
6	.____ 6	9	.9 6 ____
7	.7 6	10 — rolled again	
		10 — rolled again	
		6	.9 6 6

David was the winner.

Can you think of other ways to play this game?

336

Replace ● with <, >, or =.

1. 0.32 ● 3.2
2. 1.01 ● 1.001
3. 0.07 ● 0.3
4. 26.37 ● 2.84
5. 0.5 ● 1.0
6. 1.28 ● 1.280
7. 0.06 ● 0.2
8. 0.6 ● 0.02
9. 3.89 ● 3.809
10. 0.73 ● 0.073
11. 0.215 ● 0.215
12. 21.2 ● 18.0
13. 0.973 ● 0.839
14. 0.973 ● 8.39
15. 51.24 ● 204.1

16. 9.7 ● 6.8
17. 5.5555 ● 40.7
18. 1.4 ● 0.8
19. 0.0104 ● 0.104
20. 4.083 ● 4.07
21. 209.74 ● 142.857
22. 52.0 ● 56.0
23. 0.38 ● 0.38
24. 80.42 ● 30.42
25. 21.63 ● 21.630
26. 4.8 ● 32.7
27. 0.27 ● 0.05
28. 1.815 ● 1.158
29. 3.6 ● 2.1
30. 92.9 ● 92.009

Challenge problems

Use cents, nickels, dimes, quarters, and half dollars to
form each amount. Try to use as few coins as possible.

a. $0.57   (50) (5) (1) (1)

b. $0.80

c. $0.35

d. $0.74

e. $1.05

IRON AND GOLD Part 1

The queen of Addonia did not forget that Manolita, Mark, Ferdie, and Portia helped find her treasure on Mugg Island.

"I am very pleased," said the queen. "You helped me get the Royal Treasure back. I will give you a reward."

She called her steward and said to him, "Give these children a bag of money."

The steward sniffed. "A whole bag of money for these children? Well, all right."

"And see that it has some gold in it," said the queen.

Mark, Portia, Ferdie, and Manolita followed the steward. He set out 3 bags of money. One bag was red, 1 bag was blue, and 1 was green. "Pick the bag you want and be gone," he said.

"May we look inside?" Manolita asked.

"No," said the steward. "But you may reach in and pick up some coins to see what they are like. I will tell you this.

Every bag has some iron coins and some gold coins. And some bags have more gold coins than others."

"We'll take the bag with the most gold coins," said Ferdie. "Which one is that?"

"That's for you to figure out—if you can," said the steward, with a mean smile.

"I know," said Portia. "Let's vote! We'll each vote for the bag that we think has the most gold in it. We'll take the one that wins."

1. Why would the children want the bag that has the most gold coins in it? Why not the bag with the most iron coins?

2. Is voting a good way to decide which bag to take? Why or why not?

3. What would be a good way to choose which bag to take?

Dorothy is buying things for a birthday party. There will be 10 people at the party. She made a chart to show prices in cents and in dollars and cents.

Copy and complete the chart.

Item	Cents		Dollars and Cents	
	Price for 1	Price for 10	Price for 1	Price for 10
Balloon	7¢	70¢	$0.07	$0.70
Noisemaker	12¢	120¢	$0.12	$1.20
Kazoo	29¢	▦	▦	▦
Hat	18¢	▦	▦	▦
Skyrocket	92¢	▦	▦	▦

- Compare the 2 dollars-and-cents columns. What do you notice about the decimal point?

10 people are sharing the cost of the food for Dorothy's birthday party. They made a chart to show the prices in cents and in dollars. Copy and complete the chart.

Item	Cents		Dollars and Cents	
	Total Cost	Cost for Each Person	Total Cost	Cost for Each Person
Cupcakes	380¢	38¢	$3.80	$0.38
Ice cream	630¢	▦	▦	▦
Cookies	240¢	▦	▦	▦
Milk	180¢	▦	▦	▦

- Compare the 2 dollars-and-cents columns. What do you notice about the decimal point?

The value of a digit in its place in a number is 10 times as great as in the place to its right. So you can multiply by 10 by moving the decimal point 1 place to the right.

Examples: $10 \times 4.5 = ?$ 4.5. $10 \times 4.5 = 45$

$3.06 \times 10 = ?$ 3.0 6 $3.06 \times 10 = 30.6$

$8 \times 10 = ?$ 8.0. $8 \times 10 = 80$

Sometimes you need to write in a 0.

Multiply.

1. 10×7 3. 12×10 5. 10×60 7. 10×59

2. 10×7.2 4. 10×81.34 6. 86.29×10 8. 47.28×10

To multiply by 100, move the decimal point 2 places to the right.

Examples: $100 \times 17.15 = ?$ 17.1 5. $100 \times 17.15 = 1715$

$6.7 \times 100 = ?$ 6.7 0. $6.7 \times 100 = 670$

Multiply.

9. 100×7 11. 12×100 13. 60×100 15. 100×59

10. 100×7.2 12. 100×81.34 14. 100×86.29 16. 100×47.28

To multiply by 1000, move the decimal point 3 places to the right.

Examples: $1.9396 \times 1000 = ?$ 1.9 3 9.6 $1.9396 \times 1000 = 1939.6$

$1.07 \times 1000 = ?$ 1.0 7 0. $1.07 \times 1000 = 1070$

Multiply.

17. 1000×8 20. 1000×0.798 23. 1000×73

18. 1000×7.23 21. 50×1000 24. 1000×74.82

19. 42×1000 22. 1000×68.92 25. 479.26×100

The value of a digit in its place in a number is one-tenth the value it would have in the place to its left. So you can divide by 10 by moving the decimal point 1 place to the left.

Examples: $47 \div 10 = ?$ $4.7.$ $47 \div 10 = 4.7$

$0.7 \div 10 = ?$ $.0.7$ $0.7 \div 10 = 0.07$

$38.6 \div 10 = ?$ $3.8.6$ $38.6 \div 10 = 3.86$

Divide.

1. $38 \div 10$ 3. $0.8 \div 10$ 5. $0.9 \div 10$ 7. $5.9 \div 10$

2. $3.8 \div 10$ 4. $43.2 \div 10$ 6. $0.78 \div 10$ 8. $48.27 \div 10$

To divide by 100, move the decimal point 2 places to the left.

Examples: $545 \div 100 = ?$ $5.4.5$ $545 \div 100 = 5.45$

$65 \div 100 = ?$ $.6.5$ $65 \div 100 = 0.65$

$0.73 \div 100 = ?$ $.0.0.73$ $0.73 \div 100 = 0.0073$

Sometimes you need to write in a 0.

Divide.

9. $75 \div 100$ 11. $8390 \div 100$ 13. $7.5 \div 100$ 15. $0.98 \div 100$

10. $6.8 \div 100$ 12. $183 \div 100$ 14. $1116 \div 100$ 16. $0.756 \div 100$

To divide by 1000, move the decimal point 3 places to the left.

Examples: $45 \div 1000 = ?$ $.0.4.5$ $45 \div 1000 = 0.045$

$22 \div 1000 = ?$ $.0.2.2$ $22 \div 1000 = 0.022$

Divide.

17. $2500 \div 1000$ 20. $351 \div 1000$ 23. $14.76 \div 1000$

18. $8 \div 1000$ 21. $125.7 \div 1000$ 24. $147.6 \div 1000$

19. $51 \div 1000$ 22. $327 \div 1000$ 25. $1476 \div 1000$

Multiply.

1. 100×8.3
2. 10×90.0
3. 421.02×10
4. 10×59.3
5. 816.41×100

6. 401.1×10
7. 77×1000
8. 8.06×10
9. 100×91.011
10. 100×910.11

11. 10×88.34
12. 110.1×100
13. 384.71×100
14. 1000×62.073
15. 10×93.74

Divide.

16. $61.6 \div 10$
17. $70.04 \div 100$
18. $8.23 \div 10$
19. $0.43 \div 10$
20. $7.342 \div 1000$

21. $8971.1 \div 10$
22. $652.36 \div 100$
23. $0.06 \div 100$
24. $1.003 \div 10$
25. $900.1 \div 100$

26. $0.7 \div 100$
27. $962.1 \div 10$
28. $475 \div 100$
29. $0.67 \div 100$
30. $8.08 \div 1000$

Multiply or divide. Watch the signs.

31. 29.03×100
32. $0.507 \div 10$
33. 1000×0.301
34. 10×8.06
35. $482.1 \div 100$

36. 2.601×10
37. $0.04 \div 10$
38. $3.45 \div 100$
39. $8.066 \div 100$
40. 32×1000

41. $98.03 \div 10$
42. 437.2×100
43. 1000×0.062
44. 100×1.304
45. $3.421 \div 100$

Challenge problem

A stack of 1000 sheets of paper is 9.5 centimeters thick.
How many centimeters thick is each sheet?

9.5 cm

IRON AND GOLD
Part 2

"Before I vote on which bag to take," said Manolita, "I want to find out what kind of coins are in them."

She reached into the red bag and drew out a gold coin. Then she reached into the blue bag and drew out an iron coin. She also drew an iron coin from the green bag.

"That settles it," said Manolita. "I vote for the red bag."

"Before I vote," said Mark, "I want to take a big handful of coins from every bag."

Mark scooped a handful of coins from the red bag. He got 1 gold coin, and all the rest were iron. Next he took a handful of coins from the blue bag. They were all gold except for 1! Then he took a handful of coins from the green bag. He got 4 gold coins and 8 iron ones.

"I'm glad I did that," Mark said. "If we'd followed Manolita, we would have picked the wrong bag."

1. How is what Mark found out different from what Manolita found out?

2. If you were Manolita, would you have changed your vote after seeing Mark's results?

3. Can we be sure that Manolita voted for the wrong bag? Explain.

4. How could you be even more sure than Mark about which bag to pick?

When this ruler is unfolded, it is 1 meter long.

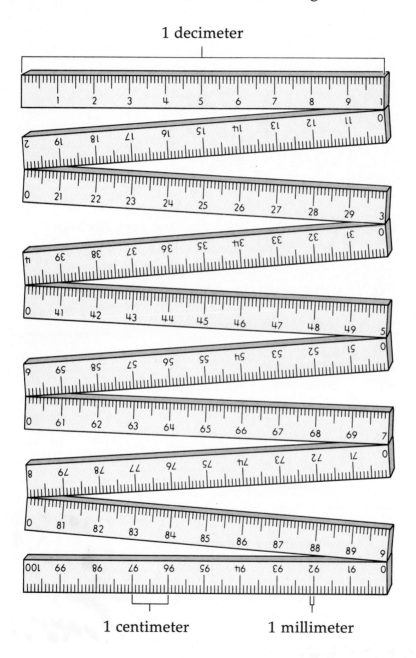

1 decimeter

1 centimeter   1 millimeter

1 meter = 10 decimeters = 100 centimeters = 1000 millimeters

About how long is a meter? Most doors are about 2 meters high. A meterstick is 1 meter long. Most classroom doors are a little less than 1 meter wide.

If a meter is divided into 10 equal parts, each part is 0.1 meter. That's also called 1 decimeter (dm).

1 dm = 0.1 m

2 of the parts (2 dm) would be 0.2 meter.   2 dm = 0.2 m

1. 3 dm = ▓ m   3. 8 dm = ▓ m   5. ▓ dm = 6 m
2. 5 dm = ▓ m   4. ▓ dm = 9 m   6. ▓ dm = 1.0 m

If a meter is divided into 100 equal parts, each part is 0.01 meter. That's also called 1 centimeter (cm).   1 cm = 0.01 m

2 of the parts (2 cm) would be 0.02 meter.   2 cm = 0.02 m

7. 7 cm = ▓ m   9. 8 cm = ▓ m   11. ▓ cm = 0.04 m
8. 27 cm = ▓ m   10. ▓ cm = 0.31 m   12. ▓ cm = 1.00 m

If a meter is divided into 1000 equal parts, each part is 0.001 meter. That's also called 1 millimeter (mm).

1 mm = 0.001 m

2 of the parts (2 mm) would be 0.002 meter.   2 mm = 0.002 m

13. 6 mm = ▓ m   16. 709 mm = ▓ m   19. ▓ mm = 0.300 m
14. 66 mm = ▓ m   17. ▓ mm = 0.004 m   20. ▓ mm = 0.305 m
15. 347 mm = ▓ m   18. ▓ mm = 0.76 m   21. ▓ mm = 1.000 m

Measure. Write each measurement in 2 ways.

Classroom   **Top of desk**

Length: ▓ cm = ▓ m   Length: ▓ mm = ▓ cm

Width: ▓ cm = ▓ m   Width: ▓ mm = ▓ cm

347

Donald measured a table and found it was 2 meters, 3 decimeters, 8 centimeters, and 5 millimeters long. There is a shorter way to report this measurement.

Change each unit to meters   **Then add**

2 m = 2 m	2.000 m
3 dm = 0.3 m	0.300 m
8 cm = 0.08 m	0.080 m
5 mm = 0.005 m	0.005 m
	2.385 m

2 m, 3 dm, 8 cm, 5 mm = 2.385 m

Write each measurement in meters only.

1. 6 m, 3 dm, 8 cm, 5 mm   5. 3 cm, 6 mm, 9 m
2. 4 m, 0 dm, 2 cm, 6 mm   6. 5 mm, 2 dm, 3 m
3. 4 m, 2 cm, 6 mm   7. 7 m, 4 cm, 1 dm, 0 mm
4. 8 mm, 9 cm, 0 dm, 2 m   8. 1 dm, 7 m, 4 cm

1000 meters is called a kilometer (km).   1000 m = 1 km
It takes about 12 minutes to walk 1 kilometer.
1 meter is 0.001 kilometer.   1 m = 0.001 km

The distance from the Bookville Library to the Fire House was measured. It was 2 kilometers, 415 meters. Write that in kilometers only.

2 km = 2 km	2.000 km
415 m = 0.415 km	0.415 km
	2.415 km

2 km, 415 m = 2.415 km

Write these measurements in kilometers only.

9. 1 km, 210 m   10. 4 km, 50 m   11. 4 km, 500 m   12. 2200 m

Tell the length or diameter of each object in millimeters,
then in centimeters.

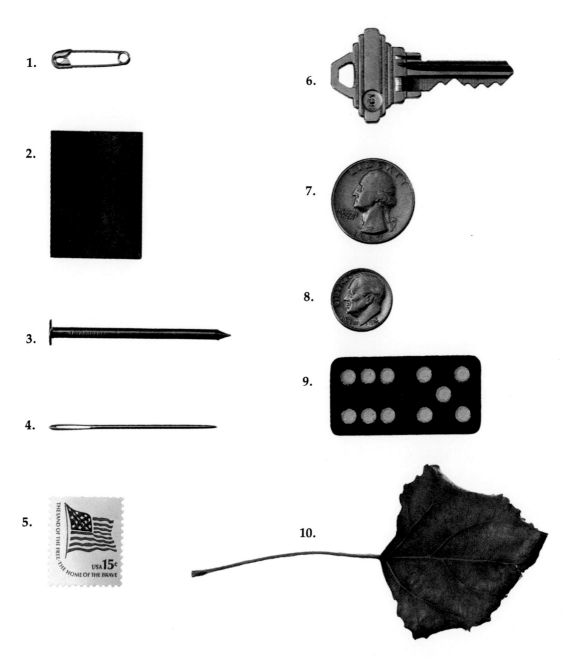

1.

2.

3.

4.

5.

6.

7.

8.

9.

10.

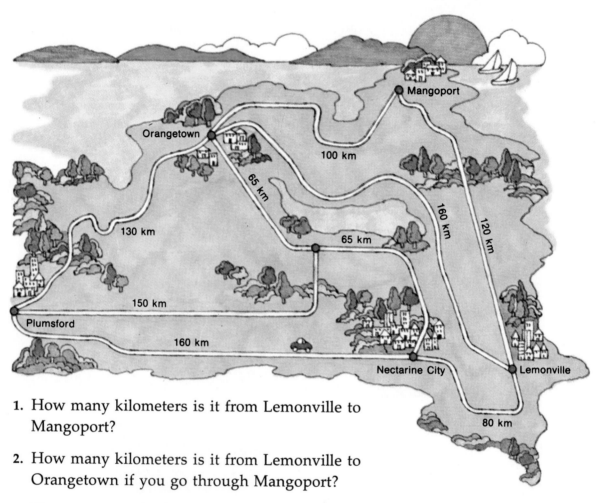

1. How many kilometers is it from Lemonville to Mangoport?

2. How many kilometers is it from Lemonville to Orangetown if you go through Mangoport?

3. If you were going from Plumsford to Lemonville, how much farther would it be to go through Orangetown?

4. Suppose you were going from Lemonville to Plumsford and wanted to visit Nectarine City and Orangetown on the way.
   a. Would it be shorter to visit Nectarine City first or Orangetown first?
   b. How much shorter?

5. Which town is closest to Lemonville?

How tall are you?

Work in groups. Measure the height of each person in your group.

Stand up straight.
Back to wall.
Put book on head.

Walk away.
Make a mark.

Measure in
centimeters.

Angela made a chart to show the height of each person in her class.

Height (cm)	Number of People
118	II
119	
120	II
121	III
122	⊬⊬⊬ I
123	⊬⊬⊬ II
124	IIII
125	
126	II
127	I

Then Angela made a bar graph so people could see the results more easily.

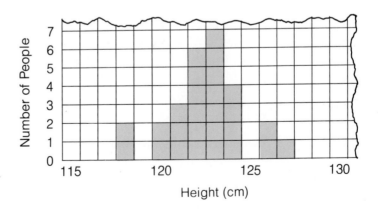

Make a chart and a bar graph to show the results for your class.

351

Ryan has $0.97. If he earns $3.75 for mowing Mr. Stern's lawn, how much money will he have?

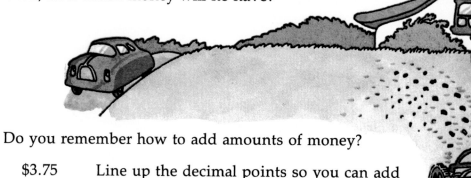

Do you remember how to add amounts of money?

$3.75   Line up the decimal points so you can add
+ 0.97 cents to cents, dimes to dimes, dollars to
$4.72   dollars, and so on.

Ryan needs $10 to buy a model rocket. How much more does he need?

Do you remember how to subtract amounts of money?

$10.00   Line up the decimal points so you subtract
− 4.72   cents from cents, dimes from dimes, dollars
$ 5.28   from dollars, and so on.

When you add or subtract decimals, line up the decimal points.

Example: 14.8 + 2.35 = ?

14.8   Line up the decimal points.
+ 2.35

14.8   If it helps, put in a 0 (since 14.8 and 14.80
+ 2.35   have the same value).

14.80   Add.
+ 2.35

Example: $8.6 - 3.25$

$$\begin{array}{r} 8.6 \\ -\ 3.25 \\ \hline \end{array}$$ Line up the decimal points.

$$\begin{array}{r} 8.60 \\ -\ 3.25 \\ \hline \end{array}$$ If it helps, put in a 0 (since 8.6 and 8.60 have the same value).

$$\begin{array}{r} 8.60 \\ -\ 3.25 \\ \hline 5.35 \end{array}$$ Subtract.

Add or subtract. Watch the signs.

1.	$\begin{array}{r} 6.72 \\ +\ 11.09 \\ \hline \end{array}$	**3.**	$\begin{array}{r} 9.5 \\ +\ 8.63 \\ \hline \end{array}$	**5.**	$\begin{array}{r} 5.2 \\ -\ 3.15 \\ \hline \end{array}$	**7.**	$\begin{array}{r} 8.2 \\ +\ 3.01 \\ \hline \end{array}$
2.	$\begin{array}{r} 8.03 \\ -\ 7.04 \\ \hline \end{array}$	**4.**	$\begin{array}{r} 3.07 \\ +\ 0.96 \\ \hline \end{array}$	**6.**	$\begin{array}{r} 4.07 \\ -\ 3.10 \\ \hline \end{array}$	**8.**	$\begin{array}{r} 5.33 \\ -\ 4.03 \\ \hline \end{array}$

Solve for n.

9. $2.36 + 6.5 = n$ **13.** $6.07 + 3.03 = n$ **17.** $10.9 - 9.01 = n$

10. $5.4 - 3.3 = n$ **14.** $2.34 - 2.09 = n$ **18.** $4.64 + 6 = n$

11. $8.26 - 8.19 = n$ **15.** $13.3 + 4.11 = n$ **19.** $25.01 + 0.6 = n$

12. $4.5 + 5.41 = n$ **16.** $18.1 - 10 = n$ **20.** $6.33 - 6 = n$

1. In the 1900 Olympics, Irving Baxter jumped 1.90 meters in the running high jump. In 1968, Dick Fosbury jumped 2.24 meters in the running high jump.
   a. Which man jumped higher?
   b. How much higher?

2. In the 1960 Olympics, Wilma Rudolph ran 100 meters in 11.0 seconds. In the same Olympics, 4 American women ran the 400-meter relay in 44.5 seconds. Was the average time for each runner in the relay faster or slower than Wilma Rudolph's time?

3. In the 1896 Olympic games, Thomas Burke ran 100 meters in 12 seconds. In the 1900 Olympic games, F. W. Jarvis ran 100 meters in 10.8 seconds.
   a. What was the difference in their times?
   b. Who ran faster?

4. In the 1968 Olympics, James Hines ran 100 meters in 9.9 seconds. By how much time did he beat 10 seconds?

5. In the 1972 Olympics, Valeri Borzov ran 100 meters in 10.14 seconds. If he ran that fast for 200 meters, how long would it have taken him to run 200 meters?

6. In the 1972 Olympics, Borzov ran 200 meters in 20.00 seconds. Was his average speed for the 200-meter run faster or slower than for the 100-meter run? Why do you think there was this difference?

7. The 10,000-meter run is an Olympic event. How many kilometers is 10,000 meters?

8. In the 1960 Olympics, Debbie Meyer swam 400 meters in 4 minutes and 31.8 seconds. In the 1924 Olympics, Johnny Weismuller swam 400 meters in 5 minutes and 4.8 seconds. By how much did Debbie Meyer beat Johnny Weismuller's time?

9. In the 1968 Olympics, Abebe Bikila ran the marathon barefoot in 2 hours, 12 minutes, and 11.2 seconds. In the 1908 Olympics, John Hayes ran the marathon in 2 hours, 55 minutes, and 18.4 seconds. In how much less time did Abebe Bikila run the marathon?

10. In the 1960 Olympics, Wilma Rudolph ran 100 meters in 11.0 seconds. Was her average speed for the race more than 10 meters per second?

11. In the 1932 Olympics, Iso-Hollo ran an extra lap by mistake in the 3000-meter steeplechase. His time for the race was 10 minutes and 33.4 seconds. In the 1936 Olympics, he ran the same race in 9 minutes and 3.8 seconds. About how long do you think it took Iso-Hollo to run the extra lap?

1. A year ago Jake bought a used car that had traveled 18,927.8 kilometers. Now the car has traveled 25,485.2 kilometers. How many kilometers has the car traveled in the past year?

2. Jan wants to ride her bike at least 50 kilometers every week. At the beginning of the week the odometer on her bike showed 143.6 kilometers. Now it shows 184.8 kilometers. How many more kilometers does she have to ride this week to meet her goal?

3. Murty had $5.81. Last week he spent $1.50 and earned $1.50 raking leaves. How much money does he have now?

4. A movie ticket costs $4.25.
   a. How much will 2 tickets cost?
   b. How much will 4 tickets cost?

5. Will the antenna touch the ceiling of the entrance?

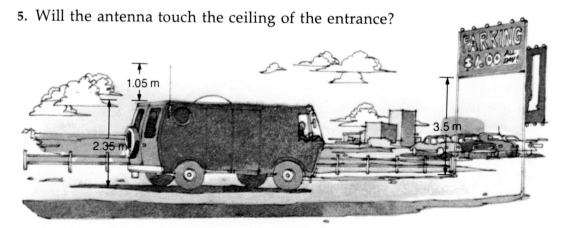

HARDER ROLL A DECIMAL GAME

Players: 2
Materials: One 0–5 cube, one 5–10 cube
Object: To get the greater total score

Rules
1. Follow rules 1 through 4 for the Roll a Decimal Game on page 336.
2. Subtract the smaller decimal from the greater decimal and award the difference to the player with the greater decimal.
3. After an agreed-upon number of rounds, add up your score.
4. The player with the greater total is the winner.

Sample Game

Round	Sara	David	Sara's Score	David's Score
1	.76	.966		.206
2	.957	.676	.281	
3	.97775	.9665	.01125	
4	.8	.9576		.1576
5	.99	.866	.124	
6	.86855	.8875		.01895
7	.7	.5	.2	
8	.775	.97755		.20255
Total			.61625	.58510

After 8 rounds, Sara was the winner.

Can you think of other ways to play this game?

Whenever Miss Taylor pays someone with a check, she keeps a record of it in her checkbook. That way she can keep track of how much money she has in her checking account.

Miss Taylor keeps the record of each check on a check stub. Look at this check stub to see what information is on it.

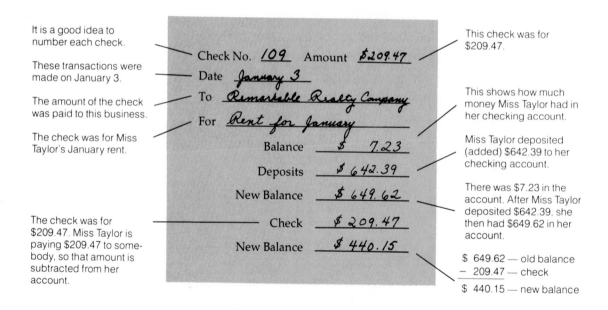

It is a good idea to number each check.

These transactions were made on January 3.

The amount of the check was paid to this business.

The check was for Miss Taylor's January rent.

The check was for $209.47. Miss Taylor is paying $209.47 to somebody, so that amount is subtracted from her account.

Check No. *109*   Amount *$209.47*
Date *January 3*
To *Remarkable Realty Company*
For *Rent for January*
　　　　　Balance　 *$　7.23*
　　　　　Deposits　 *$ 642.39*
　　　New Balance　 *$ 649.62*
　　　　　　Check　 *$ 209.47*
　　　New Balance　 *$ 440.15*

This check was for $209.47.

This shows how much money Miss Taylor had in her checking account.

Miss Taylor deposited (added) $642.39 to her checking account.

There was $7.23 in the account. After Miss Taylor deposited $642.39, she then had $649.62 in her account.

$ 649.62 — old balance
− 209.47 — check
$ 440.15 — new balance

Every month Miss Taylor gets a statement from her bank. The statement shows the bank's records of her account. The statement for January said that Miss Taylor had $7.23 in her account on January 3 and $54.85 at the end of the month. This did not agree with her records.

Look at Miss Taylor's checkbook on the next page. Did she make an error on these check stubs? If she did, correct the error so that her records show the same balance at the end of the month as the bank statement shows.

Miss Taylor's Checkbook

Check No. _109_ Amount _$209.47_
Date _January 3_
To _Remarkable Realty Company_
For _Rent for January_

Balance	$ 7.23
Deposits	$642.39
New Balance	$649.62
Check	$209.47
New Balance	$440.15

Check No. _112_ Amount _$34.26_
Date _January 14_
To _Better Butter Boutique_
For _Pants_

Balance	$306.96
Deposits	
New Balance	
Check	$ 34.26
New Balance	$273.70

Check No. _110_ Amount _$50.00_
Date _January 8_
To _Cash_
For _____

Balance	$440.15
Deposits	
New Balance	
Check	$ 50.00
New Balance	$390.15

Check No. _113_ Amount _$110.85_
Date _January 16_
To _Callous Clothing_
For _Jacket_

Balance	$273.70
Deposits	
New Balance	
Check	$110.85
New Balance	$162.85

Check No. _111_ Amount _$83.19_
Date _January 12_
To _Pooper Power Company_
For _Electricity_

Balance	$390.15
Deposits	
New Balance	
Check	$ 83.19
New Balance	$306.96

Check No. _114_ Amount _$107.00_
Date _January 28_
To _Terrific Travel Agency_
For _Bus tickets_

Balance	$162.85
Deposits	
New Balance	
Check	$107.00
New Balance	$ 55.85

IRON AND GOLD

"Have you decided now which bag to take?" the steward asked, with his evil grin.

"Yes," said Mark, "we'll take the blue bag. It has the most gold coins in it."

"Wait a minute," said Ferdie. Then he whispered to the other children. "I think the man is trying to trick us. He doesn't want us to get much gold. Let me try something different."

Ferdie took a handful of coins from each bag, but he didn't do it the way Mark did. Instead of scooping the coins from the top of the bag, he reached all the way to the bottom of each bag and took the coins from there.

From the bottom of the red bag Ferdie got 5 gold coins and 3 iron ones. From the bottom of the blue bag he got only iron coins.

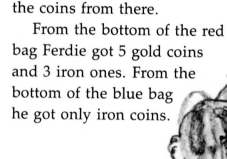

And from the bottom of the green bag he got
4 gold coins and 4 iron ones.

"I was right," said Manolita. "The red
bag is best."

"I think something funny is going on
here," said Mark.

"I told you," Ferdie said. "The
steward was trying to trick us."

1. Why does Manolita think she was right?

2. What reason does Ferdie have to say the steward was
   trying to trick them?

3. How could Ferdie and Mark get such different results?

Jenny is selling tickets to her school play for $1.35 each. Mrs. Baker wants to buy 7 tickets. How much should Jenny charge her?

To find out, you would multiply $1.35 by 7.
Mrs. Baker told Jenny that 7 × $1.35 was $9.45.
Can that be right? Why or why not?

You could do the problem in cents. Multiply 135¢ by 7.

$$
\begin{array}{r}
135 \\
\times\ 7 \\
\hline
945
\end{array}
\qquad 945¢ = \$9.45
$$

So Jenny should charge 945¢, or $9.45.
Mrs. Baker was right. 7 × $1.35 is $9.45.

Let's look at the 2 multiplications side by side.

$$
\begin{array}{rr}
135 & 1.35 \\
\times\ 7 & \times\ 7 \\
\hline
945 & 9.45
\end{array}
$$

The problems and the answers are the same, except for the decimal point.

• Can you figure out a simple rule for deciding where to put the decimal point in the answer?

362

To multiply a decimal by a whole number:
A. Multiply as you would with 2 whole numbers.
B. Put the decimal point in the answer as many places from the right as it is in the decimal factor.

Example A: 2.3×514

```
    514        Multiply as you would with 2 whole
  × 2.3        numbers.
  1 5 4 2
1 0 2 8
1 1 8 2 2
```

```
    514        Then place the point in the answer.
  × 2.3  ──── The point is 1 place from the right.
  1 5 4 2
1 0 2 8
1 1 8 2.2 ──── So put the point 1 place from the
              right in the answer.
```

Example B: 73×0.375

```
  .3 7 5       Multiply as you would with 2 whole
  × 7 3        numbers.
  1 1 2 5
2 6 2 5
2 7 3 7 5
```

Then place the point in the answer.

```
  .3 7 5  ──── The point is 3 places from the right.
  × 7 3
  1 1 2 5
2 6 2 5
2 7.3 7 5 ──── So put the point 3 places from the
              right in the answer.
```

Remember

```
  4.0 7 —— The point is 2 places
  ×  1 2      from the right.
  8 1 4
  4 0 7
  4 8.8 4 —— Place the point 2
              places from the right.
```

```
  3 5 7    ╱ The point is 3 places
  ×.0 0 6 ╱   from the right.
  2.1 4 2 —— Place the point 3
              places from the right.
```

Multiply.

1. 3.07×11
2. 82×0.03
3. 127×0.007
4. 385×1.2
5. 39×2.25
6. 1008×0.009
7. 673×5.6

8. 7198×0.09
9. 6.8×13
10. 5.23×0.1
11. 1.05×0.06
12. 256×1.2
13. 8.2×7.9
14. 617×2.5

15. 71.3×85.2
16. 2.306×1528
17. 0.83×22
18. 97.8×79
19. 451×82.3
20. 19.84×17.76

21. Bart is the manager of a baseball team. His team needs 13 new bats. Each bat costs $7.29. Bart has $75. Does he have enough money?

22. Myrna wants to buy 2 boards. One is 3 meters long and the other is 4 meters long. A board costs $4.05 per meter. How much will the 2 boards cost?

23. Mr. Washington is building a house. He needs 27 electrical outlets. Each outlet costs $2.71. Will that cost more than $100?

24. The Speedee Publishing Company ships an average of 751 books a week. It costs 13¢ to mail each book. How much does mailing cost, on the average, for the week?

1. If a snail can crawl 0.6 meter a day, how far can it crawl in a week? In a month (31 days)? In a year (365 days)?

2. Otis wants to tile his kitchen floor. Each tile covers 0.34 square meter. Otis ordered 60 tiles. Each tile cost $0.89. How much did he pay for the tiles?

3. Mrs. Khan bought 15 cases of soft drinks for a party. Each case cost $4.89. How much did she pay?

4. Albert wants to call his mother long distance. He does not want to spend more than $4 for the call. Each minute costs 31¢. Can he talk for 15 minutes?

In each problem, 2 of the answers are clearly wrong and 1 is correct. Choose the correct answer.

5. 8 × 1.7	a. 19.6	b. 13.6	c. 7.6
6. 6 × 2.4	a. 10.4	b. 22.4	c. 14.4
7. 4.9 × 5	a. 28.67	b. 259.7	c. 24.5
8. 0.5 × 9	a. 34.5	b. 4.5	c. 45
9. 8.73 × 9	a. 71.07	b. 78.57	c. 83.67
10. 20 × 5.1	a. 102	b. 94.2	c. 98.2
11. 16 × 3.28	a. 52.48	b. 42.48	c. 72.48
12. 33.51 × 2	a. 67.02	b. 47.14	c. 105.2
13. 70 × 67.3	a. 4971.0	b. 47,111	c. 4711.0
14. 59 × 53.12	a. 1712.58	b. 3134.08	c. 3629.08
15. 79 × 61.07	a. 2824.53	b. 7842.13	c. 4824.53

IRON AND GOLD   Part 4

"The blue bag has the most gold on the top, and the red bag has the most gold on the bottom," said Mark. "Portia, why don't you take coins from the middle of each bag? That way we can find out which has the most gold there."

"I have a different idea," said Portia. She reached into each bag and stirred and stirred until the coins were all mixed up. Then she took a big handful from each bag. From the red bag she got 3 gold coins and 13 iron ones. From the blue bag she got 4 gold coins and 11 iron ones. From the green bag she got 9 gold coins and 7 iron ones.

"Oh, no!" said Manolita. "First the red bag wins. Then the blue bag wins. Then the red bag wins again, and now the green bag wins! How can we ever tell which bag to take?"

"I guess we'd better take the red bag," said Ferdie. "It won twice."

"I say the blue bag," said Mark. "I got almost all gold coins when I took a handful from it."

"I vote for the green bag," said Portia.

"Me too," said Manolita.

"Oh, well," said the steward. "Democracy wins again!"

1. Which bag do you think is the best choice? Why?

2. About what fraction of the coins in the green bag do you think are gold?

3. What would be a reason for mixing up the coins in each bag, the way Portia did?

4. What do you think the steward did to trick the children 2 ways?

The gram and the kilogram are units of weight.
About how much is 1 gram?
Two paper clips weigh about 1 gram (1 g).
A marble weighs about 5 grams (5 g).
A man's shoe weighs about 500 grams (500 g).

1 kilogram is 1000 grams.   1 kg = 1000 g

1 gram is one-thousandth of a kilogram.   1 g = 0.001 kg

1. 2 g = ▓ kg	5. 805 g = ▓ kg	9. 0.05 kg = ▓ g
2. 40 g = ▓ kg	6. 900 g = ▓ kg	10. 0.005 kg = ▓ g
3. 88 g = ▓ kg	7. 0.3 kg = ▓ g	11. 25 kg = ▓ g
4. 620 g = ▓ kg	8. 8 kg = ▓ g	12. 2.5 kg = ▓ g

• How are kilograms and grams like kilometers and meters?

The liter and milliliter are units of volume.
About how much is 1 liter?
This container can hold about 1 liter (1 L) of milk.

There are 1000 milliliters in 1 liter.   1000 mL = 1 L

1 milliliter is one-thousandth of a liter.   1 mL = 0.001 L

13. 3 mL = ▓ L	17. 500 mL = ▓ L	21. 0.025 L = ▓ mL
14. 63 mL = ▓ L	18. 758 mL = ▓ L	22. 0.725 L = ▓ mL
15. 40 mL = ▓ L	19. 0.002 L = ▓ mL	23. 2.5 L = ▓ mL
16. 409 mL = ▓ L	20. 0.02 L = ▓ mL	24. 5 L = ▓ mL

• How are liters and milliliters like meters and millimeters?

Work in groups with a set of containers and a balance. Measure the weights of various volumes of water, in grams.

Luisa made a chart to show the weight of each volume of water. Make a chart to show your results or copy and complete Luisa's chart.

Volume of Water in Container (millimeters)	Weight of Empty Container (grams)	Weight of Container with Water (grams)	Weight of Water (grams)
0	8	8	0
10	8	18	▪
20	8	27	▪
40	8	47	▪
50	8	57	▪
0	10	10	▪
60	10	71	▪
80	10	91	▪
100	10	110	▪
0	21	21	▪
120	21	141	▪
140	21	163	▪
160	21	185	▪

Luisa made a line graph to show her results. Make a graph of your results. If you haven't done the experiment, make a graph of Luisa's results.

The cubic centimeter is a unit of volume.
This cube has a volume of 1 cubic centimeter.
1 cubic centimeter is the same volume as 1 milliliter.

Find the volume of each box in cubic centimeters by
figuring out how many cubes there are.

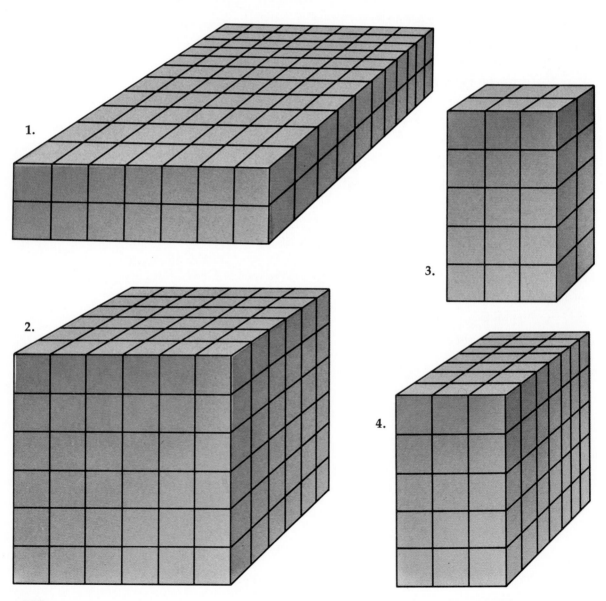

1.

2.

3.

4.

1. A 1-liter container is half filled with water. How many milliliters of water are in the container?

2. Which is a better buy, a 1.5-liter can of pineapple juice for $0.80 or two 700-milliliter cans of the same juice for $0.40 each?

3. A liter of water weighs 1.00 kg. How much do each of these weigh?
   a. one-half liter of water
   b. 0.5 liter of water
   c. 100 milliliters of water
   d. 0.1 liter of water

4. An empty jar weighs 100 grams. When filled with water, the jar weighs 500 grams.
   a. How much does the water in the jar weigh?
   b. How many milliliters of water does the jar contain? (Remember, 1 liter of water weighs 1 kilogram.)

5. Lila is making pancakes. She has a recipe for 20 pancakes but wants to make 40. The recipe calls for 400 milliliters of milk. How much milk should she use to make 40 pancakes?

6. Seth weighed 100 marbles. Altogether they weighed 490 grams. On the average, how much does each marble weigh?

7. Lina wants to go fishing. She has $4. Casting flies cost 73¢ each. Does she have enough money to buy 4 casting flies?

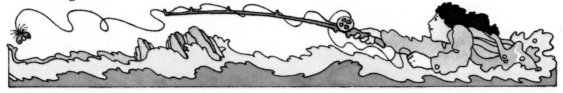

$\frac{2}{3}$ of 24 = ? ————————

Divide 24 into 3 equal parts. $3\overline{)24}$ ———

Then take 2 parts. $2 \times 8 = 16$ ———

So $\frac{2}{3}$ of 24 is 16.

Remember: The bottom part (denominator) of a fraction tells how many equal parts to divide something into. The top part (numerator) of a fraction tells how many of those parts to take.

2 — numerator
3 — denominator

1. Pearl has gone about $\frac{1}{4}$ of the way to Toptown, a distance of 120 kilometers. About how many kilometers is that?

2. Mr. Barclay is reading a magazine that is 75 pages long. He has read 55 pages. Has he read more than $\frac{2}{3}$ of the magazine?

3. A radio that usually sells for $24 is on sale for $\frac{1}{3}$ off.
   a. How much is $\frac{1}{3}$ of 24?
   b. What is the sale price of the radio?

4. A jar that can hold 300 milliliters of water is about $\frac{2}{3}$ full. About how many milliliters of water are in the jar?

Solve.

5. $\frac{1}{2}$ of 12   8. $\frac{1}{4}$ of 20   11. $\frac{1}{5}$ of 100   14. $\frac{3}{10}$ of 100   17. $\frac{2}{3}$ of 24

6. $\frac{1}{3}$ of 9   9. $\frac{1}{2}$ of 20   12. $\frac{3}{5}$ of 100   15. $\frac{3}{10}$ of 50   18. $\frac{1}{8}$ of 24

7. $\frac{2}{3}$ of 9   10. $\frac{3}{4}$ of 20   13. $\frac{1}{6}$ of 36   16. $\frac{2}{3}$ of 30   19. $\frac{3}{8}$ of 24

FRACTIONS OF 60 GAME

Players: 2 or more
Materials: Two 0–5 cubes
Object: To score a total of 150 or more

Rules
1. Roll both cubes. Combine the numbers rolled to make a fraction no greater than 1.
2. Find that fraction of 60 and write the answer.
3. Add the answer to your last score.
4. If you roll one 0, your score for that turn is 0.
5. If you roll two 0s together, roll both cubes again.
6. The first player whose score totals 150 or more is the winner.

If you rolled:	You would take:	Your answer would be:
2 3	$\frac{2}{3}$ of 60	40
0 4	$\frac{0}{4}$ of 60	0
2 2	$\frac{2}{2}$ of 60	60

Other Ways to Play This Game

1. Try to score a different total.
2. Change the game to Fractions of 120 or Fractions of 30.
3. Use one 0–5 cube and one 5–10 cube.

Can you think of other ways to play this game?

Jimmy and Naomi are rolling a 0–5 cube. Jimmy wins if a 0 is rolled. Naomi wins if a 1, 2, 3, 4, or 5 is rolled.

- Who do you think will win more often?
- What fraction of the time do you think Jimmy will win?
- If they roll the cube 6 times, how many times would you expect Jimmy to win? What is $\frac{1}{6}$ of 6?
- Would you be surprised if Jimmy did not win exactly 1 time out of 6 tries?

A **probability** is a number that tells what fraction of the time something is expected to happen.

Jimmy's probability of winning is $\frac{1}{6}$.

- What is Naomi's probability of winning?

If something cannot happen, the probability is 0.
If something is certain to happen, the probability is 1.

Here's an experiment Jimmy did with his class. Each student rolled a 0–5 cube 6 times. Each person kept track of how many times he or she rolled 0 in the 6 tries. Then Jimmy made a chart to show how many people didn't roll a 0 at all, how many rolled one 0, and so on.

Number of Times 0 Was Rolled in 6 Tries	Number of People
0	10
1	12
2	6
3	2
4	0
5	0
6	0

- How many people took part in Jimmy's experiment?
- How many people in the class rolled a 0
  - a. 0 out of 6 times?
  - b. 1 out of 6 times?
  - c. 2 out of 6 times?
  - d. 3 out of 6 times?
  - e. 4 out of 6 times?
  - f. 5 out of 6 times?
  - g. 6 out of 6 times?

Try an experiment like Jimmy's in your class. But use a 5–10 cube instead. Each person should roll the cube 6 times and write down how many times he or she rolled an 8. Then put the results on a chart like Jimmy's.

1. Does your chart look exactly like Jimmy's?
2. In what ways is your chart similar to Jimmy's?
3. How many people in Jimmy's class rolled a 0 either 4, 5, or 6 times?
4. How many people in your class rolled an 8 either 4, 5, or 6 times?
5. More than $\frac{2}{3}$ of the people in Jimmy's class rolled a 0 either 0 times or 1 time. Did most of the people in your class roll an 8 either 0 times or 1 time?

1. The city council can vote only if at least $\frac{5}{6}$ of its members are present. The city council has 18 members. How many members must be present for a vote to take place?

2. About $\frac{1}{7}$ of the total population is left-handed. There are 21 students in Mary Ellen's class.
   a. About how many students in her class might be left-handed?
   b. Would you be surprised if you were not exactly right?

3. $\frac{2}{3}$ of Winston's cousins are boys. He has 9 cousins. How many of his cousins are girls?

4. Laverne can save $\frac{1}{4}$ of the cost of a model airplane if she waits until after Christmas to buy it on sale. How much will an $8 airplane cost on sale?

5. Chip's doctor said that $\frac{3}{5}$ of all schoolchildren get 2 colds every winter.
   a. How many children in a class of 30 might Chip expect to have 2 colds this winter?
   b. Could Chip be sure of exactly how many classmates would have 2 colds?

6. What is $\frac{2}{3}$ of 30?   9. What is $\frac{1}{6}$ of 30?   12. What is $\frac{5}{6}$ of 30?

7. What is $\frac{3}{3}$ of 30?   10. What is $\frac{3}{6}$ of 30?   13. What is $\frac{6}{6}$ of 30?

8. What is $\frac{0}{3}$ of 30?   11. What is $\frac{4}{6}$ of 30?

- Compare your answers to problems 6 and 11. Why are they the same?

- Are some other answers the same? Why?

ANYTHING BUT 10 GAME

Players: 2 or more
Materials: One 0–5 cube, one 5–10 cube
Object: To score a total of 100 or more

Rules

1. Roll both cubes. Find the sum of the 2 numbers rolled.
2. If the sum is not 10, you get the number of points you rolled. You may keep your turn and roll again, or you may stop and add those points to your score.
3. On each turn you may have as many rolls as you like until you either roll a sum of 10 or choose to stop.
4. When you roll a sum of 10, you lose your turn and you lose any other points you may have had on that turn.
5. The first player to score 100 or over is the winner.

Sample Game

Round	Janice Rolls:	Sum	Score	Pete Rolls:	Sum	Score
1	7 5	12		9 4	13	
	5 4	9		6 2	8	21
	10 5	15	36	Stops		
	Stops					
2	8 3	11		10 4	14	
	7 0	7		8 3	11	
	6 4	10	36	7 1	8	54
	Loses turn			Stops		

After 2 rounds, Pete is ahead.

Andre and Marilyn are rolling a 0–5 cube. When it shows
0 or 1, Andre wins. When it shows 2, 3, 4, or 5, Marilyn wins.

1. What is the probability that Andre will win?
2. What is the probability that Marilyn will win?
3. Suppose Andre and Marilyn play their game 120 times.
   a. About how many times would you expect Andre to win?
   b. About how many times would you expect Marilyn to win?
   c. Would you be surprised if Andre did not win
      exactly 40 times?

They change their game so that Marilyn wins if the cube
shows 5, 4, or 3. Andre wins if it shows 2, 1, or 0.

4. What is the probability that Marilyn will win?
5. What is the probability that Andre will win?
6. Suppose they play the new game 120 times.
   a. About how many times would you expect Marilyn to win?
   b. About how many times would you expect Andre to win?
   c. Would you be surprised if Marilyn did not win
      exactly 60 times?

Hans and Merika flip a coin. Hans will win if it lands
heads. Merika will win if it lands tails.

7. What is the probability that Hans will win?
8. If they play 120 times, about how many games would
   you expect Hans to win?
9. Compare your answers for problems 6 and 8.
   (Compare $\frac{3}{6}$ of 120 and $\frac{1}{2}$ of 120.)
10. Which probability is greater, $\frac{3}{6}$ or $\frac{1}{2}$?
11. What is the probability of landing on red if you
    a. spin spinner A?   b. spin spinner B?
12. Which spinner gives you a better chance of landing on red?

A

B

What fraction of the circle is shaded?

1.
2.
3.
4.

5. Which is greater, $\frac{1}{4}$ of the circle or $\frac{1}{2}$ of the circle?
6. Which is greater, $\frac{3}{4}$ of the circle or $\frac{1}{2}$ of the circle?

What fraction of the rectangle is shaded?

7.
8.
9.

Draw 5 rectangles that are each 4 centimeters long and 3 centimeters wide.

10. What is the area of each rectangle you drew?

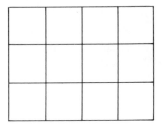

Shade $\frac{1}{2}$ of each rectangle in a different way.

11. What is the area of the shaded part of each rectangle?

Draw 3 more rectangles that are each 4 centimeters long and 3 centimeters wide. Shade $\frac{2}{4}$ of each rectangle in a different way.

12. What is the area of the shaded part of each rectangle?
13. Why do you think the answers to questions 11 and 12 are the same?

Show which fraction of the circle is larger or whether they are the same. Replace ● with >, <, or =.

1. $\frac{2}{4}$ ● $\frac{3}{4}$ 6. $\frac{5}{12}$ ● $\frac{1}{2}$

2. $\frac{2}{4}$ ● $\frac{1}{2}$ 7. $\frac{1}{2}$ ● $\frac{6}{12}$

3. $\frac{3}{4}$ ● $\frac{1}{2}$ 8. $\frac{6}{12}$ ● $\frac{2}{4}$

4. $\frac{1}{3}$ ● $\frac{5}{6}$ 9. $\frac{1}{6}$ ● $\frac{1}{4}$

5. $\frac{7}{12}$ ● $\frac{1}{4}$ 10. $\frac{5}{6}$ ● $\frac{2}{4}$

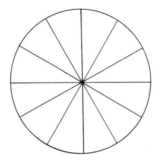

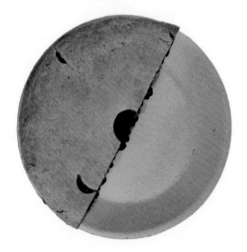

11. Which is bigger, $\frac{1}{2}$ of the big pie or $\frac{1}{2}$ of the small pie?

12. Nell and Jeremy want to share a pizza sliced into 12 pieces. If Nell eats 5 pieces, will she have eaten more or less than $\frac{1}{2}$ of the pizza?

13. Ricky read about $\frac{2}{3}$ of a 250-page book, and Ramona read $\frac{2}{3}$ of a 150-page book.
    a. Who read more pages?
    b. Who read more words?

1. Sherman can save $2 each week. How much can he save in 1 year (52 weeks)?

2. Conchita can save $4 each week. How much can she save in 1 year?

3. Lance has $10.00. He wants to buy a sweater for $8.57 and a scarf for $2.00. Does he have enough money?

4. Noelle has 35 meters of fencing. If she builds a garden with an area of 36 square meters, is it possible that she has enough fencing to enclose it?

5. Spencer has a stack of baseball cards. Eve has a stack 4 times as high as Spencer's. How many baseball cards does Spencer have?

6. Brent's garden is shaped like a rectangle. It is 10 meters long and 8 meters wide. Denise's garden is shaped like a square. Each side measures 9 meters.
   a. Whose garden has the larger area?
   b. How much larger?

7. Floyd earns $4.75 per hour. He works 40 hours each week. How much money does he earn in 1 year (52 weeks)?

8. A show takes 2 hours and 35 minutes. If the show starts at 8:15 P.M., what time will it end?

9. Half the children in Jordan's class are girls. How many children are in his class?

10. Virginia has $239.40 in her checking account. She deposited $148.00 and then wrote a check for $239.40. How much money is left in her account?

Mr. Cheng baked four loaves of bread. His children ate half of one loaf. Mr. Cheng had three and one-half loaves left.

Before   **After**

We can write three and one-half as $3\frac{1}{2}$.

Shana is slicing cucumbers for a salad. She started with six cucumbers. She had sliced four whole cucumbers and one-third of another when the doorbell rang. She had one and two-thirds cucumbers left to slice when she returned to the kitchen.

Before   **After**

We can write one and two-thirds as $1\frac{2}{3}$.

Miss Batra bought five packages of popcorn for her movie theater. Last night she used three whole packages and three-fourths of another. Miss Batra had one and one-fourth packages left.

Before   **After**

How would you write the number of packages she has left?

Write a mixed number to show how many.

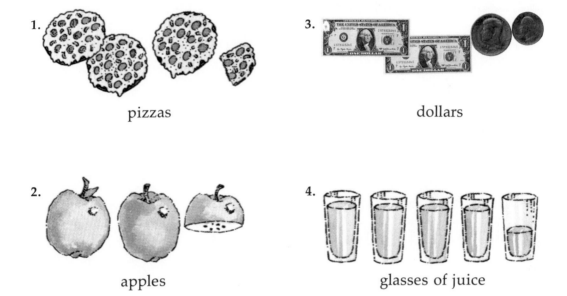

1.

pizzas

3.

dollars

2.

apples

4.

glasses of juice

In each case, write **yes** if the last sentence is true.
Write **no** if it isn't.

5. Walter has guitar lessons at 5:30 P.M. At 3:00 P.M. he
said, "My guitar lesson starts in $2\frac{1}{2}$ hours."

6. A can of frozen orange juice makes enough juice for 6
glasses. Deborah made a pitcher of orange juice. She
drank $3\frac{1}{2}$ glasses for breakfast. There are $3\frac{1}{2}$ glasses of
orange juice left.

7. DeDe works $3\frac{3}{4}$ hours every day at a hardware store.
Today she worked 2 hours before dinner and $1\frac{3}{4}$ hours
after dinner.

8. Sonia told Jay to meet her in $1\frac{1}{2}$ hours. 90 minutes later
Jay showed up on time.

This pencil is between 3 and 4 inches long.
It is almost halfway between 3 and 4 inches. It is about
$3\frac{1}{2}$ inches long.

This piece of chalk is between 2 and 3 inches long. It is
about $2\frac{3}{4}$ inches long.

This marker is between 4 and 5 inches long. It is about
$4\frac{7}{8}$ inches long.

Remember: 12 inches = 1 foot
36 inches = 3 feet = 1 yard

Estimate the length.

Then measure to the nearest $\frac{1}{8}$ inch.

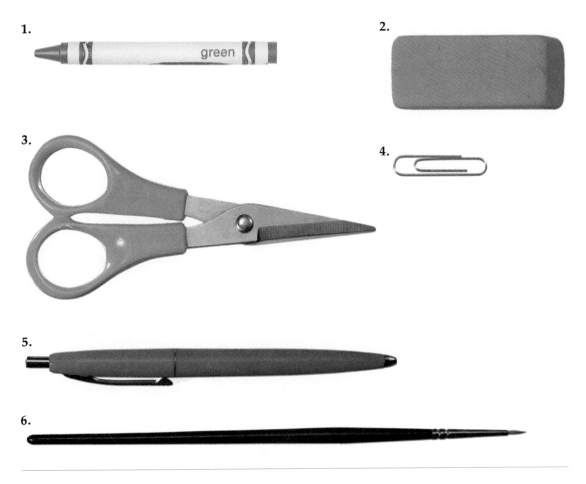

1.

2.

3.

4.

5.

6.

Measure.

- How long is your classroom in yards and feet? In feet only?
- How wide is your classroom in yards and feet? In feet only?
- How long is your desk in feet and inches? In inches only?
- How wide is your desk in feet and inches? In inches only?
- How long is the cover of your mathematics book in inches?
- How wide is the cover of your mathematics book in inches?

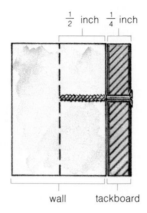

$\frac{1}{2}$ inch $\frac{1}{4}$ inch

wall   tackboard

Mr. Murphy is putting a tackboard on his wall. The tackboard is $\frac{1}{4}$ inch thick. He wants the screws to go about $\frac{1}{2}$-inch into the wall. How long a screw should he use?

Measure to check.

$\frac{1}{2}$ inch $\frac{1}{4}$ inch

Is this $\frac{3}{4}$ inch long?

Mr. Murphy has a $\frac{3}{4}$-inch wooden plug to fill a hole $\frac{1}{2}$ inch deep. How much must be cut off so that no wood sticks out of the hole?

Measure to check.

$\frac{3}{4}$ inch

$\frac{1}{2}$ inch

Is this $\frac{1}{4}$ inch?

Figure out the answer. Then draw line segments
and measure to check.

1. $\frac{1}{4}$ inch + $\frac{1}{4}$ inch

2. $\frac{3}{8}$ inch + $\frac{3}{8}$ inch

3. 2 inches − $\frac{1}{4}$ inch

4. 1 inch − $\frac{5}{8}$ inch

5. $1\frac{1}{2}$ inches + $1\frac{1}{8}$ inches

6. $\frac{3}{4}$ inch + $\frac{1}{2}$ inch

7. Kurt sailed for 2 hours yesterday and $\frac{3}{4}$ hour today.
How many hours did he sail during the past 2 days?

8. Eleanor placed a box that is $\frac{3}{4}$ foot tall on another box that is
$\frac{1}{4}$ foot tall. How tall are the 2 boxes together?

9. Cathy Jo had $2\frac{1}{2}$ dollars. She gave a shiny quarter to
Warren. How much money does Cathy Jo have now?

10. Pauline had $1\frac{1}{2}$ pounds of coffee beans. She gave her
sister $\frac{1}{4}$ pound. How much did she have left?

11. Ben had 3 dollars. He spent half a dollar for a comic
book and a dollar for a kite. How much did he have then?

12. Andrea ran 2 miles on Monday and $2\frac{1}{2}$ miles on
Wednesday. How many miles did she run in those 2 days?

IRON AND GOLD

"I was hiding behind the door," said the queen. "And I saw what the steward did. He was trying to cheat you. Now I know that he has been cheating me too, and stealing money from the Royal Treasury. I will see that he pays for his crimes. But now I want to give you another reward."

The queen set out some glass jars filled with jewels. "The red jewels are rubies and the clear ones are worthless glass," said the queen. "You may each choose 1 jewel, but you will be blindfolded so that you can't tell if you are taking a ruby or a piece of glass. I will shake up the jar before you draw, so that you can't remember where a ruby is and reach for it."

These are the first 2 jars she showed them:

Ferdie got the first turn. "I want to draw from the full jar," he said, "because it has the most rubies in it." Ferdie wasn't so lucky, however. He drew a piece of glass.

These are the jars that Portia could choose from:

"I don't think it matters which jar I draw from," Portia said. She drew from the jar that had only 2 jewels in it, and she got the glass jewel.

These are the jars Mark got to draw from:

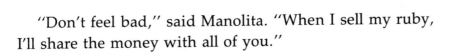

"I know for sure which jar to choose from," Mark said. "I'm sure to get a ruby." He picked the jar with only 8 jewels. The queen blindfolded him. Then she shook the jar. Mark reached into it—and got a glass jewel. "Impossible," he said.

These are the jars Manolita got to choose from:

"Don't feel bad," said Manolita. "When I sell my ruby, I'll share the money with all of you."

1. Did Ferdie choose the right jar to draw from? Why or why not?

2. Why would Portia say it didn't matter which jar she drew from?

3. Why might Mark be so sure he would get a ruby?

4. If Mark chose the right jar, how could he fail to get a ruby?

5. Could Manolita be sure she would get a ruby? How?

6. Of all the children, who had the best chance of getting a ruby? Who had the next best chance? Who had the poorest chance?

1. Kay's road repair crew used $\frac{1}{4}$ barrel of tar yesterday and $\frac{1}{2}$ barrel today. How many barrels did they use in these 2 days?

2. Maurice lives $3\frac{1}{2}$ blocks from his school. How many blocks does he have to walk to school and back?

3. Mr. Moore drove from his home to Last Gulch. When he left home, he had about $\frac{3}{4}$ of a tank of gasoline in his car. When he arrived in Last Gulch, he had only $\frac{1}{4}$ of a tank.
   a. What fraction of a tank of gas did Mr. Moore use up on the trip to Last Gulch?
   b. Can Mr. Moore drive back home without getting more gasoline?
   c. What fraction of a tank of gasoline does Mr. Moore need to fill up his tank in Last Gulch?
   d. If Mr. Moore fills up his tank in Last Gulch, about how full will it be when he gets home?
   e. How many tanks of gasoline does Mr. Moore use on a trip to Last Gulch and back?
   f. Can you make a good guess of how many kilometers it might be from Mr. Moore's home to Last Gulch?

Multiply or divide. Watch the signs.

1. 100×3.5
2. $5.7 \div 1000$
3. $14.3 \div 10,000$
4. 10×15.576
5. $1,000,000 \times 6.5591$
6. $56.227 \div 100,000$
7. 100×323.75
8. $10,000 \times 46.5$
9. $237.39 \div 1000$
10. 75.19×100

11. $100,000 \times 394.565$
12. 10×36.237
13. $101.6761 \times 1,000,000$
14. $55.107 \div 100$
15. 1000×53.45
16. $10,000 \times 89,065.339$
17. $84.6 \div 100$
18. $60.273 \div 10,000$
19. 10×9.78
20. 100×8959.7766

Multiply.

21. 4×3.5
22. 17.95×6
23. 7×59.106
24. 53×5.467
25. 37×4.86
26. 40.5×67
27. 82.7×17
28. 36×67.3
29. 76.3×325
30. 63×36.7

31. 76.39×91
32. 327×9.37
33. 3.1×872
34. 124×0.47
35. 53.15×79
36. 102×9.14
37. 2.208×7129
38. $32,153 \times 6.15$
39. 15.08×717
40. 2585×7.12

41. Valerie wants to buy 3 new books that cost $3.25 each. To raise money, she is selling some of her old books for $0.49 each.
    a. If she sells 25 of her old books, how much money will she take in?
    b. Will that be enough to pay for the new books?

Copy, but replace each ⬤ with <, >, or =.

1. 0.7 ⬤ 0.07
2. 0.14 ⬤ 0.32
3. 0.2 ⬤ 0.09
4. 0.325 ⬤ 0.096
5. 0.40 ⬤ 1.22
6. 0.0005 ⬤ 0.008

Multiply or divide.

7. 1000 × 1.257
8. 35.298 × 10
9. 100 × 0.037
10. 4.73 × 1000
11. 3.996 ÷ 10
12. 100,000 ÷ 10

Remember: 1 meter = 10 decimeters = 100 centimeters = 1000 millimeters
1 m = 10 dm = 100 cm = 1000 mm

13. 3 dm = ▨ m
14. 100 cm = ▨ m
15. 35 mm = ▨ m
16. 6 dm, 3 cm, 9 mm = ▨ m
17. ▨ mm = 0.650 m
18. ▨ cm = 0.45 m

Give the length of each object to the nearest centimeter.

19. ▨ cm

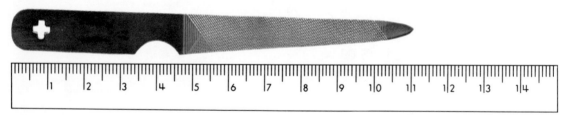

20. ▨ cm

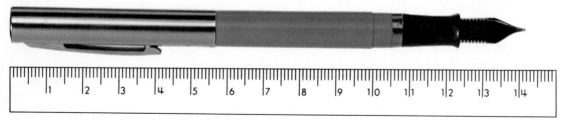

Add or subtract.

21. $3.6 + 1.5$ **26.** $15.17 - 13.29$

22. $6.2 - 2.7$ **27.** $90.528 - 18.016$

23. $12.2 - 8.9$ **28.** $0.03 + 0.31$

24. $20.13 + 9.18$ **29.** $24.26 - 24.01$

25. $3.11 + 20.26$ **30.** $0.15 + 1.45$

Multiply.

31. 6×3.5 **35.** 3.425×50 **38.** 5.316×90

32. 60×3.5 **36.** 7×0.152 **39.** 63.587×2

33. 0.37×8 **37.** 400×1.8 **40.** 3×0.084

34. 5.41×300

What fraction of each figure is shaded?

41. 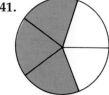   **42.** 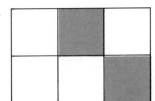   **43.**

Solve for n.

44. $\frac{1}{3}$ of $12 = n$ **46.** $\frac{0}{4}$ of $80 = n$ **48.** $\frac{1}{2}$ of $44 = n$

45. $\frac{4}{5}$ of $20 = n$ **47.** $\frac{6}{6}$ of $180 = n$ **49.** $\frac{4}{10}$ of $100 = n$

If a 0–5 cube is rolled, what is the probability of

50. rolling a 2?

51. rolling a 0 or a 1?

52. rolling a 0, 1, 2, 3, 4, or 5?

53. rolling an even number?

54. If you roll a 0–5 cube 300 times, about how many times would you expect to roll a 3?

55. Irma bought 2 kilograms of popcorn. She popped half of it last week. How much popcorn is left?

56. Wayne had $342.38 in his checking account. He wrote a check for $37.49. How much did he then have in his account?

57. Priscilla bought some nails and screws at the hardware store. The bill came to $2.47. How much change should she get if she gives the clerk a $5 bill?

58. Which has more juice, a 1.4-liter can of juice or two 750-milliliter cans of juice?

59. 10 copies of a book weigh 45 kilograms. How much does each copy of the book weigh?

60. Julius took 36 foul shots and made 20 of them. Did he miss more than $\frac{1}{4}$ of the shots?

Copy, but replace each ● with <, >, or =.

1. 0.3 ● 0.4
2. 0.2 ● 0.02
3. 0.2 ● 0.003
4. 0.07 ● 0.007

5. 0.65 ● 0.6
6. 0.55 ● 0.60
7. 0.15 ● 0.07
8. 0.9 ● 0.99

9. 0.67 ● 0.33
10. 0.305 ● 0.810
11. 0.265 ● 0.260
12. 0.5 ● 0.050

Remember: 1 meter = 10 decimeters = 100 centimeters = 1000 millimeters

1 m = 10 dm = 100 cm = 1000 mm

13. 100 cm = ■ m
14. 400 cm = ■ m
15. 1 dm = ■ m
16. 5 dm = ■ m

17. ■ mm = 1 cm
18. ■ cm = 1 dm
19. ■ dm = 1 m
20. 45 mm = ■ m

21. 3 dm, 2 cm, 5 m = ■ m
22. 2 dm, 0 cm, 6 mm = ■ m
23. 6 dm, 5 mm = ■ m
24. 8 cm, 5 mm = ■ m

25. Draw a circle. Shade $\frac{2}{4}$ of it. Then shade another $\frac{1}{4}$ of it.

26. Draw another circle just like the one you drew in problem 25. Shade $\frac{3}{4}$ of it.

27. What is $\frac{1}{4} + \frac{2}{4}$?

28. Draw a rectangle. Shade $\frac{3}{4}$ of it. What fraction is **not** shaded?

29. What is $\frac{4}{4} - \frac{3}{4}$?

Solve for n.

30. $n = \frac{1}{2}$ of 24
31. $n = \frac{3}{4}$ of 24
32. $n = \frac{3}{8}$ of 24
33. $n = \frac{1}{4}$ of 32

34. $n = \frac{1}{8}$ of 32
35. $n = \frac{1}{3}$ of 30
36. $n = \frac{2}{3}$ of 60
37. $n = \frac{1}{6}$ of 30

38. $n = \frac{2}{6}$ of 30
39. $n = \frac{2}{4}$ of 24
40. $n = \frac{6}{8}$ of 24
41. $n = \frac{2}{4}$ of 32

1. Selena has $15.00 in her checking account.
   a. She deposits $5.00. How much does she now have in her account?
   b. She writes a check for $8.00. How much does she now have in her account?

2. Bruce had 2 quarters and 2 dimes. Then his mother gave him a $1 bill. How much money does he have?

3. Maya bought some fruit. The grocer charged her $1.74. If Maya pays with a $5 bill, how much change should she get?

4. It is 1.4 kilometers from Daisy's house to the library. How far is it there and back?

5. The doorway in Makio's classroom is 85 centimeters wide. Can a table that is 1 meter wide fit through the doorway without being tilted?

6. Janis says she is 140 centimeters tall. Grace says she is 1.35 meters tall.
   a. Who is taller?
   b. By how much?

7. Callie wants to find out the weight of a paper clip. She weighs 100 clips and finds out they weigh 50 grams. How much does 1 paper clip weigh?

8. In the running broad jump, Bennett jumped 6.21 meters. His opponent, Judd, jumped 6.16 meters.
   a. Who won?
   b. By how many centimeters?

Do the following experiments with 2 friends. One of you keeps records, one flips the coins or rolls the cubes, and the third person keeps track of the total number of rolls or flips. Take turns doing each job.

1. Flip a coin 100 times. How often did it land heads? About what fraction of the time did it land heads? (Pick the answer that's closest to your result.)

   a. None of the time   **c.** $\frac{1}{2}$ of the time   **e.** All the time

   b. $\frac{1}{4}$ of the time   **d.** $\frac{3}{4}$ of the time

2. If you flip a coin once, what is the probability that it will land heads?

Roll a 0–5 cube 120 times. Keep track of the number of times you get each number.

3. About what fraction of the time did you roll a 0? a 5?

   a. $\frac{0}{6}$ **b.** $\frac{1}{6}$ **c.** $\frac{2}{6}$ **d.** $\frac{3}{6}$ **e.** $\frac{4}{6}$ **f.** $\frac{5}{6}$

4. How many times did you roll an even number?

- If you flip a penny and a nickel (or any 2 coins) together 100 times, how many times do you think you'll get 0 heads? 1 head? 2 heads? Think carefully. Then put your predictions on a chart like the one shown.

- Now try it. Keep a tally. You can change your predictions after a few flips.

- Were your predictions close?

Heads	How Many Times in 100 Flips	
	Predicted	Actual
0		
1		
2		

Copy, but replace each ● with <, >, or =.

1. 0.04 ● 0.3   **3.** 1.5 ● 1.06   **5.** 0.025 ● 0.007
2. 0.08 ● 0.003   **4.** 0.75 ● 0.80   **6.** 0.750 ● 1.000

Multiply or divide.

7. 10×1.3 **9.** 1000×1.3 **11.** 100×0.14
8. $12.07 \div 10$ **10.** $3.821 \div 100$ **12.** $5.329 \times 10,000$

Remember: 1 meter = 10 decimeters = 100 centimeters = 1000 millimeters
1 m = 10 dm = 100 cm = 1000 mm

---

13. ▨ dm = 0.3 m   **15.** ▨ cm = 0.4 m
14. 65 mm = ▨ m   **16.** 2 dm, 5 cm = ▨ m

Give the length of each object to the nearest centimeter.

17.

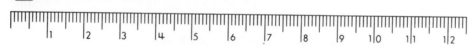

18.

Add or subtract.

19. $40.53 + 40.85$ **22.** $30.0 - 0.0345$ **25.** $4.57 + 63.97$
20. $26.47 - 16.18$ **23.** $16.774 + 28.845$ **26.** $15.62 - 1.80$
21. $0.051 + 27.754$ **24.** $8.5 - 7.9$

Multiply.

27. 2 × 7.2   **30.** 40 × 2.3   **33.** 40,000 × 8.73

28. 0.241 × 70   **31.** 27.38 × 600   **34.** 7.49 × 30

29. 300 × 5.11   **32.** 4.0 × 10

What fraction of each figure is shaded?

35. 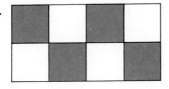   **36.**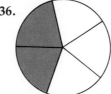

Solve for *n*.

37. $\frac{1}{2}$ of 62 = *n*   **40.** $\frac{5}{6}$ of 42 = *n*   **43.** $n = \frac{1}{4} + \frac{2}{4}$

38. $\frac{2}{3}$ of 45 = *n*   **41.** $\frac{1}{3}$ of 90 = *n*   **44.** $n = \frac{5}{8} - \frac{2}{8}$

39. $\frac{3}{10}$ of 1000 = *n*   **42.** $\frac{1}{10}$ of 50 = *n*   **45.** $n = \frac{3}{6} + \frac{3}{6}$

46. If you are rolling a 5–10 cube 1 time, what is the probability of rolling an odd number?

47. If you roll a 0–5 cube 600 times, how many times would you expect to roll a 4?

48. Millie has 3 quarters and 3 dimes. How much more money does she need to buy a book that costs $1.25 with tax included?

49. Rodney lives on a block that is rectangular. It is 0.25 kilometer long and 0.10 kilometer wide. How far does Rodney jog when he jogs around the block once?

50. It takes Edie $\frac{1}{2}$ hour to walk home from school. If she leaves school at 3:30, when will she get home?

Metric System

Length	Weight (mass)	Liquid Volume (capacity)
millimeter (mm) 0.001 m **centimeter** (cm) 0.01 m decimeter (dm) 0.1 m **meter** (m) dekameter (dam) 10 m hectometer (hm) 100 m **kilometer** (km) 1000 m	**milligram** (mg) 0.001 g centigram (cg) 0.01 g decigram (dg) 0.1 g **gram** (g) dekagram (dag) 10 g hectogram (hg) 100 g **kilogram** (kg) 1000 g	**milliliter** (mL) 0.001 L centiliter (cL) 0.01 L deciliter (dL) 0.1 L **liter** (L) dekaliter (daL) 10 L hectoliter (hL) 100 L kiloliter (kL) 1000 L

Units of area are derived from units of length.

square centimeter (cm²)   1 cm² = 0.0001 m²   The area of this square is 1 square centimeter.

square meter (m²)   1 m² = 10,000 cm²   A square 1 meter on a side has an area of 1 square meter.

hectare (ha)   1 ha = 10,000 m²   A square 100 meters on a side has an area of 1 hectare.

square kilometer (km²)   1 km² = 1,000,000 m²   A square 1 kilometer on a side has an area of 1 square kilometer.

Units of volume can also be derived from units of length.

cubic centimeter (cm³)   The volume of this cube is 1 cubic centimeter.

cubic meter (m³)   1 m³ = 1,000,000 cm³   A cube 1 meter on a side has a volume of 1 cubic meter.

Descriptions of some common units:

kilometer   You can walk a kilometer in about 12 minutes.

meter   Most classroom doors are about 1 meter wide.

centimeter   This line segment is 1 centimeter long.   ——

millimeter   This line segment is 1 millimeter long.   –

liter   Four average-size glasses hold about 1 liter of liquid.

milliliter   This cube holds about 1 milliliter.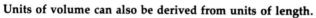

kilogram   A pair of size-10 men's shoes weighs about 1 kilogram.

gram   A nickel (or a marble) weighs about 5 grams.

400

Traditional System

Length

inch (in) $1 \text{ in} = \begin{cases} \frac{1}{12} \text{ ft} \\ \frac{1}{36} \text{ yd} \end{cases}$

foot (ft) $1 \text{ ft} = \begin{cases} 12 \text{ in} \\ \frac{1}{3} \text{ yd} \end{cases}$

yard (yd) $1 \text{ yd} = \begin{cases} 36 \text{ in} \\ 3 \text{ ft} \end{cases}$

mile (mi) $1 \text{ mi} = \begin{cases} 5280 \text{ ft} \\ 1760 \text{ yd} \end{cases}$

Liquid Volume (capacity)

fluid ounce (fl oz) $1 \text{ fl oz} = \frac{1}{8} \text{ cup}$

cup (c) $1 \text{ c} = \begin{cases} 8 \text{ fl oz} \\ \frac{1}{2} \text{ pt} \end{cases}$

pint (pt) $1 \text{ pt} = \begin{cases} 16 \text{ fl oz} \\ 2 \text{ c} \\ \frac{1}{2} \text{ qt} \end{cases}$

quart (qt) $1 \text{ qt} = \begin{cases} 32 \text{ fl oz} \\ 4 \text{ c} \\ \frac{1}{4} \text{ gal} \end{cases}$

gallon (gal) $1 \text{ gal} = \begin{cases} 128 \text{ fl oz} \\ 16 \text{ c} \\ 8 \text{ pt} \\ 4 \text{ qt} \end{cases}$

Area

square inch (sq in or in²)
square foot (sq ft or ft²) $1 \text{ ft}^2 = 144 \text{ in}^2$
square yard (sq yd or yd²) $1 \text{ yd}^2 = 9 \text{ ft}^2$
acre (A) $1 \text{ A} = 4840 \text{ yd}^2$
square mile (sq mi or mi²) $1 \text{ mi}^2 = 640 \text{ A}$

Volume

cubic inch (cu in or in³)
cubic foot (cu ft or ft³) $1 \text{ ft}^3 = 1728 \text{ in}^3$
cubic yard (cu yd or yd³) $1 \text{ yd}^3 = 27 \text{ ft}^3$

Weight

ounce (oz) $1 \text{ oz} = \frac{1}{16} \text{ lb}$

pound (lb) $1 \text{ lb} = 16 \text{ oz}$

ton (T) $1 \text{ T} = 2000 \text{ lb}$

Glossary

addend A number that is added to another number to make a sum. For example:

$$35 \text{ — addend}$$
$$\underline{+\ 48} \text{ — addend}$$
$$83 \text{ — sum}$$

$$7 + 8 = 15 \text{ — sum}$$

addend   addend

algorithm A step-by-step procedure for solving a certain type of problem.

approximation An answer to a mathematical problem that is not precise but is close enough for the purpose. Sometimes an approximate answer is more appropriate than a precise answer. (See *estimate*.)

arrow operation A notation for showing an action of a function machine. In 7 —(×8)→ 56, 7 goes in and is multiplied by 8 to give 56. The *function rule* in this case is ×8. In the operation 6 ◄—(−5)— 11, 11 goes in and 5 is subtracted from it to give 6. The function rule in this case is −5.

average A number that can sometimes be used to describe a group of numbers. To find the average of a set of numbers, add the numbers and divide the sum by how many numbers were added. The average of 5, 6, 6, 8, and 10 is 7 (5 + 6 + 6 + 8 + 10 = 35 and 35 ÷ 5 = 7). (Also called *mean*.)

axes (of a graph) The two zero lines of a graph that give the coordinates of points. The horizontal axis is the *x*-axis. The vertical axis is the *y*-axis.

balance 1. The amount of money remaining in an account. 2. A double-pan balance is an instrument used to measure weight.

bound A number that an answer must be greater than or less than. For example, 36 × 21 must be less than 40 × 30, or 1200. So 1200 is an *upper bound*. The answer to 36 × 21 must be greater than 30 × 20, or 600. So 600 is a *lower bound*.

circle A figure (in a plane) in which all the points are the same distance from a point called the center. In this figure, for example, points A,

B, and C are the same distance from point O, the center of the circle:

composite function A function with two or more operations.
For example: x —(×3)→ n —(+5)→ y

composite number A whole number with factors other than 1 and itself.

coordinates Numbers that give the position of a point on a graph.

In the figure shown, for example, the coordinates of point A are (2, 3). 2 is the *x*-coordinate. 3 is the *y*-coordinate.

decimal point A dot used to separate the ones digit from the tenths digit.

denominator The part of a fraction written below the line. The part written above the line is called the *numerator*. The denominator tells how many equal parts something is divided into; the numerator tells how many of those parts are being referred to. In the fraction $\frac{3}{4}$ the denominator (4) indicates that something is divided into four equal parts. The numerator (3) says to consider three of those parts.

diameter A line segment, going through the center of a circle, that starts at one point on the circle and ends at the opposite point on the circle. (Also, the length of that line segment.) AB is a diameter of this circle:

difference The amount that one number is greater or less than another. For example:

$$43 \text{ — minuend}$$
$$\underline{-\ 16} \text{ — subtrahend}$$
$$27 \text{ — difference}$$

$$10 - 7 = 3 \text{ — difference}$$

   subtrahend
   minuend

digit Any of the numbers 0, 1, 2, 3, 4, 5, 6, 7, 8, and 9. The two digits in 15 are 1 and 5.

dividend A number that is divided by the divisor. For example:

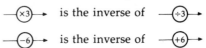

$$6 \div 3 = 2 \text{ — quotient}$$

divisor A number that the dividend is divided by. (See *dividend*.)

equilateral triangle A triangle with all three sides the same length. For example:

equivalent fractions Fractions that have the same value. $\frac{2}{6}$, $\frac{4}{12}$, and $\frac{1}{3}$ are equivalent fractions.

estimate A judgment about the size or quantity of something. (Also, to make such a judgment.) Sometimes it is more appropriate to make an estimate than to measure or count precisely. (See *approximation*.)

even number Any multiple of 2. 0, 2, 4, 6, 8, and so on are even numbers.

fraction $\frac{1}{2}$, $\frac{3}{4}$, and $\frac{7}{8}$ are examples of fractions. The fraction $\frac{3}{4}$ means that something is divided into four equal parts and that we are considering three of those parts. (See *denominator* and *numerator*.)

function machine A device (sometimes imaginary) that does the same thing to every number that is put into it. (See *arrow operation*.)

function rule See *arrow operation*.

hexagon A polygon with six sides.

hundredth If a whole is divided into 100 equal parts, each part is one-hundredth of the whole.

inequality A statement that tells which of two numbers is greater. For example: 4 > 3 is read "4 is greater than 3." 3 + 6 < 10 is read "3 plus 6 is less than 10."

intersecting lines Lines that meet. In this figure, lines AB and CD intersect at point E:

inverse operation An operation that "undoes" the results of another operation. Multiplication and division are inverse operations; addition and subtraction are inverse operations.

isosceles triangle A triangle with two equal sides. These are isosceles triangles:

line segment A part of a line with two endpoints. For example, AB is a line segment; points A and B are its endpoints.

mean See *average*.

minuend A number from which another number is subtracted. (See *difference*.)

mixed number A number made up of a whole number and a fraction. $1\frac{1}{2}$, $2\frac{3}{4}$, and $7\frac{7}{8}$ are mixed numbers.

multiple A number that is some whole number of times another number. 12 is a multiple of 3 because $3 \times 4 = 12$.

multiplicand A number that is multiplied by another number, the multiplier. For example:

5 — multiplicand
× 3 — multiplier
15 — product

$3 \times 5 = 15$ — product
multiplicand
multiplier

The multiplier and multiplicand are also called the factors of the product.

multiplier See *multiplicand*.

numerator The part of a fraction written above the line. (See *denominator*.)

octagon A polygon with eight sides.

odd number A whole number that is not a multiple of 2. All whole numbers that are not even are odd. 1, 3, 5, 7, 9, 11, and so on are odd numbers.

ordered pair Two numbers written so that one is considered before the other. Coordinates of points are written as ordered pairs, with the *x*-coordinate written first. For example: (3, 4). (See *coordinates*.)

parallel lines Lines in a plane that do not intersect.

Lines AB and CD are parallel:

Lines EF and GH are not parallel:

parentheses A symbol ( ) used to show in which order operations should be done. For example: (3 × 5) + 7 says to multiply 5 by 3 and then add 7; 3 × (5 + 7) says to add 5 and 7 and then multiply by 3.

partial product The product that comes from multiplying the multiplicand by one of the digits of the multiplier. For example:

```
  36   ┌ This partial product comes from
× 12  /└ multiplying 36 by 2 ones.
  72 ´ ┌ This partial product comes from
  36 ─└ multiplying 36 by 1 ten.
 432 ┌ The product comes from adding the
     └ partial products.
```

pentagon A polygon with five sides.

perimeter The distance around a figure. The perimeter of this rectangle is 6 cm:

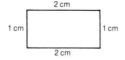

perpendicular lines Lines that intersect at right angles.

These lines are perpendicular:

So are these: But these are not:

place value The value of a digit in a number. The value of 7 in 27 is 7 ones; in 74 its value is 70, or 7 tens; in 726 its value is 700, or 7 hundreds.

polygon One of a certain type of figure. These figures are polygons:

These are not:

These are not:

Here are the names of some common polygons and the number of sides:

Number of Sides	
3	triangle
4	quadrilateral
5	pentagon—a regular pentagon has five equal sides:

6	hexagon—a regular hexagon has six equal sides:

8	octagon—a regular octagon has eight equal sides:

prime number A whole number divisible only by 1 and itself.

probability How likely something is to happen. The probability that some particular thing will happen is a fraction in which the denominator is the total number of possible things that can happen and the numerator is the number of ways this particular thing can happen. The probability that an ordinary coin will show heads when flipped is about $\frac{1}{2}$.

product The result of multiplying two numbers together. (See *multiplicand*.)

profit In a business the money that is left after all expenses have been paid.

quadrilateral A polygon with four sides.

quotient The result (other than the remainder) of dividing one number by another. (See *dividend*.)

radius A line segment that goes from the center of a circle to a point on the circle. (Also, the length of such a segment.) OA is a radius of the circle shown here. The radius of this circle is 1 centimeter.

rectangle A quadrilateral in which all four angles are right angles.

regroup To rename a number to make adding and subtracting easier.

Example of regrouping in subtraction:

$$\begin{array}{r} {\scriptstyle 1\ 15} \\ \cancel{2}\ \cancel{5} \\ -\ 1\ 7 \\ \hline 8 \end{array}$$
(To subtract in the ones column, 2 tens and 5 is regrouped to 1 ten and 15.)

Example of regrouping in addition:

$$\begin{array}{r} {\scriptstyle 1} \\ 2\ 9\ 6 \\ +\ 4\ 4\ 2 \\ \hline 7\ 3\ 8 \end{array}$$
(After adding the tens column, 13 tens is regrouped to 1 hundred and 3 tens.)

relation signs The three basic relation signs are > (greater than), < (less than), and = (equal to). (See *inequality*.)

remainder A number less than the divisor that remains after the dividend has been divided by the divisor as many times as possible. For example, when you divide 25 by 4, the quotient is 6 with a remainder of 1:

$$\begin{array}{r} 6\ \text{R1} \\ 4\overline{)25} \\ 24 \\ \hline 1 \end{array}$$

right angle An angle that forms a square corner.

These are right angles: These are not:

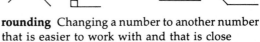

rounding Changing a number to another number that is easier to work with and that is close enough for the purpose. (See *approximation*.)

square A quadrilateral with four equal sides and four equal angles.

subtrahend A number that is subtracted from another number. (See *difference*.)

sum The result of adding two or more numbers. (See *addend*.)

tenth If a whole is divided into 10 equal parts, each part is one-tenth of the whole.

triangle A polygon that has three sides.

unit cost The cost of one item or one specified amount of an item. If 20 pencils cost 40¢, then the unit cost is 2¢ for each pencil. If dog food costs $9 for 3 kilograms, then the unit cost is $3 per kilogram.

whole number The numbers that we use to show how many (0, 1, 2, 3, and so on). 3 is a whole number, but $3\frac{1}{2}$ and 4.5 are not whole numbers.

zero The number that tells how many things there are when there aren't any. Zero times any number is zero; zero plus any number is that number: $0 \times 3 = 0$, $0 + 3 = 3$.

Index